ON WILLIAM STAFFORD

UNDER DISCUSSION

Donald Hall, General Editor

On William Stafford

The Worth of Local Things

Edited by Tom Andrews

Ann Arbor

THE UNIVERSITY OF MICHIGAN PRESS

First paperback edition 1995
Copyright © by the University of Michigan 1993
All rights reserved
Published in the United States of America by
The University of Michigan Press
Manufactured in the United States of America
1996   1995   4   3   2   1

Library of Congress Cataloging-in-Publication Data

On William Stafford : the worth of local things / edited by Tom
    Andrews.
        p.   cm. — (Under discussion)
    Includes bibliographical references.
    ISBN 0-472-10424-1 (alk. paper). — ISBN 0-472-08321-X
        (pbk. : alk. paper)
    1. Stafford, William, 1914–   —Criticism and interpretation.
    I. Andrews, Tom, 1961– . II. Series.
    PS3537.T143Z8   1994
    811'.54—dc20   93-34665
                                                            CIP

A CIP catalogue record for this book is available from the British Library.

For Stuart and David

Preface

A great deal has been written about William Stafford, as a glance at the selected bibliography that closes *On William Stafford: The Worth of Local Things* will indicate. This book could easily have been twice its current length. Still, I hope that the book, in its present form, provides a fair and interesting overview of the critical response to Stafford's work.

Stafford's work has been used—as a foil or as a positive example—in some of the livelier debates in poetics of the past few decades. In editing *On William Stafford* I have tried to reflect these debates. Thus, the many criticisms of Stafford's "process-rather-than-substance view of writing" (in Stafford's phrase) are countered with Judith Kitchen's defense of it in the last chapter of her *Understanding William Stafford*. Bob Perelman's provocative reading, in "The First Person," of "Traveling Through the Dark" as a "voice" poem, in which the speaker is "firmly in control of all the meaning" and therefore "in a privileged position, unaffected by the words," is addressed by Dick Barnes in "The Absence of the Artist." Paul Zweig's critique, in "The Raw and the Cooked," of Stafford's "conversational style," with its "deliberate naïveté" and "coy sentimentality," is taken up by David Young in "'1940': Shivers of Summer Wind." I have also tried to include essays that raise fundamental questions about Stafford's work even as they find much of value in it. Such an essay, for example, is William Heyen's "William Stafford's Allegiances," which gives a fair assessment of Stafford's remarkably prolific output, another issue critics have been divided about, as *On William Stafford* makes clear.

On William Stafford is divided into four parts. Parts 1 and 2 collect book reviews and general essays, respectively, arranged chronologically. A special feature of the book is part 3, which collects essays by poets on particular Stafford poems as well as John Haines's critique of "A Way of Writing," perhaps Stafford's best-known articulation of his theory of writing. These essays are arranged according to the original chronology of the poem or article being discussed. With the exceptions of Haines's essay,

Leonard Nathan's "One Vote," and Frank Steele's "William Stafford's 'Mornings,'" all of the essays in part 3 were originally published as a symposium in *Field* in the fall of 1989. I am very grateful to *Field*'s editors, Stuart Friebert and David Young, for allowing me to reprint the Stafford symposium (and several other essays) and for their work with *Field*. *Field* began twenty-three years ago with three Stafford poems leading off the first issue and has been a forum for Stafford's work ever since. To Stuart and David I gratefully dedicate this book.

Part 4 consists of the jurors' citation written on the occasion of the Lifetime Achievement in Poetry Award given to Stafford at the 1992 Western States Book Awards. Because it articulates so well the unusual combination of virtues in Stafford's poems and makes clear why one would wish to spend time with them, the citation seems an especially fitting piece with which to end this book.

I would like to thank William Stafford himself, who answered my questions with characteristic generosity and patience. I also thank Bruce Carlson, chair of the Ohio University Research Committee; Steve Flaherty, who made available the interlibrary loan operations at Ohio University's Lancaster Campus; Mara Holt, David Lazar, James Pirie, and Warren Slesinger, who took time out from their busy schedules to answer questions; and Jeff Gundy of Bluffton College, who made available his essay "Without Heroes, without Villains: Community and Identity in *Down in My Heart*," which appears in print for the first time here. As far as I have been able to determine, *Down in My Heart* received no reviews when it was published by the Brethren Publishing House in 1947 nor when it was reprinted by the Bench Press in 1985. Gundy's essay fills that unexpected void and shows how Stafford's concerns in *Down in My Heart* resonate throughout his long career. Finally, I wish to thank Donald Hall and LeAnn Fields for their enthusiastic support of this project, and my wife Carrie for her help and understanding and much, much more.

Contents

Part Two   General Essays

Part Three   Essays on Particular Poems or Articles

Part Four   Conclusion

PART ONE   *Book Reviews*

JAMES DICKEY

William Stafford

There are poets who pour out rivers of ink, all on good poems. William Stafford is one of these. He has been called America's most prolific poet, and I have no doubt that he is. He turns out so much verse not because he is glib and empty, but because he is a real poet, a born poet, and communicating in lines and images is not only the best way for him to get things said; it is the easiest. His natural mode of speech is a gentle, mystical, half-mocking and highly personal daydreaming about the landscape of the western United States. Everything in this world is available to Mr. Stafford's way of writing, and I for one am very glad it is. The things he chooses to write about—I almost said "talk"—seem in the beginning more or less arbitrary, but in the end never so. They are caught up so genuinely and intimately in his characteristic way of looking, feeling, and expressing that they emerge as fresh, glowing creations; they *all* do, and that is the surprising and lovely fact about them:

> The well rising without sound,
> the spring on a hillside,
> the ploughshare brimming through deep ground
> everywhere in the field—
>
> The sharp swallows in their swerve
> flaring and hesitating
> hunting for the final curve
> coming closer and closer—
>
> The swallow heart from wing beat to wing beat
> counselling decision, decision:

Review of *West of Your City,* from *Virginia Quarterly Review* 37, no. 4 (Autumn 1961): 640. Also published in *Babel to Byzantium: Poets and Poetry Now* by James Dickey. Copyright © 1961, 1968 by James Dickey. Reprinted by permission of Farrar, Straus & Giroux, Inc.

> thunderous examples. I place my feet
> with care in such a world.

Let Mr. Stafford keep pouring it out. It is all good, all to his purpose.

LOUIS SIMPSON

From "Important and Unimportant Poems"

The present disparity between performance and reputation is appalling. Take William Stafford, for example. Is Stafford really so far inferior to Robert Lowell that Lowell should be treated as a classic, and Stafford virtually unknown? I have the greatest respect for the author of *Lord Weary's Castle*—clearly he is one of the few significant poets of the age—but when I read the poems of Stafford, I must respect him also, and yet who, outside of a few readers, is aware of Stafford? What a concatenation of critics, what sheer ignorance, must control the American literary scene, for such a disparity to exist!

This is a poem from Stafford's *West of Your City:*

AT THE BOMB TESTING SITE

At noon in the desert a panting lizard
waited for history, its elbows tense,
watching the curve of a particular road
as if something might happen.

It was looking at something farther off
than people could see, an important scene
acted in stone for little selves
at the flute end of consequences.

There was just a continent without much on it
under a sky that never cared less.
Ready for a change, the elbows waited.
The hands gripped hard on the desert.

Review of *West of Your City,* from *Hudson Review* 14, no. 3 (Autumn 1961): 461–70. Also published in *A Company of Poets* by Louis Simpson (Ann Arbor: University of Michigan Press, 1981), 657–75.

Stafford's subject matter is usually important in itself. (The theory that subject matter is nothing, the treatment everything, was invented to comfort little minds.) Also, he deals with his subject directly; that is to say, he has a personal voice. Contrary to what many poets believe nowadays, it is not necessary to spill your guts on the table in order to be "personal," nor to relate the details of your aunt's insanity. What is necessary is originality of imagination and at least a few ideas of your own. Another point in favor of Stafford is that he actually writes about the country he is living in; all sorts of ordinary places, people, and animals appear in his poems, and not as subjects of satire, but with the full weight of their own existence. As we read Stafford we are aware of how much has been omitted from modern American poetry only because it is not literary, or because it springs from the life of ordinary, rather than "alienated" people. An observer from another country would be struck by the absence from American poetry of the American landscape; he would find, also, that the language of our poetry is not the language of our real thoughts; and he might wonder at the psychic disorder this indicates. As for history—it seems we are trying to forget it. But Stafford is one of the few poets who are able to use the landscape and to feel the mystery and imagination in American life.

> Light wind at Grand Prairie, drifting snow.
> Low at Vermilion, forty degrees of frost.
> Lost in the Barrens, hunting over spines of ice,
> the great sled dog Shadow is running for his life.

He is a poet of the people in the deepest and most meaningful sense. And a poet of nature—in a time when poets claim our attention because they are unnatural, pitiable, demoralized. His poems are strong and true; rightly understood, they will enrich our lives.

ROBERT HUFF

From "Design and Matter"

West of Your City is a different matter, and a glance at the table of contents clearly indicates that *matter* is the springboard for Mr. Stafford's poetry. In addition to the title poem, we find pieces entitled "A Visit Home," "At the Salt Marsh," "Weather Report," "The Gun of Billy the Kid," "By the Snake River," and "On the Glass Ice." These titles suggest that Mr. Stafford is concerned with the everyday, with the immediate—that he has selected these poems for his first volume implies that his concern is deep. The worst books of this kind offer catalogues of frequently loud sentimentalities; the best present poems in which an individual's relationship with his actual environment is given significantly human utterance. Luckily for Mr. Stafford and for us, *West of Your City* is an exceptionally fine first volume. Readers of his widely published work are not surprised. Many agree with Louis Simpson that there is really not so great a distance between the work of William Stafford and the products of the new "establishment" as fashionable critical response and major literary awards would suggest.

Perhaps because Mr. Stafford writes a great deal without pushing or pulling too hard he almost always writes well. His idiom is deceptively casual. When he says in "One Home" (and, as with Robert Frost, Mr. Stafford says poems) "The sun was over our town; it was like a blade," his pace tells me that he does not feel life is cutting him up, rather that "Wherever we looked the land would hold us up." Note how much the rhythm of the poem "Ceremony" has to do with our believing it. Otherwise stated, how easily an account of this ritual might become completely fake.

> On the third finger of my left hand
> under the bank of the Ninnescah
> a muskrat whirled and bit to the bone.
> The mangled hand made the river red.

Review of *West of Your City,* from *Prairie Schooner* 36, no. 1 (Spring 1962): 80–83.

That was something the ocean would remember:
I saw me in the current flowing through the land,
rolling, touching roots, the world incarnadined,
and the river richer by a kind of marriage.

While in the woods an owl started quavering
with drops like tears I raised my arm.
Under the bank a muskrat was trembling
with meaning my hand would wear forever.

In that river my blood flowed on.

I'm willing to pay the price of Mr. Stafford's self-conscious "the world incarnadined" for the experience of this poem. Although "The Move to California" is a very different poem in which the casual pace becomes off-hand, it is a convincing observation. We are told in a subtitle that one section of the piece was "Written on the Stub of the First Paycheck," and I believe it may have been. Even at his best, Mr. Stafford gives me the impression that he's practicing all the time—that he simply needs to throw fewer efforts away each year because he is one of the few people alive who see life from the point of view of a poet.

Whatever their limitations, poets don't happen every year. I have read few first volumes of the order of *West of Your City* since the appearance in 1955 of John Woods's *The Deaths at Paragon, Indiana*. Our nationally acknowledged "younger poets," academic and beat, exhibit a virtuosity of controlled expression or no control at all. Essentially either of these fashionable modes is primarily concerned with the expression of thematic abstractions. For Mr. Stafford, social, religious, and philosophical meanings hover around the poem. They are radiations only. The westerly direction is not for him an outdated answer to the contemporary predicament. It offers no honey in the horn. But it is the spiritual focus which gives this volume unity and which makes William Stafford a poet of integrity. His intention is consistently to find the formal voice of his immediate experience. The poem "On the Glass Ice" indicates how successfully he fulfills his intention.

It was time. Arriving at Long Lake the storm
shook flakes on the glass ice, and the frozen fish
all lay there surprised by February.

I skated hard in the beginning storm
in order to meet every flake. Polished,
the way rich men can't wait for progress, the lake waited.

It got a real winter blanket—the day
going and the white eye losing downward,
the sky deeper and deeper. No sound.

In deep snow I knew the fish were singing.
I skated and skated till the lake was drowned.

PETER DAVISON

From "The New Poetry"

Of all the poets reviewed here, William Stafford shows the greatest promise of major stature. His first book, *West of Your City,* was published very prettily in 1960 by one of those small private presses which can bring a book to print but have trouble causing it to be noticed or read. This book is already unavailable. The second collection, *Traveling Through the Dark,* contains too many new poems of lower energy than Stafford's remarkable best, and it seems a pity that this new volume could not have been arranged to include the best poems from *West of Your City* instead. Yet the first long section has many rich poems in it—robust, mystical, sensuous, witty, wealthy with the rhythms of everyday speech. Stafford brings to his poetry a really good mind, a highly developed eye for landscape, a broad frame of reference, a maturity about joy and trouble, and a natural unforced talent that may one day make him the envy and despair of his contemporaries.

In the best poems of *Traveling Through the Dark* you find yourself plunged happily into the middle of a poem's experience before you know how you have got there. In the less good poems you tend to be aware of a bustle of preparation, but the lesser poems are simply a little less intense, less striking. Among the finest poems, as in the first book, are those dealing with the patterns behind landscape; but you will also find quizzical poems on the nature of thought and understanding, on the meaning of natural disasters, on the discrimination between the large and the small, on the exchange between one generation and the next, or on the place of poetry. No narrowness here. One poem, called "The Job," is the best I know about the profession of teaching. Another, "The Thought Machine," gives sheer delight in the reading and the rereading, as it relates, with humor and justice, man to machine. The best sample short enough to be quoted here in its entirety is a rueful one called "Parentage":

Review of *Traveling Through the Dark,* from *Atlantic Monthly* 210 (November 1962): 88.

My father didn't really belong in history.
He kept looking over his shoulder at some mistake.
He was a stranger to me, for I belong.

There never was a particular he couldn't understand,
but there were too many in too long a row,
and like many another he was overwhelmed.

Today drinking coffee I look over the cup
and want to have the right amount of fear,
preferring to be saved and not, like him, heroic.

I want to be as afraid as the teeth are big,
I want to be as dumb as the wise are wrong:
I'd just as soon be pushed by events to where I belong.

If William Stafford can discipline himself to print only the very best of his poems, watch out. He is a poet with something to say, who can transcend his human limitations and perform the poet's highest task by clarifying the world around us. As a sample of his prophetic quality, here is a short poem from *West of Your City* which in its way has the power of Yeats's "The Second Coming." This one is called "At the Bomb Testing Site."

At noon in the desert a panting lizard
waited for history, its elbows tense,
watching the curve of a particular road
as if something might happen.

It was looking at something farther off
than people could see, an important scene
acted in stone for little selves
at the flute end of consequences.

There was just a continent without much on it
under a sky that never cared less.
Ready for a change, the elbows waited.
The hands gripped hard on the desert.

ROBERT CREELEY

From "'Think What's Got Away . . .'"

The poems of William Stafford are, in some contrast, much quieter in tone. But, despite the frequent colloquialisms, an equally conscious rhetoric seems to me at work. For example, it is present I think in this kind of balance of manners: "no acrobat of salvation, / I couldn't help seeing. . . ." Stafford familiarizes his reality, makes it often subject to a "we," generalizing in that way the personal insight. The primary tones of his work are those of nostalgia, of a wry wit, often, which can make peace with the complexities of times and places. He says "that some kind of organization / is the right way to live." The danger is simply that things will become cozy ("The earth says have a place . . ."), and that each thing will be humanized to an impression of it merely. When the irony can outwit this tendency, then an active intelligence comes clear. In the following poem I am put off by the personifications of the first verse, but, in fairness, they do underline what becomes the point of the second:

FOUND IN A STORM

A storm that needed a mountain
met it where we were:
we woke up in a gale
that was reasoning with our tent,
and all the persuaded snow
streaked along, guessing the ground.

We turned from that curtain, down.
But sometime we will turn

Review of *Traveling Through the Dark,* from *Poetry* 102, no. 1 (April 1963): 42–48. Also published in *The Collected Essays of Robert Creeley.* Copyright © 1989 The Regents of the University of California.

back to the curtain and go
by plan through an unplanned storm,
disappearing into the cold,
meanings in search of a world.

STANLEY MOSS

Country Boy

When the poets have significantly recreated a country, that country may be said to have a culture. It was in this context that Valéry replied to his own question, "Who is the greatest French poet?" by answering, "France." America has not and will not produce a single great man of genius who speaks for all of us. (In relatively homogenous France, whoever succeeds de Gaulle to the Elysée Palace, whether of the left or of the right, will no doubt keep on the cook.) In America, our tastes and religions are too diverse, the classes too fluid, for a single poet to celebrate. The American Jerusalem is being built like the fortress-monasteries of old Spain, by artisans who contribute a single signed stone, perhaps several. Nobody builds a wall.

William Stafford comes from Hutchinson, Kansas. During high school years his family pushed west. He speaks for himself and small-town people. With irony as thin as Bible paper he takes this position:

> Mine was a Midwest home—you can keep your world.
> Plain black hats rode the thoughts that made our code.
> We sang hymns in the house; the roof was near God.

In the poem "Fifteen," Stafford recalls an incident behind the willows of his boyhood. He comes across a fallen motorcyclist. Shocked by the bruised and bleeding stranger, young Stafford helps the man back on the machine, and the motorcyclist roars away. Such intrusions are infrequent. Stafford tries to avoid encounters with the "left-handed world that other people see."

> But where I come from withdrawal is easy to forgive.

He ends this poem, saying:

Review of *The Rescued Year*, from *New Republic*, 19 November 1966, 23–24.

Forgive me these shadows I cling to, good people:
Trying to hold quiet in my prologue.
Hawks cling the barrens wherever I live.
The world says, "Dog eat dog."

You read from one "ordinary" setting to the next until suddenly
you realize that someone like the bleeding motorcyclist crashes
into almost all of Stafford's poems. And that motorcyclist is the
poet himself. Take this "simple" poem rescued in this volume
from his first unavailable collection:

OUR PEOPLE

Under the killdeer cry
our people hunted all day
greying toward winter, their lodges
thin to the north wind's edge.

Watching miles of marsh grass
take the supreme caress,
they looked out over the earth,
and the north wind felt like the truth.

Fluttering in that wind
they stood there on the world,
clenched in their own lived story
under the killdeer cry.

Stafford wants us to read the line "under the killdeer cry" twice.
Why the choice of "killdeer," the bird overhead whose very
name evokes death and states the action? Note the hunters, "our
people," are touched by the truth. The poet stands a distance
apart; the distance between "our people" and my people. The
poet himself is the casualty of the poem, the motorcyclist, the
element that doesn't fit. Rhymes, rightly, are imperceptible: cry/
day, grass/caress, earth/truth.

Stafford can be his opposite; not simple but complex, not with-
drawn, but engaged in a battle for his soul. He is closer to Faust
than to Job. Halfway into *The Rescued Year*, Stafford, who began by
writing: "Mine was a Midwest home—you can keep your world,"
writes, "Ours is a low, curst, under-swamp land," and concludes
almost sensuously, "And if we purify the pond, the lilies die."

Nature for Melville was malignant, for Frost almost indifferent. Stafford uses nature like a real son of the wheat belt: he cultivates her. Under a simple sketch from nature, one may find a complex moral study. Take the fine poem "A Human Condition." Stafford exposes the impossibility of really domesticating the human animal. He opens by saying:

> If there is a forest anywhere
> the one you live with whimpers in her
> sleep or construes a glance wrong.

I cannot imagine a European poet, or even a poet of the eastern coast of the United States using nature in such a way, as Stafford does in the final beautifully tortuous stanza:

> But there are farms—to see them in the evening
> extends your breath; you hover their hills
> with regard for a world that offers human beings
> a lavish, a deepening abode, in the evening,
> like them. These places could have been home,
> are lost to you now. They are foreign but good.
> There are these farms.

Toward the close of this extraordinary volume one comes across two companion poems: "Once Men Were Created" and "The Animal That Drank Up Sound." Here, Stafford deserts his eyes; he moves into the echoing canyons of the west and listens like a blind animal given at once the gift of deafness and perfect pitch. His language moves into a high frequency that almost hurts the ear, not because of its beat but because of sharp changes in altitude, the speed with which the reader goes back and forth between the real objects and things infinite.

> Some thought it was only morning, or water;
> a few held their ears and ran, but it just got louder.
> One hoped and flooded his head and welcomed
> every leaf and tap and the whole siren of the world.
> But they all crazed fell,
> checked and crystallized and cold.

In the course of this volume, Stafford moves from half-innocence to experience to loneliness.

ADRIANNE MARCUS

From "Five Poets"

William Stafford's new collection, *The Rescued Year*, is a decep-
tive book. On first glance it may appear somewhat colorless. It is
simple and direct. It lacks clutter. Mr. Stafford has no need of
frothy garnish, hysterical adjectives, or gimmicks. The poems
communicate. With a distinct, sure voice, Stafford takes his direc-
tion from the opening poem, "The Tulip Tree":

> Only pale by the evergreen,
> hardly distinguished by leaf or color,
> it used to slide a little pale from other trees
> and—no great effect at our house—
> it sustained what really belonged,
> but would, if severely doubted,
> disappear.

Most of the poems are direct confrontations with "The small
event." Value judgments are carefully weighed and, for the most
part, calmly asserted. The poems reestablish the valid relation-
ship between the speaker and his surroundings. As such, what
could be ground into sentimentality in the hands of a lesser poet
assumes, in Mr. Stafford's hands, a force that goes beyond the
poem. We are immediately inside and outside the poem, as in
"Vacation":

> One scene as I bow to pour her coffee:—
>
> > Three Indians in the scouring drouth
> > huddle at a grave scooped in the gravel,
> > lean to the wind as our train goes by.
> > Someone is gone.
> > There is dust on everything in Nevada.
>
> I pour the cream.

Review of *The Rescued Year*, from *Shenandoah* 18, no. 3 (Spring 1967): 82–84.

Summoned by his own uncertainties, the poet proceeds by tentative steps. There are no shouting protests of scattered rage. Instead, the poet examines a directed purpose that might qualify as a route, as in "Doubt on the Great Divide":

Better to stand in the dark of things and crash,
hark yourself, blink in the day, eat bitter bush
and look out over the world. A steadfast wire
shaking off birds into paralyzed air
crosses the country; in the sound of noon you stand
while tethers whisper out and come to their end.

Mountains that thundered promises now say something small—
wire in the wind, and snow beginning to fall.

The poems go beyond the limit of the page to a country that has its own kind of music.

Listeners, I have come far to keep it from
making a difference whether I lie or
tell the truth: if incidents of my journey
sing right for you, then my mouth can abide
this communion, or I can gnaw other bones.

("Glimpses in the Woods")

The legend repeats itself:

So, the world happens twice—
once what we see it as;
second it legends itself
deep, the way it is.

("Bi-Focal")

Mr. Stafford reasserts his balance with the land, the delicate balance that exists between writer and ecology. He learns to live by its demand, and to adapt. The poetry speaks for itself, there is no easy paraphrase:

You have to take the road seriously
even if it promises only perspective,
and listen . . .

("Prologue")

Listening is an action in these poems. It is an involvement.

As I said, this appears deceptively simple. For those interested in obscure puzzles, indirect communication, this is not their book. But for those who know simplicity and individual perception are the hardest and most elusive qualities a poet can attempt, this book will be read and reread. Its language is exact and beautiful, inviting the reader to an involvement with words and silence. Here is poetry, written with a knowledge that goes beyond mere craftsmanship. I come away richer having read *The Rescued Year.*

LAURENCE LIEBERMAN

From "The Expansional Poet:
The Return to Personality"

William Stafford's grip is always loose, his touch light—almost
feathery. Often a very good poem slips through his fingers,
slides away from him in the closing lines; and this is the risk he
takes by his unwillingness to tighten his hold to protect his
interests. If the reader feels let down, disappointed, he also senses
the poet is content to have lost the poem to save the quiet tender-
ness of the human voice weaving through it. If we read on, we
learn that a few poems end with a magic and bewitching mysti-
cism that is a perfect arrival, a blossoming and fulfillment of the
poet's voice, one of the strangest in our literature:

> So I try not to learn, disengage because reasons
> block the next needed feeling. While others
> talk, all of my tentative poems begin
> to open their eyes, wistful . . .

These intensely memorable lines are of a quality we have seen
nowhere else. All of Stafford's poems may be viewed as hopeful
voyages toward those few deeply religious moments. His best
lines don't necessarily have the ring of inevitability: rather, they
are on exactly the right wavelength, in the right tone of voice.
They could as easily have been other lines, we feel, but we know
they have been intimately listened—not worried!—into being:

> Today drinking coffee I look over the cup
> and want to have the right amount of fear,
> preferring to be saved and not, like him [his father], heroic.

Review of *The Rescued Year,* from *Yale Review* 57, no. 2 (Winter 1967): 258–71.
Also published in *Unassigned Frequencies: American Poetry in Review, 1964–1977* by
Laurence Lieberman (Urbana: University of Illinois Press, 1977), 263–71. Re-
printed by permission.

In these lines from "Parentage," there is a cautiousness, an apparent narrowing and reduction of soul response, that is deceptive. Actually, it is the fixing of a scale of thinking that will allow Stafford's deeper mind to move steadily—if carefully, safely—into the dark reality behind experience: a reality in the world and in the mind. The scale chosen may disturb the reader, since it automatically restricts itself to the limitations of a softly whispered one-man's viewing, but we are never led to doubt that Stafford has perfectly secured his most telling angle of vision. The style of seeing is usually the mover behind the poem's subject, not the reverse; and the poem becomes a way of creating a sensibility, not just discovering one already inherent in himself: a way of shaping a manner of feeling, wording inner responses and fitting them to the world. There is a religion here of the right response: the poem is praying for feelings, lines, ideas, phrases, that are true to the mind's touch:

> Reader, we are in such a story:
> all of this is trying to arrange a kind of a prayer for you.
>
> Pray for me.

Not accidentally, these lines end the book.

But it is the sequence "Following the *Markings* of Dag Hammarskjöld" that radically extends Stafford's personality outward, for the first time perhaps, by absorbing and transmitting through his own mental apparatus the mystical workings—*Markings*—of the mind of a magnificent human Other being. In most of his poems, it appears that Stafford has let himself become somewhat too rigidly, or programmatically, confined to a studiedly low-keyed temperament:

> In scenery I like flat country.
> In life I don't like much to happen.
>
> In personalities I like mild colorless people.
> And in colors I prefer gray and brown.

But as he self-mockingly reveals later in the same poem ("Passing Remark"), he also has an ungovernable weakness for his colorful opposites:

My wife, a vivid girl from the mountains,
says, "Then why did you choose me?"

Mildly I lower my brown eyes—
there are so many things admirable people
do not understand.

And it is not so much his attraction to his opposites as his greater resiliency, in recent poems, to allow himself to be sympathetically drawn into the mind of another person for whom he feels great spiritual affinity, that saves him from a protective insularity of being.

His poems to his father, some of which are re-collected in this volume from his first book *West of Your City,* demonstrate his early leanings in this direction; but his father's mind is too much an incorporated part of his own personality for the experience of identification to extend the boundaries of his immediate consciousness very much. However, merging his thought with the mind and spirit of Dag Hammarskjöld lifts him entirely out of that insular self and expands his personality as never before. I can imagine Stafford training and disciplining his mind for months— patiently quieting and muffling his mental habits of years, to prepare a fertile mental soil in which seeds wafted from the mental field of his newly adopted alter ego, Dag Hammarskjöld, firmly took root. How else can he so decisively and conclusively have expanded himself? I have to strongly differ with the critic Hazard Adams, who admonishes Stafford to adhere, fixedly, to writing poetry in a nostalgic personal mode. I agree most of his best work has been done in that mode, but that mastery is precisely the reason it is time to go beyond.

VICTOR HOWES

"Quiet as All Books"

William Stafford's allegiances are to the simple things of earth. Born and raised in Kansas, he has the feel of a locale in his metaphors, but, like the New England's Robert Frost, he has a grasp of the universe in his meanings. What he says of the explorer Sublette is true of Mr. Stafford himself, and his poems:

> You were the one who always began on the level part,
> forth on a line trued for accepted real things,
> looking across the prairies a rod of steady light.

Mr. Stafford's lines, "trued for accepted real things," are paradigms of the way local occasions generate larger connectedness. His Kansas opens on the world, or as he puts it with characteristic understatement in "Stories from Kansas":

> Carelessly the earth
> escapes, loping out from the
> timid little towns
> toward Colorado.

No more time-bound than he is bounded by space, Mr. Stafford nevertheless has a special feeling for time. He hears clocks "chip" at the long spangled seconds. "The ratchet of time" takes him "a step toward here, now, and this look back through the door that always closes." Thinking back on his sophomore class picnic, blossoming in "ribbons and watermelons," he recognizes how time has taken its "innocent swimmers" into the world they studied: "It opened its afternoons deep as a pond."

His poems are frequently sharp, cold, clear epiphanies of a past recaptured, rescued, as it were, from time. In the amber of poem after poem he preserves the memory of a western past that

Review of *Allegiances,* from *Christian Science Monitor,* 28 September 1970, 9. Reprinted by permission from *The Christian Science Monitor.* Copyright © 1970 The Christian Science Publishing Society. All rights reserved.

is part of American history. The grief of the grandfather of Crazy Horse recounts the tragedy of the plains Indians. Mr. Stafford's depiction of wise old guides like Logue who closes camp before the winter storm, "when the wolves get the mountain back," and his portrayal of the street-corner preacher who admits "Many a time it's bad . . . I've wanted to find a hole and pull the hole / in after me"—his portraits of men who endure hardships, and survive them, perpetuate the spirit of the men who built the country.

A brief review can hardly begin to rehearse the special pleasure to be found in William Stafford's sense of the otherness of animals, his delight in weathered things, his lively awareness of scene. Such a review can only suggest that, if you have been wondering where the articulate, readable poems have gone in the last third of the twentieth century, you might start with Stafford. "Quiet as all books," he invites,

> I wait, and promise
> we'll watch the night: you turn a page;
> winter misses a stride. You see
> a reason for time, for everything in the sky.
> And into your eyes I climb, on the strongest
> thread in the world, weaving the dark and the cold.

GERALD BURNS

A Book to Build On

William Stafford's reputation needs no defense; it's just that more people should know he has one. *Allegiances* is a book for the mountain cabin, to shelve beside *Robinson Crusoe, Pilgrim's Progress,* and the Bible. It's designed to be part of the furniture—there when you want it.

Even in the Vietnam sixties, when all poets were drunk on the possibility of making meaningful statements and the luxury of being listened to, the war for Stafford was never a compelling object of the imagination but, rather, a criminal distraction from the important business of being human. The waste and distress of living in the world is inescapable; our information service is now too good for us to go back to the comfy village ethic in which women belong in kitchens and blacks in woodpiles. Further, it is very hard to be a citizen now, engaging in rational discourse to persuade our fellows the way Aristotle says we should. This has consequences for poets, who have always wanted to think they wrote for everybody. What if everybody includes the disadvantaged, the culturally deprived? Can verse afford to entertain in a world bursting with sin and sorrow? The suggestion is that we sell the rare ointment and give the *money* to the poor. The temptation is to become a wholly public voice, like Sandburg, or chuck poetry and join Vista.

Stafford is three very hard things to find in America: an adult, a poet, and an adult poet—and he does a very hard thing in *Allegiances*. He drops out. He can afford to; in his case it's being a good citizen. *Traveling Through the Dark* and *The Rescued Year* are what we have come to think of as archetypal Stafford—wise, witty observations in plain, rich verse at once sustaining and confection, like a kuchen. While I wouldn't like to say that these two are a necessary preface to *Allegiances,* the new book will strike many as more like edible lichen. When I leafed through it in a shop it seemed thin. In fact the poems are very dense, I think the most deliberate I ever read. Reading them slowly is almost

Review of *Allegiances*, from *Southwest Review* 55, no. 3 (Summer 1970): 309–10.

frightening because you see how thoroughly they are *meant*. It isn't "sincerity," which is meaning what one says (and has nothing to do with art), but a trick he's developed of signaling that the act of saying is meant too.

Though Stafford's poems show up in prominent journals of opinion, *Allegiances* is beneath that level of dogfighting. Like Frost, he's more interested in griefs than grievances. Stein once said that American buildings look temporary. Our architecture makes it look as if we don't really think we'll always be here; a white wood church is as transient as a tepee. What Stafford has done since "Lake Chelan" is dig in—sit quiet and feel out what relation is possible between us and the frightening land buried under all that asphalt, and how such a peculiar people as ourselves can live together with something like dignity. To do this you have to get away from the movers ("Deerslayer's Campfire Talk"):

> Wherever I go they quote people
> who talk too much, the ones who
> do not care, just so they take the center
> and call the plans.

There are Indians all over the place in *Allegiances,* people in an organic relation to land, being destroyed by people who aren't. Geronimo is us in "The Last Day," and Crazy Horse's grandfather in "A Sound from the Earth." There are no cowboys, but there is an adult poem called "Texas—," a geographical analogue to Pound's (not so adult) coming to terms with Whitman. "Behind the Falls" and "Quiet Town" define the quality of life we endure and "The Gift" tells us what to do, or what will happen anyway (see "Note").

In terms of content, *Allegiances* is the most dangerous American book since *Walden*. In terms of art, particularly as a work to hearten other artists who wonder whether fribble and propaganda exhaust the choices, it is of inestimable value. I should say that *at least* from a writer's point of view Stafford has given us a country to write in and write about, which is to say he is for us a kind of Hesiod. To *review* an achievement that important would be an impertinence, to reward it honorable.

PAUL ZWEIG

From "The Raw and the Cooked"

As with any language which settles into a code and a set of conventions, the conversational style of the 1960s has gradually discovered its limits. All too often "honesty" has become a formula, slack rhythms a vehicle for unfocused energy, smallness of perception a form of avoidance. The enormous release which many poets experienced in the early 1960s has been replaced by mannerisms of release.

This weakening of the language is apparent in William Stafford's new book, *Someday, Maybe*. Stafford is one of the finest poets of the conversational style. His poems are limpid and controlled, with a sort of narrative plainness that recalls Robert Frost. Like Frost too, he writes out of an experience of America, in particular of the American Northwest, though rarely with the insistent localism which characterized other poets of the 1960s, who loaded their poems with folk history and picturesque placenames. For Stafford the American landscape is the embodiment of a way of seeing. It supplies a solitary vastness crossed by languages which reach from one blind place to another; not only human languages, confined to the long loops of telephone wire which appear so often in Stafford's poems, but natural languages spoken by snowflakes, by echoes, by tumbleweed. Stafford's "language of hearts" speaks across the distance which separates man from his own created objects, and from nature, as in this poem from *The Rescued Year*:

> Some catastrophes are better than others.
> Wheat under the snow lived by blizzards
> that massacred stock on Uncle George's farm.
> Only telephone poles remember the place, and the wire
> thrills a mile at a time into that intent blast
> where the wind going by fascinated whole
> millions of flakes and thousands of acres of tumbleweeds.

Review of *Someday, Maybe*. "The Raw and the Cooked" by Paul Zweig first appeared in *Partisan Review* 41, no. 4 (1974).

These connections come easily to Stafford. He perceives them with a child's immediacy, but a child who has grown older and learned to understand the irremediable quality of distance. When he is at his best, Stafford's plain style has some of the feeling of folk stories and myth: it does not need complexities of language in order to create its vision, because the vision belongs to the world the poet sees, and not to the poet himself.

These marvelous qualities are only sparsely present in *Someday, Maybe*. Instead, the simple language has become a mannerism. The transparent sense of myth or folktale has become a deliberate naïveté. There are too many lines in the book like these:

> A person mixing colors bends low
> when we walk there. "Why are you
> so intent on that bottle you are stirring?"
> And then I know: in that little bottle
> he has the sky.

and

> But many things in the world
> haven't yet happened. You help
> them by thinking and writing and acting.
> Where they begin, you greet them
> or stop them. You come along
> and sustain the new things.

This sounds like the sort of idea an adult would mistakenly invent to amuse a child. But the child would miss the point, because the images do not have the innocence of something "seen" for the first time. Although they try for that quality, they come up instead with commonplace statements and coy sentimentality. Much of *Someday, Maybe* fails in the same way. Here is another example of what I mean:

> One day Sun found a new canyon.
> It hid for miles and ran far away,
> then it went under a mountain. Now Sun
> goes over but knows it is there. And that
> is why Sun shines—it is always looking.
> Be like the sun.

The attempted myth creates no echoes here. The strained simplicity of the poem chokes it off before it can gather resonance. One need only recall Stafford's extraordinary myth poem in *The Rescued Year*, "The Animal That Drank Up Sound," to see how powerfully this mode has worked for him in the past. But in *Someday, Maybe* the ideas fall limply on the page. One has the sense of a formula being offered, instead of a perception still damp with its birth-water.

But Stafford is too good a poet to be defined by his failures, even in a book as disappointing as *Someday, Maybe*. Here and there one comes upon poems which are as quietly startling as any Stafford has written. In the end, one feels that *Someday, Maybe* represents not so much a flagging of Stafford's powers as an editorial mistake, made all too easily because the convention of simple talk lay at hand, ready to speak on when the poet himself had fallen silent. Here is one of the wholly lovely poems in the book which must be added to the number of Stafford's finest; it is entitled, "The Widow Who Taught at an Army School":

> She planted bullets in a window box,
> lead tips up like a row of buds,
> and she told the children: "Every charge
> the Indians made was a dance for their horses,
> but serious men made the Gatling gun;
> its bullets come true forever—you go
> mad from shooting the gun.
>
> "From east of the mountains, from Daylight Lake,
> morning begins," she said,
> "and it loves us all; its edge opens the field.
> Children, let's sing 'Rescue Me, Day,'
> for we are all prisoners here."
>
> There are windows like that in many schools,
> and officers with eyes like badges
> that follow a look past the window box,
> ready for a dance but mad from the gun,
> and stare out over the field.

DABNEY STUART

Someday, Maybe

Too often in American poetry the *program for* the poem gets most of what attention is paid, the poem itself little. William Stafford, however, has no program: I will honor that by using no reviewer's categories for this, the fifth of his best books, by saying only *Attend these poems.*

> Each place out of the wind has a name
> so swift it escapes your lips when you
> enter. You say it like the password God
> already knows at His altar.

Or:

> Where we live, the teakettle whistles out
> its heart. Fern arrives to
> batter the window. Every day gets lost
> in a stray sunset and little touches of air.
> Someone opens a door. It is this year.

Yes it is, and richer, more various, more possible because of these poems.

Library Journal, 1 June 1973, 1824.

LAURENCE LIEBERMAN

From "The Shocks of Normality"

The shocks of normality. Of healthiness. To be an ordinary man today. To be alive now, to spring awake in the night, what a lucky coincidence! It is the great reward, the greatest privilege of all:

> Sometimes we wake
> in the night: the millions better than we
> who had to crawl away! We borrow their
> breath, and the breath of the numberless
> who never were born.

In William Stafford's poems, the shocks of steadiness, the great stillnesses of his quiet, reserved voice—innocently surprised at its own depths of silence—are just one step, one line of verse, one breath away from registering the whole earth's shudder as our own:

> When the earth doesn't shake, when the sky
> is still, we feel something under the earth:
> a shock of steadiness. When the storm is gone,
> when the air passes, we feel our own
> shudder—the terror of having such a great
> friend, undeserved.

One of the rich, unexpected rewards of Stafford's maturity was the discovery that the many years of cultivating a bare, plain idiom capable of the widest range of expressiveness in the lowest registers of the quiet tones of language—the low-pitched key of our human voice (consider the narrow range of the bass viol, but the unearthly overtones sung by the instrument in the hands of a virtuoso performer!)—have produced a medium in which his own great calm would be a fit conductor for violent hidden

Review of *Someday, Maybe*, from *Yale Review* 63, no. 3 (Spring 1974): 453–73. Also published in *Unassigned Frequencies: American Poetry in Review, 1964–1977* by Laurence Lieberman (Urbana: University of Illinois Press, 1977), 272–83. Reprinted by permission.

movements of the earth, quaking in concert with deep temblors of the human spirit. Stafford celebrates the common bonds—the mediating site—between the earth and the single frail human vessel, astonished to find that any one of us in depths of "our stillness" can *contain* such magnitude of subterranean currents:

> We know the motions of this great friend,
> all resolved into one move, our stillness.

Stafford is inundated with the ecstasy of beautiful surging communion with the land, and he is so stubbornly committed to thinking himself an average simple person, his experience ordinary and shared by everyone, by anyone else—any reader, certainly—why, he petitions, isn't each one of us this very moment out running on the hills of night, of day, to become swept up into this love affair with our great benefactor, this marriage to our most faithful patron:

> Why is no one on the hills where they
> graze, the sun and the stars, no one
> clamoring north, running as we would
> run to belong to the earth. We come, we
> celebrate with our breath, we join on the curve
> of our street, never lost, the surge of the land
> all around us that always is ours,
> the beginning of the world and the end.

Stafford's voice is so quiet, so low-keyed, that his taciturnity may be mistaken for frailness, timidity; his humble cries for self-diminishment, or self-depreciation. Yet he makes the highest possible claims for his humanity and his art. He is a man who knows how to stand utterly alone and let the heart of the world shudder through him. In the most intimate communion between one soul and the earth, there is no friend, no companion, no beloved who can follow or accompany this pilgrim, "*Oh friends, where can one find a partner / for the long dance over the fields?*" That path is immitigably a lonely one (this is his poem "So Long" in the earlier volume *Allegiances):*

> At least at night, a streetlight
> is better than a star.
> And better good shoes on a
> long walk, than a good friend.

Often in winter with my old
cap I slip away into the gloom
like a happy fish, at home
with all I touch, at the level of love.

No one can surface till far,
far on, and all that we'll have
to love may be what's near
in the cold, even then.

This poem is aimed at the unpeopled zones of the planet. There is an arctic chill lining the verses. In this book, as in the others before it, Stafford is of two minds: a loving, generous, outgoing brother to all human fellows, dear ones and strangers alike—not accidentally, he addresses remarks in his poems to *friend,* or *stranger,* by turns; or a militiaman of the wilds, a guerrilla woodsman constantly in training to *provide, provide* for a foreseen era of extreme shortages of supplies, an age of severe poverty and drought (guess how soon, reader). On one wavelength, all the saying favors a life of giving and belonging to the human community. On the other, he would give himself up irrevocably to the wilderness:

At caves in the desert, close
to rocks, I wait. I live
by grace of shadows. In moonlight
I hear a room open behind me.

At the last when you come
I am a track in the dust.

Stafford's enduring resources of human warmth and personal intimacy are revealed in the short masterful poem, "Father and Son":

No sound—a spell—on, on out
where the wind went, our kite sent back
its thrill along the string that
sagged but sang and said, "I'm here!
I'm here!"—till broke somewhere,
gone years ago, but sailed forever clear
of earth. I hold—whatever tugs
the other end—I hold that string.

The kite metaphor skillfully mediates between the worlds of paternity and authorship. In so few lines, aptly low-keyed, undertoned, Stafford merges the two aesthetics—the siring of poems, of sons—and demonstrates with effortless grace and agility the stark interwovenness of his vision. The trick is to keep holding the string years and years after it breaks, and to keep feeling the infinitesimally faint—but invaluable—tugs from the lost kite of fatherhood through the feeble, paltry conductor of thin air. To continue to traverse that gap across a near-vacuum in the thinning filial atmosphere is a feat of mental radar, thoughts and feelings so delicately balanced and held by so light a grasp, contact with the other being—father to son, writer to reader—is maintained by subtle echo-location.

A large unwritten chapter of the book of our "Origins" is locked in the racial memory of our hands—the key site, or locus, of our body's subconscious mind passed over by Jungian psychologists:

> So long ago that we weren't people then
> our hands came upon this warm place on a rock
> inside a high cave in the North, in the wilderness.
> No light was there, but "Homeland" glowed in that dark. . . .
> Now along walls, over quilts, by locks, our hands
> retell that story. Wherever touch finds hope again,
> these hands remember that other time: they are lost;
> they hunt for a place more precious than here.
> *Who will accept us wanderers? Where is our home?*

In many new poems, Stafford explores the frontiers of the hands' powers of remembering. A friend of mine, an expert craftsman of the short story, doggedly insists on the rule of thumb—not of tongue—"I never know what I think about anything until my hand tells me." Stafford is a poet who espouses that aesthetic. His art is lavishly extemporaneous and unpremeditated. He is poetry's zealot of improvisation. Moreover, with a childlike innocence, he profoundly trusts what his hand tells him is true:

> This is the hand I dipped in the Missouri
> above Council Bluffs and found the springs.
> All through the days of my life I escort
> this hand. . . .

Summits in the Rockies received this diplomat.
Brush that concealed the lost children yielded
them to this hand. Even on the last morning
when we all tremble and lose, I will reach
carefully, eagerly through that rain, at the end—

Toward whatever is there, with this loyal hand.

Stafford's lines of verse are felt to be a perfect extension of his hand's natural moves and gestures, as exhalations of our breath are inescapably tinged with our lungs' odor. The lines charmed and escorted across the page by the maestro's conducting hand are the intensest and most irreducible expression of our human reality. They are *the authentic:*

> The authentic is a line from one thing
> along to the next . . . It holds
> together something more than the world,
> this line. And we are your wavery
> efforts at following it. Are you coming?
> Good: now it is time.

To live well in the world, to write the poem that rings true, follow the hand's right leads, the hand's wisdom. Aristotle was a great thinker because he correctly assessed the hand's sensitive intelligence. Its genius inheres in its flexibility, the instinctive rightness of its moves, not in its power—athletic or military prowess, a lesson which his student, Alexander, failed to learn (from *Allegiances*):

> Aristotle was a little man with
> eyes like a lizard. . . .
>
> He said you should put your hand out
> at the time and place of need:
> strength matters little, he said,
> nor even speed.
>
> His pupil, a king's son, died
> at an early age. That Aristotle spoke of him
> it is impossible to find—the youth was
> notorious, a conqueror, a kid with a gang,
> but even this Aristotle didn't ever say.

35

William Stafford has continued, unwaveringly, for the last thirteen years, following the publication of his first volume of poetry at age forty-six, to develop and refine one of the most delicate supersensitive recording instruments in our poetry. He has been training himself to hear and feel his way back in touch with distant places, ages, epochs. Like some stones, there are men "too quiet for these days," and a part of themselves hangs back, lingers, dreams its way to other eras, universes. But it's not bodiless imagination, pure enchanted spirit, that negotiates the leaps across thousands of years, billions of miles. It is, rather, an act of the senses, a superkeen listening, a reaching of the hand via its magical powers of touching for immanent—but deeply buried—crypts of reality hidden in the rock, the walls of a cave:

TOUCHES

Late, you can hear the stars. And beyond them
some kind of quiet other than silence, a deepness
the miles make, the way canyons
hold their miles back: you are in the earth and
it guides you; out where the sun comes
it is the precious world.
There are stones too quiet for these days,
old ones that belong in the earlier mountains.
You put a hand out in the dark of a cave and
the wall waits for your fingers. Cold, that stone
tells you all of the years that passed without knowing.
You think of caves held in the earth, no mouth,
no light. Down there the years have lost their way.
Under your hand it all steadies,
is the world under your hand.

It is the transcendent grace of the hand's gentlest touch, and of the listener's marvelously intense hearing, that achieves penetration into spheres of reality the mind cannot enter. The hand's touch can recover any lost world.

Touches. The shocks of a normal hand. In our homes and families, by common daily routines, we connect with the spirit of all that lives across the planet ("At the sink I start / a faucet; water from far is / immediate on my hand"), the whole world rescued and transmitted in each natural human gesture, and these are the events most worth publishing to a readership; the simple motions of our body's saying them at home are the true miracles, the noteworthy headlines of each day's life. The poem aspires to catch the exact uniquely marvelous twist of each never-to-be-repeated human event of watching this bird now, glimpsing the moon between buildings at a special new angle, improvising a new story to a child at bedtime, seeing the light (". . . any light. Oh—any light.") come on again in the child's eyes, or in his late father's intricately remembered words. These occurrences, then, are Stafford's alternative to what newsprint "an eighth of an inch thick" offers as world news (from *Allegiances*):

> That one great window puts forth
> its own scene, the whole world
> alive in glass. In it a war happens,
> only an eighth of an inch thick.
> Some of our friends have leaped
> through, disappeared, become unknown
> voices and rumors of crowds.
>
> In our thick house, every evening
> I turn from that world,
> and room by room I walk, to
> enjoy space. At the sink I start
> a faucet; water from far is
> immediate on my hand. I open our
> door, to check where we live.
> In the yard I pray birds,
> wind, unscheduled grass,
> that they please help to make
> everything go deep again.

Stafford chronicles *his* global highlights in the form of lean verses, messages offered to the world for minimal daily unction, so many "small acts of honesty, to use like / salt pills, one at a time, at need." Stafford always localizes himself by starting from the small indigenous happenstance whereby he feels solidly anchored and centered in his person (from *Allegiances*):

> Like a stubborn tumbleweed I hold,
> hold where I live. . . .
>
> We ordinary beings can cling to the earth and love
> where we are, sturdy for common things.

If the poem always stays within hand's-reach of pedestrian daily events, it finds its life mainly in collecting the inner resonances. How quickly and adroitly Stafford can step back from the life of action, himself the tree abruptly engulfed in fog, given over completely to the inner storm of mirrorings and reverberations ("that far flood / Inside"), without losing his grasp of the bare, plain, earthy quantities—mortal or inanimate particularities—that touched off the inner chain of correspondences (from *Allegiances*):

IN FOG

In fog a tree steps back.

Once gone, it joins those hordes
blizzards rage for over tundra.

With new respect I tell
my dreams to grant all claims;

Lavishly, my eyes close between
what they saw and that far flood

Inside: the universe that happens
deep and steadily.

Stafford's calm, mild-mannered voice dances lightfootedly, the nimble steps half-masking the scrupulous rigor of his thought and toughness of his vision. Many readers fail to grasp how much concentrated force of mind—a shrewd, energetic intelligence—is mobilized to support his mild soft-spokenness, those lines that would "breathe a harmless breath." Stafford would make his lines imitate the effortless floating ease and drift of the falling snowflake ("what snowflake, even, may try / today so calm a life, / so mild a death?"). Words and phrases, as in a dance by Fred Astaire, swish and glide and float across the page—lightest footfalls, a delicate, thin, relaxed saying that approaches a condition of pure breath, all easefulness:

This whole day is your gift:
hold it and read a leaf at a
time, never hurried, never waiting,
Step, step, slide; then turn,

> dance on the calendar,
> reach out a hand, give lavish
> as anyone ever gave—all.

The lines imitate the smooth, easy gestures of a dancer, or those
of any great musical performer whose instrument—violin, pi-
ano, cello, his own body or voice—seems to vanish, to disappear,
to melt away into the serene flow of pure, entranced rhythm.
There is a quality of relaxed arbitrariness by which Stafford laz-
ingly coaxes—or coaches—so many of his best lines and images
out of the depths of his solitude, such that the lines seem to lean
backward, half-clinging still to the lovely voiceless silence of his
frequent late-night strolls. By a most rigorous artifice, he estab-
lishes the fleetingly accidental human impulse, the feeling of this
moment, as *the* viable human occasion most tractable for grafting
into his art: he celebrates, above all, each accidental next passing
fancy, notion, hunch, guess, chance remark. He must learn to be
always on the alert, on his mental toes so to speak, to select fertile
items from the always available and swiftly unfolding agendas of
sensory and cerebral data that flicker upon the screen of his rich
imaginative life, and he proceeds with an unprecedented good
faith that the inexhaustible stockpile of such treasures of informa-
tion is readily accessible to the poetry-making process at any
moment of our waking lives, and it will be fully replenished
every next moment. Luck is a helpful catalyst which we can train
ourselves—always on the run, in the midst of flow—to seize
upon as an indispensable ally to creation, and some moments are
inherently more propitious to the creative eye than others.

We are persuaded by the sheer weight of swiftly mounting
evidence, as we move from poem to poem, that William Staf-
ford's day-to-day life is perennially aglow with constellations of
tiny momentous events, meetings, exchanges, transferrals of
mystical energies between Stafford and the world. We witness in
him a chosen person whom the world makes thousands of care-
ful moves daily to reward:

> Oh, I thought, how hard the world has tried
> with its wind, its miles, its blundering
> stumbling days, again and again, to find my hand.

To receive the many gifts, he need only restore in himself daily
the condition of availability and receptiveness.

In the Staffordian psychic Elysium, it appears that anyone

who simply cultivates the spirit of lowliness, one who trains daily the faculty of bowing down before the world's delicate beauties ("'A great event is coming, bow down.' / And I, always looking for something anyway, / always bow down"), enhances the world's power to bestow them. Stafford is not, as might appear to some, offering himself as a candidate for sainthood; speaking for the common chosenness in us all, he locates and canonizes a site in himself that is shared by all of common humanity, and perhaps this is why William Stafford, to a keener pitch than any other American contemporary, raises in his voice the accents of a statesman's speech. He would re-endow our poetry with a Frostian vernacular, a level directness of delivery of sufficient plainness to win back to the reading of verse a wide readership of unsophisticated caring humans. He is a civic manager legislating urban renewals of the heart. Stafford is our poetry's ambassador to the provinces.

RICHARD HOWARD

Someday, Maybe

In 1970, on the jacket of *Allegiances,* probably the best of his five
books written from and about

> the hard country
> no one can misjudge, where we survive
> our indulgences and mean just the earth again,

a book given over to "weaving the dark and the cold" into a
texture of losses, till the poet had "woven a parachute out of
everything broken; my scars my shield," William Stafford, in
one of his rare critical pronouncements, remarked that he was
interested in what he called "incremental progression in single
works . . . a level delivery of non-rhetorical poems." *Single
works,* I believe, because, as Stafford also moralized, in one of the
poems, "we are led *one thing at a time* through gain / to that pure
gain—all that we lose." (Italics mine.)

That is, certainly, a relation of consequence between the rejec-
tion of "rhetoric" and the refusal of cumulative structure. The
poems in all Stafford's work come at us in the register of winter,
"the great repeated lesson," and as he says of the creatures of
earth, "everything cold can teach, they learn." Cold can teach
everything except one thing—how to structure. There is no
articulation, no development in this determinedly erasing voice;
determined, I mean, to abide by the provisional and the negative:

> our work is to forget in time what if remembered might block
> that great requirement which waits on its wide wings: the
> wilderness.

So the poems accumulate but they do not *grow;* they drift like
snowflakes into a great and beautiful body of canceling work

Parnassus 2, no. 2 (Spring–Summer 1974): 213–20. Reprinted by permission of
Atheneum Publishers, an imprint of Macmillan Publishing Company, from
Alone with America: Essays on the Art of Poetry in the United States since 1950 by
Richard Howard. Copyright © 1974 by Richard Howard.

("You wake / from dreams and hear the end of things: No One, No One, No One," or again, "At the end we sense / here none of you, one of us—no one"), for Stafford is, in all of his determinations, minor. A reader confronted by two poems of his of equal merit—and there are a great many poems of equal and enormous merit—but written at different times cannot immediately say which was written first, cannot settle their chronology on the basis of the poems themselves. That is the world of minor poetry, but it is, as Stafford says, "a good world to be lost in," and if it is predictable ("we follow by going ahead of what we know is coming"), it is never assertive or greedy ("I beg of the wind: *Read my lips, forget my name*"), and over and over, instance after instance, or ecstasy after ecstasy, as we do what he says, as we "let that—the nothing, the no one, the calm night—often recur," we feel that "in what he says a giant is trying to get out."

The giant does not get out very far in Stafford's new book, *Someday, Maybe,* partly because of the minority determinations I speak of, the insistence on no more than one damned thing after another—"the authentic is a line from one thing / along to the next"—and partly because in order to achieve his remarkable effect, the effect of discursive purity untempered by social compromise, Stafford relies upon and requires the mediate, the entrapped, the contingent language: "we study how to deserve / what has already been given us. . . ." All society, in Stafford, is in the past, remembered, elegized; in the present is solitude, "a calm face against the opening world"; and in the future, only death. The allegiances are unwavering—

> I will reach
> carefully, eagerly through the rain, at the end—
> toward whatever is there with this loyal hand.

The hand is loyal to water, to sources, to the perishable clay and the imperishable changes. These poems are brief, they do not take more than a page to make their stoic observances (hence they have appeared in forty-seven periodicals), and in the wars between movement and stillness they constitute little more than a brief joust, "a sound like some rider saying / the ritual for help, a chant or a song." They do not concern themselves much with the world of culture, which is the world of memory, except to cross it out. A wonderful poem, "Ozymandias's Brother," is a rare instance, the canyon tomb making "about the right degree of assertion, holding forth / what there is, no despair": Shelley's overthrown idol summoned up and dismissed to a superior negation. These are poems of chthonic release, their weather is storm, their season winter, their time of day darkness, and Stafford reaches for no more of what he calls "his grabbed heritage" than, in a rustling, subversive breviary of estrangements, these "close reliable friends / in the earth, in the air, in the rock."

It is mistaken, then, as I have been mistaken, to call *Allegiances* a "better" book than *Someday, Maybe;* to credit one way of putting it:

> we live in that cold range now
> where the temporary earth tries
> for something greater, with the keen air's aid,
> and more, where the world perishes
> day by day in the tall winter beyond any range.

as superior, as in any way higher in aspiration or reach than any other way of putting it:

> we come, we
> celebrate with our breath, we join on the curve
> of our street, never lost, the surge of the land
> all around us that always is ours,
> the beginning of the world and the end.

For William Stafford, the important thing, the ineluctable thing, is that one poem be written in that *level delivery* of his, and then that another poem be written, that the poems keep coming, replacing each other, like leaves released from the tree at the start of winter—is the leaf that will come *better* than the life discarded? more nearly the *right leaf?* The point is all in the process, the seasonable realization until, as Stafford says in his extraordinary diction of some three hundred words, the voice never raised above the sound of one man talking to one other man at nightfall outdoors, no one word given more energy or pitched higher than any other word, no one poem enhanced by the glamors of compositional stress beyond any other poem—until

> unbound by our past we sing
> wherever we go, ready or not,
> stillness above and below, the slowed
> evening carried in prayer toward the end.

RALPH J. MILLS, JR.

Like Talk

This gathering of work from books dating back to the author's first collection in 1960 makes available in one volume the substantial achievement of a truly vigorous, independent American poet. William Stafford was born in Kansas in 1914, schooled in the Middle West, and received a doctorate from the University of Iowa; he was a conscientious objector during World War II, and held intermittent construction and oil refinery jobs before becoming a teacher in several colleges, settling at last in 1948 at Lewis and Clark in Portland, Oregon, where he has remained. In his life and in his writing he has looked constantly westward or to the northwest; only his deep ties to the past bind him to the Middle Western towns he recalls in many poems. Of the Eastern states, of our swollen urban areas, he does not write, though his work and attitudes say a good deal indirectly about contemporary modes of living that have lost touch with the earth and what it has to teach. He is a regional poet in the best, rather than the narrow sense: he uncovers and keeps alive strata of experience and knowledge that his readers are in grave danger of losing, and without which, Stafford keeps saying, they will forget how "To walk anywhere in the world, to live / now, to speak, to breathe a harmless / breath."

Stafford's poems reflect an unshakable predilection for a certain number of themes, which at his best he can explore over and over, finding something new in them or reasserting—and he is not afraid of doing so—their persistent validity or pertinence. These themes include his family, the life of small towns and their inhabitants, and—underlying and pervading everything—nature, which he sees with an extraordinarily perceptive attention to all its manifestations, habits, patterns, and minor fluctuations. For him, the best qualities of man are integral with his instinctive responsiveness to and harmony with physical

Review of *Stories That Could Be True: New and Collected Poems,* from *New York Times Book Review,* 1 January 1978, 11. Copyright © 1978 by the New York Times Company. Reprinted by permission.

surroundings: weather, seasons and landscape. "History," he writes, "is a story God is telling, / by means of hidden meanings written closely / inside the skins of things." Indians and pioneers possess this awareness in some of the poems; so does Stafford's father, whose uncanny wisdom and perceptual powers recur as a subject:

> My father could hear a little animal step,
> or a moth in the dark against the screen,
> and every far sound called the listening out
> into places where the rest of us had never been.

The son inherits this talent, discovers in it a way for reading the significance of the apparently insignificant, as in this passage from the aptly titled "Things That Happen":

> We were back of three mountains called
> "Sisters" along the Green Lakes trail
> and had crossed a ridge when that
> one little puff of air touched us,
> hardly felt at all.
>
> That was the greatest event that day;
> it righted all wrong.
> I remember it, the way the dust moved there.
> Something had come out of the ground
> and moved calmly along.
>
> No one was ahead of us, no one
> in all that moon-like land.
> Oh, I thought, how hard the world has tried
> with its wind, its miles, its blundering
> stumbling days, again and again, to find my hand.

Immediate detail, then, is always important to Stafford; but as a reader of signs and traces, of the authentic and veracious elements in existence (always against the inauthentic, the mechanistic, the facelessly bland, if only by implication), he is relentlessly a poet of memory and reminiscence. He revisits the past to bring to life again not only his mother or father, or an occasional historical figure such as Crazy Horse or Daniel Boone, but also people from his youth, his schooldays, the little towns he knew so intimately: these nearly anonymous persons he delineates with understanding and compassion, locating their singularity and dignity. He writes of the "girl in the front row who had no mother / and went home every day to get supper," or, in "Remembering Althea":

> When you came out of your house
> and put your hand on the August day,
> walls of the barn delicate in the light
> began the season that would ribbon away
> all that we saw and blow it past the world. . . .

Stafford's sense of writing and of the poem, he has indicated in some of his prose pieces, lays stress on process, on the continuous activity or gesture, rather than the intentional arrival at specific ends or products. The "slow girl in art class, / less able to say where our lessons led" of one of his poems is correspondingly the wiser; and this aesthetic attitude matches his questing attitude toward life, "hunting our own kind of deepening home." Or, as he tells us in "An Introduction to Some Poems": "The authentic is a line from one thing / along to the next." This favoring of process may perhaps account for poems that are careless or slight or awkwardly handled, and for an occasional unfinished feeling about some of them. But these lesser or unsatisfactory pieces are a small price to pay for the force of genuineness of so many fine ones. Besides, there is a conscious roughness, oddity (the word is Stafford's), dominant in the work. "It is much like talk, with some enhancement," he has said, noting his "most congenial poetry landmark" as Hardy (which seems to me right), but observing that the voice he usually hears in his poems is his mother's voice.

This volume includes the contents of five previous books, in addition to quite a few new poems. The familiar anthologized poems are here, beautiful and satisfying; but Stafford is a poet to be read in bulk, to be reread thoughtfully. Then his strengths emerge; his vision captures us; he becomes one of our indispensable poets.

WILLIAM H. PRITCHARD

From "Expressing the Difference"

Whether or not it is correct to say that William Stafford also deserves more American readers than he has at present, I note that even an intelligently managed operation like the *Norton Anthology of Modern Poetry* has no room for him, which surely doesn't help things. The appearance, then, of these new and collected poems should be an occasion to salute him as a valuable resource, though the best poems in the collection are not his newest ones but are to be found in the three volumes from the 1960s: *Traveling Through the Dark* (1962), *The Rescued Year* (1966), and *Allegiances* (1970). Like James Richardson, Mr. Stafford is an elegiac poet who has surely written the most quiet poems of any recent American. He seldom rhymes, seldom if ever depends on tight stanzaic structures to snap the reader along. One should not (I found out, going through the collected volume) read too many poems at the same sitting, else they blur into one another. The range of Stafford's voice is narrow; like Randall Jarrell, though with less variation of tone, he works with a rich vein of nostalgia, and whatever one's attitude toward that mode of feeling—mine is shamelessly sympathetic—the attractiveness of his poetry importantly depends upon it.

Consider the beginning of the title poem from *The Rescued Year:*

> Take a model of the world so big
> it is the world again, pass your hand,
> press back that area in the west where no one lived,
> the place only your mind explores. On your thumb
> that smudge becomes my ignorance, a badge
> the size of Colorado: toward that state by train
> we crossed our state like birds and lodged—
> the year my sister gracefully
> grew up—against the western boundary
> where my father had a job.

Review of *Stories That Could Be True,* from *Poetry* 132, no. 4 (July 1978): 230–38.

Time should go the way it went
that year: we weren't at war, we had
each day a treasured unimportance;
the sky existed, so did our town;
the library had books we hadn't read;
every day at school we learned and sang,
or at least hummed and walked in the hall.

Later in the poem, memory of a particular evening asserts itself:

I walked out where a girl I knew would be;
we crossed the plank over the ditch
to her house. There was popcorn on the stove,
and her mother recalled the old days, inviting me back.
When I walked home in the cold evening,
snow that blessed the wheat had roved
along the highway seeking furrows,
and all the houses had their lights—
oh, that year did not escape me: I rubbed
the wonderful old lamp of our dull town.

There was such a year in *my* dull town too, and part of the
success with which Stafford rubs the lamp in this longish (for
him) poem lies in his daring to make the verse line a little flat,
eschew "lively" effects, and try to lay out things as they hap-
pened, as if no rhetoric, no underlining or swelling were neces-
sary. I am charmed by the anticlimactic way of following (in the
first passage quoted) the line about learning and singing in school
with the casual corrective, "Or at least hummed and walked in
the hall"; or in the latter passage, as he walks home through the
drifted snow, observing only that "and all the houses had their
lights." That "had" quietly says it all, only and wholly sufficient
unto themselves.

It is true that sometimes Mr. Stafford rubs the lamp of dullness
and nothing much appears; true also that an Easterner like me may
be too ready to plug in romantic responses to "Western" leanness,
dryness, spareness. In some ways a Selected rather than Collected
Stafford would be to the point, might focus more sharply this
particular talent, as it is most sharply focussed in the wonderful
"Lake Chelan" ("They call it regional, this relevance— / the deep-
est place we have . . .") written out of deepest Stafford. Its speech
is just indirect and subtle enough to tease the reader into attention:

Suppose a person far off to whom this lake
occurs: told a problem, he might hear a word
so dark he drowns an instant, and stands dumb
for the centuries of his country and the suave
hills beyond the stranger's sight.

Is this man dumb, then, for whom Chelan lives
in the wilderness?

Yes and no, but we are asked to take seriously whatever deepest
place *we* have, and thereby effect a renewal of spirit:

Permissive as a beach, he turns inland,
harks like a fire, glances through the dark
like an animal drinking, and arrives along that line
a lake has found far back in the hills
where what comes finds a brim gravity exactly requires.

Here is a short list of Mr. Stafford's poems which will con-
tinue to be read, along with the two just mentioned: "Traveling
Through the Dark," "Elegy" (for his father), "In Dear Detail by
Ideal Light," "The Animal That Drank Up Sound," "Bess," "A
Gesture toward an Unfound Renaissance," "Observation Car
and Cigar." And "At Our Home," which is short enough to
quote in its entirety:

Home late, one lamp turned low,
crumpled pillow on the couch,
wet dishes in the sink (late snack),
in every child's room the checked,
slow, sure breath—

Suddenly in this doorway where I stand
in this house I see this place again,
this time the night as quiet, the house
as well secured, all breath but mine borne
gently on the air—

And where I stand, no one.

This seems to me exactly right, and piercing.

LAWRENCE KRAMER

From "In Quiet Language"

In a recent poem, William Stafford has his "sisters never born" address him from within the trees:

> *Brother of Air, Brother of Sun,*
> *please tell our story, that we*
> *may live in the brief wind.*

("Always")

These quiet lines hide a startling extravagance of trust in the poet and his language. The poet with whom an unrealized reality pleads is the brother of air and sun by virtue of the words with which he tells their story. The words, with the potency of The Word, give life; they bear so fully on reality that they alter it, or even contain it; and they release the "brief wind" of inspiration, the primal breath or pneuma, rather than being released by it. But the most striking thing about these lines is the quiet, calm unassertiveness with which the poetry offers its credo. Stafford's trust in his language is clearly an absolute; and as the overtones of Saint Francis in the first line suggest, the way to understand it is as an analogue to religious faith.

Such a radical faith in the power of language to implicate reality has been the religion of American poetry for at least a century. When Emerson wrote, "Bring me wine, but wine which never grew / In the belly of the grape," he was calling for a sacrament of inscription, by which he could write his "old adventures" with the "pen" of creation—the pen which "on the first day drew . . . / The dancing Pleiads and eternal men." Later poets have frequently attenuated the Prometheanism of this position, but the basic impetus has always survived; Williams's *Paterson,* for example, is composed in obedience to Emerson's demand, as it literally tries to write an eternal man who is also a city. Recently, as I have argued elsewhere,[1] the American poet's

---

Review of *Stories That Could Be True,* from *Parnassus* 6, no. 2 (Spring–Summer 1978): 101–17.

trust in language has shown itself as a "letting go" of what seem to be the recognized constraints of writing: a release of potentialities that are latent in the language one sets down. This letting go produces a text that half seems to write itself, or that can be trusted to write itself in a way that dissolves or blurs the boundaries between language and its referents. The poet's role in this process is to originate it and give it contour: to let his language speak through him, as if he were a kind of modern Ion, inspired not by divine madness but by the intrinsic sanity of the word. In the case of a poet like A. R. Ammons the act of letting go discloses an almost physical force operating between phrases, a force that corresponds to the strain between perception's effort to unify objects in nature and the objects' own tendency toward dispersal. W. S. Merwin's work shows the reverse of this process. It tries—with scant success—to let a fragmentation and attenuation of language intimate a thinning-out of the world into a plane surface with few objects and no boundaries. Another instance, perhaps the one most thoughtful and innovative, is provided by John Ashbery's uncanny ability to coax a text out of its own beginnings, to make poetic language a continual unfolding of its own implications, which gradually reveal themselves as the implications of the self. Ashbery's referents are internal rather than external, and are commonly said to be obscure; but his poems are actually marked by an extreme lucidity that appears as strangeness precisely because the shifts and dodges of subjectivity that he captures are stranger than most poets' words would know how to tell.

As Ashbery, Ammons, and Merwin show, there is no central or privileged form for the American poet's trust in language. One kind of trust, however, does seem to show itself widely, and perhaps even approximates a contemporary norm. William Stafford's volume of collected poems, *Stories That Could Be True,* develops it searchingly, as do Wendell Berry's recent volumes, *Three Memorial Poems* and *Clearing.* It also appears in Eugene Ruggles's impressive first volume, *The Lifeguard in the Snow,* and in Gerald Stern's new book, *Lucky Life.* I am tempted to call this trust quietistic, partly because it leads to a language that does not seek to transform itself, and partly because the vision that this language supports is curiously muted in its terms of desire, even when the desire itself is intense. This mode of trust, which is sometimes simply quiet and sometimes genuinely quietist, is paradoxical by nature. Quiet trust in language is an extreme trust so strong in the intrinsic hold of language on reality that the poetic language it produces is the reverse of extreme. Simple, direct, rooted in observation, this language is free to cross the borders of common discourse, but rarely finds the need to. Poetry written with a quiet trust in language invests extraordinary power in simple statement, and understands the possibilities of complex figuration as resources which need be used only in the unusual situations in which reality proves especially evasive. The language of quiet poetry works on the world not by adding to it but by selecting from it; when the language is "let go," it defines itself as much by what it declines to do as by what it does, and is in that sense ascetic. Poetry written in this mode does not try to interpret reality, much less transform it, but simply to record or inscribe it, as if fact were the sweetest dream that the poem's labor knew. The language is as neutral as it can make itself, with a neutrality like a snapshot's, its presence a frame thrown around an event; if the event is something remarkable, so should the picture be. Meaning should be implicit in the fact, not in the word:

> One thing work gives
> is the joy of not working,
> a minute here or there
> when I stand and only breathe,
> receiving the good of the air.
>
> (Berry, "Reverdure")

Language like this calls attention to itself as static in relationship to its own possibilities. It is ascetic about figures, especially about metaphor, which is a sign of special intensity in quiet poetry; and it attempts to be descriptive even as it edges away from descriptiveness, as Berry does here with his final phrase, "receiving the good of the air." Speaking generally, such quiet poetry is an attempt to heighten the language of common writing, much as earlier poetry has often been an attempt to heighten the language of common speech. The distinction is an essential one, since casual writing can assume a certain complexity without seeming unusual, which casual speech can do only to a limited degree. In the excerpt from Berry's "Reverdure," the first four lines approximate speech norms, but the last line changes the tenor of the whole passage and exchanges speech for writing as its model. Moreover, it is just this allusion to another form of writing that gives the key to the basic impetus behind quiet poetry, its reverence for reality, its modesty of creative impulse:

for quiet poems derive from the same impulse embodied in those scraps of paper one finds in old drawers or stuck in old books, which record moments of experience or insight so striking that one just had to write them down.

The quiet in the poetry of William Stafford is the product of Stafford's poetics of desire. Like many modernist poems, Stafford's center on a moment of fruition or fulfillment, but unlike its modernist counterparts, Stafford's privileged moment is neither sublime nor transcendental; nor, for the most part, is it even epiphanic. Stafford acknowledges the appeal of the "dread and wonder" of the modernist moment, and even the necessity for tasting its "far streams," but he serenely puts it aside for a change that leaves us "safe, quiet, grateful" in common reality ("Allegiances"). Stafford's desire selects a moment of felt integration with the land to which he belongs, which is the West; but the texture of the moment is like the strange silence that follows the cessation of a sound one was not conscious of hearing. Often retrospective, and rarely the apparent object of a desire projecting into the future, Stafford's "moment" combines a sense of peace or calm, a stillness, and a sense that the self's presence is permitted or acknowledged by presences external to it.

To record such moments, or the void left by their absence, Stafford has developed a language of radical "quiet," but also of great clarity, like a whisper without the hoarseness. Consider this stanza from his first volume (1960); "there" is a mountain summit:

> As we stopped there, neutral,
> standing on the Great Divide,
> alpine flora, lodgepole pine
> fluttering down on either side—
> a little tree just three feet high
> shared our space between the clouds,
> opposing all the veering winds.
> Unhurried, we went down.
>
> ("Summit")

This stanza records two simultaneous definitions of Stafford's privileged moment: first, a transfer of the plurality of significant presences in both the human and the natural worlds into a miraculous singularity, the "little tree just three feet high"; and second, a movement of the self from a position of emptiness or neutrality—being "stopped" on a threshold, the Great Divide—

to a position of assurance, in which the threshold can be crossed unhurriedly. The blending together of these definitions is the subject of the stanza: for the moment at which the self finds its neutrality passing into peace is the moment in which the little tree accepts the intrusion of human presence and opposes the winds both for itself and for the human intruders. Stafford's way of inscribing this process is to describe it as simply as possible, forbearing either to interpret it or to subject it to figuration. The stanza edges toward symbolism in several of its details—the shared space between the clouds, the tree's opposition to the veering winds—but curtails its symbolic impetus by refusing to intimate anything that might be symbolized. It is as if the poet were repaying the landscape for accepting his intrusion by refusing to intrude on it a second time. The moment on the summit was radically simple; the poem is able to recapture it because it knows how not to violate that simplicity.

Stafford's poems are not written, as a rule, wholly from within a steady quiet. More often than not, the quiet is their goal, and they find it after a wandering movement in which the language moves well outside the boundaries of ordinary writing. Usually, the quiet achieved in this way focuses itself on a singularity, like the little tree: a something or someone that the poem's language recalls but does not interpret, because interpretation would be false while mere acknowledgment is in some sense true. "Homecoming," from *The Rescued Year* (1966), is an instance of this process by which ordinary writing evolves from something more remote:

> Under my hat I custom you intricate, Ella;
> at homecoming I glance and remember your street.
> "What happened to Ella," they ask, asking too fast;
> so I fold them off, thousands of answers deep.
>
> "Nobody saw her after the war." We are driving;
> in front of the Union building we stop and get out.
> You balanced one night on that step, then leaned.
> "There's Potter's Lake." And there goes our path down straight.
>
> (1–8)

The linguistic distortions of the first stanza have two motives, which run counter to each other. From one point of view, they are an attempt to defend Ella, who is the poem's term of desire, its animating singularity—later she is said to have "brightened all our class"—from the insensitive questions of the poet's classmates, who ask "too fast" about her. By addressing the absent Ella in an intricate language, the poet can signify his difference from the others, who ask their questions conversationally, and he can also seem to justify his claim that his awareness of Ella respects the intricacy that belongs to her. But from a second perspective, the poet's difficult language is not a defense of Ella but a defense against the admission that she is gone from his life. His awareness of her, as it turns out, is not intricate at all, but extremely simple; the only concrete recollection of her that the poem records is of her balancing on the steps of the Union building. This is stated with naked simplicity, in a single line that amounts to an isolated moment of quiet: "You balanced one night on that step, then leaned." The recollection briefly restores the moment, with its precarious grace, but it also firmly sets Ella in the past tense, and betrays the inauthenticity of the poem's earlier intricacy. Having remembered Ella simply, and acknowledged her absence by doing so, the poet can no longer bury her "thousands of answers deep" from the fact of her absence, no longer insist on the primacy of interpretation (the thousands of answers) when he has been moved by the primacy of fact (the balancing and leaning).

From this point on, the poem opposes the empty simplicity of the others' questions, not by an empty complexity, but by a chastened simplicity of its own that seeks to acknowledge the void left by Ella's absence: "I shake. They sing an old song. I hunt a face" (11). In its desolate close, the poem repeats its difficult first line ironically. The poet now accuses rather than praises himself for another intricate customing—not of Ella this time but of her loss, as he goes about "passing the places, betraying them all with a wave, / adding past dates and jobs that led us apart . . . 'till I've / Lost you" (18–21). Yet this penitential reenactment of loss as complexity leads to a final acknowledgment of loss as terrible simplicity, and one that appears in the simplest possible language: "What happened to Ella?" The question has been asked, "too fast," by the others; but the poet's asking it transforms the question into an echo of genuine emptiness, because he has matured it out of a progressive simplification of both his knowledge of Ella and his language about her. Moreover, the poet's asking of this question not only transvalues it for him, but for the others, too. As the poet echoes them, the others' "yelling" voices appear as signs of unconfessed anguish: sounds to set against the silence of past time metonymized by Ella's absence, and phrases whose conventional emptiness—

"'It's been a long time'"—is, at second glance, full of painful truth.

Stafford's poetry is full of moments in which the poet is instructed by others' voices, almost always remembered voices which the poet transcribes. The act of writing the voices down combines the features of celebration and recognition; sometimes, too, of translation, because the voices often come not from persons but from nature:

> I found so misty a trail
> that all not you cried, "You!"
> like a wedding bell.
>
> ("Hunting")

These voices always draw the poet close to the center of his vision, and what they say is always quiet, in the special sense I have tried to give the word. Perhaps all of Stafford's work tries to approach this moment of transcription, even when the only "voice" it involves is his own. His poetry consummates its efforts by evoking or achieving the muted, simple statement in which the special unity that he seeks appears to speak for itself, whether to tell of its arrival or departure. The language of this unity is almost painfully plain, and the poetry accommodates it by turning away from the resources of figuration—suppressing, renouncing, or muting them, as the poem's language becomes the language of its object. At its most extreme, the poem's opening into this quiet mode, this writing down of the voice of something other, turns to a genuine quietism, in which the poet's self is absorbed or dispelled:

> These places could have been home,
> are lost to you now. They are foreign but good.
> There are these farms.
>
> ("A Human Condition")

> Staccato silences
> measure out the hours: "Where does the wind
> end?" "What can the rain give?"
>
> ("Room ooo")

Stafford's achievement in his chosen domain is distinctive. It is good to have his collection. A poet who insists on listening as much as "speaking," who writes down the speech of the real, is worth attending to. Yet there are serious limits here as well. Stafford's eloquent simplicities are not immune from sententiousness and sentimentality, and when his modulations into quiet are ineffective, they appear as an evasive way to find closure for the complexities his poems have wandered into. More serious than these occasional falterings, however, is the problem inherent in Stafford's very virtue: the passivity of self implied by his quietism. With few and rather splendid exceptions ("Earth Dweller," for instance), Stafford's poetry refuses the risks of high intensity, of powerful demand and powerful disappointment. Fear in him rarely becomes terror; loss shrinks from grief to nostalgia; and privileged moments are rewarding rather than exalting, soothing rather than exacting. Ultimately, the self in Stafford's work is just too small—too willing to rest in the given, too wary of desire and inner turbulence; and this makes his various submissions to otherness less significant than they should be, wonderful as many of them are. The self, perhaps, is a surplus commodity in American poetry, from Whitman and Dickinson on down, but Stafford's attempt to modulate its claims denies its energies instead of restructuring them. Even so, this is the kind of demurral that can only be made against a poet whose vision is moving enough and persuasive enough to be troubling; and Stafford is certainly that.

NOTE

1. Lawrence Kramer, "The Wodwo Watches the Water-Clock," *Contemporary Literature* 18, no. 3 (1977): 319–42.

G. E. MURRAY

From "Poets on Poetry"

William Stafford's *Writing the Australian Crawl,* for one, is the
first volume in a University of Michigan Press series designed to
articulate the views of prominent poets on the writer's vocation.
As such, Stafford in his inaugural work gathers together articles,
lectures, addresses and interviews on matters of poetic inspira-
tion, composition, technique and purpose. Now this brand of
book is not unusual. It is a relatively contemporary practice for
writers, in effect, "to clean out their desks" by assembling odds
and ends of their works, superimposing an order of sorts, and
giving it a catchy title. The result is an instant book. To some
extent, this is the pattern Stafford follows. However, what distin-
guishes *Writing the Australian Crawl* is the engaging, emerging
profile of Stafford as creator and personality.

Ever since his 1963 National Book Award collection, *Traveling
Through the Dark,* Stafford generally has been appreciated as a
plain talking but remarkably effective and influential American
poet, one who has paradoxically fashioned a part of the main-
stream of American poetry by keeping apart from its trends and
politics. And this is the Stafford we discover in this collection of
creative position and premise.

On the basics of poetry, for example, Stafford comments: "If
you analyze it away, it's gone. It would be like boiling a watch to
find out what makes it tick." And later, he notes:

> Poems don't just happen. They are luckily or stealthily related
> to a readiness within ourselves. When we read or hear them,
> we react. We aren't just supposed to react—any poem that
> asks for a dutiful response is masquerading as a poem, not
> being one. A good rule is—don't respond unless you have to.
> But when you find you do have a response—trust it. It has a
> meaning.

Review of *Writing the Australian Crawl,* from *National Forum* 60, no. 4 (Fall 1980):
50–51.

Read that passage again. This isn't cracker-barrel wisdom. Stafford is offering anyone who wants to learn their way around a poem some mighty substantial advice. In a similar vein, when asked during an interview, "When did you first realize that you wanted to become a poet?" Stafford responds with an interesting reversal of position:

> My question is "when did other people give up the idea of being a poet?" You know, when we are kids we make up things, we write, and for me the puzzle is not that some people are still writing, the real question is why did the other people stop?

This is not to suggest anything naive or fanciful about Stafford. When he admits that "for me poetry seems like a conversation that has a lot of luck in it," he is stressing the concept of poetry as a process of intuition and opportunity:

> A writer is not so much someone who has something to say as he is someone who has found a process that will bring about new things he would not have thought of if he had not started to say them. That is, he does not draw on a reservoir; instead, he engages in an activity that brings to him a whole succession of unforeseen stories, poems, essays, plays, laws, philosophies, religions.

Stafford continues:

> When I write, grammar is my enemy; the materials of my craft come at me in a succession of emergencies in which my feelings are ambivalent; I do not have any commitments, just opportunities. Not the learning of methods, not the broadening of culture, not even the preserving of civilization (there may be greater things than civilizations), but a kind of dizzying struggle with the Now-ness of experience, that is my involvement in writing.

It is this spirit of disciplined association, of struggling for imaginative opportunities, that has served this poet's work so well. Stafford has suggested that making a poem is like starting a car on ice. *Writing the Australian Crawl* provides vision into how the poet negotiates that risk. It's a book that offers valuable sustenance and direction for poets and poetry readers alike.

STEPHEN COREY

From "Lives on Leaves"

For Stafford, the minimal becomes primarily a matter of subject, and as the title of *Things That Happen Where There Aren't Any People* announces, the poet looks for simplification through a version of a most fundamental Romantic theme: uncorrupted and primitive Nature as a wellspring of wisdom and love. This is no new theme for Stafford; in fact, his insistent returns to this idea have been almost pathological. The first poem in his first book, *West of Your City* (1960), concludes,

> Cocked in that land tactile as leaves
> wild things wait crouched in those valleys
> west of your city outside your lives
> in the ultimate wind, the whole land's wave.
> Come west and see; touch these leaves.

The penultimate poem in his newest volume begins,

> Try it, being still in the mountains. They wait.
> And where ferns have taken their kind of green
> stillness you learn the slow steps of daylight.

A more pragmatic Emerson might have written these lines, or a less allegorical Thoreau. But Stafford's dogged faith in the teaching power of Nature has been matched by his persistent demand for a plain-spoken poetry—even, at times, a bardic poetry—and in this respect he is more like Whitman than like any other American Romantic. While stylistic comparisons of Stafford and Whitman could not be carried very far, there are certain points in *Things That Happen* where the Gray Poet's rolling voice of the open road cannot be missed. In one poem Stafford addresses "Nobody," the Everyman of an empty landscape:

Review of *Things That Happen Where There Aren't Any People*, from *Virginia Quarterly Review* 57, no. 4 (Autumn 1981): 732–43.

> I looked far ahead
> and saw you making the tracks in the snow that
> I was walking faster and faster to fill.
> After I catch up and we travel on together
> you will no longer need to make those tracks in the snow.

The poet as wise and loving comrade—who else but Whitman? Elsewhere in the volume, in "Address to the Vacationers at Cape Lookout," we hear another of Whitman's tones, that of the earthy seer distraught by the blindness of men: "this place is too real for that blame / people pin on each other, for honor or dishonor." This is the Whitman of "The Animals" in *Song of Myself*: "They do not sweat and whine about their condition, / They do not lie awake at night and weep for their sins."

Stafford must abandon man in order to see him again. In a way Stafford's landscape is full of people but not in the usual sense. Rather the people are there as spirits invited to renew themselves at the altar of Nature. These poems are written *for* those not present *in* the poems. "An Offering," the last piece in *Things That Happen*, addresses beautifully just this notion of Nature as renewing force. Stafford begins by asserting that we have built-in protections against adversity:

> Had you noticed—a shadow
> that saves us when day stares
> too hard?—inside our eyes
> there's this shadow?

The best such protection, the finest shadow of them all, is the one cast by Nature, and this is the one Stafford offers as his final gift:

> And there is one shadow so great
> we live inside it our whole life long.
> And it is here right now.
> These poems are for that shadow.

Whitman spent his entire career rewriting a single volume of poems, and I have mentioned already the unity that Stafford's canon exhibits. Such persistency and constancy can be the marks of a major poet but can also carry dangers, and these two poets share flaws as well as strengths: recurrent ideas can become repetitive poems, and plain-speaking can become flat poetry. The first of these potential weaknesses threatens *Things That Happen* most often, and Stafford may be countering the problem of repetitiveness when he emphasizes the omnipresence of the natural world's power:

> You can't give away, or buy,
> or sell, or assign these hills—
> they hold what they always held.
>
> And it's the same all over the world—
> any tree, any rock, any hill.

But still the poet must give new words to the old ideas, and by the time we reach the title poem at mid-volume, we feel we have already been there. In short, Stafford's collection may have too much unity for its own good, so that respectable poems pale beside finer poems on the same subject.

Stafford is willing to have his language collapse at times as the price paid for building a voice virtually ungirded by poetic gestures. When this voice is clear and fresh, the result is marvelous, as when he describes glaciers in "The Early Ones":

> They carved on the rocks—these are what stay,
> hardly worn at all if sheltered, some
> broken and all of them gray, that distant
> gray that clouds have, or storms that moan
> at the coast. They carved and went away.

But there are times when freshness departs from Stafford's writing, and we are left only with the clarity of easy statements. There is a note in Stafford's natural songs which tends toward the sentimental ("little animals call / us, tiny feet whisper"), and another note which sings clichéd philosophies ("it's alive, the whole world's alive," or "sometime the truth will come").

Things That Happen has fine moments, but it shows Stafford eliminating too many of his strengths in single-minded pursuit of his vision of the natural world. Empty lands have always been his subject, but so have people, and many of his finest poems in earlier volumes have brought individuals to life with precise, loving detail. A poem late in *Things That Happen* concludes, "What disregards people does people good," but while Stafford often convinces us of this truth as we read his new collection, there are times when we would wish people back into this landscape—people who would regard us, and whom we would regard, in ways that would also do us good.

PETER STITT

From "A Remarkable Diversity"

William Stafford's new book, *A Glass Face in the Rain,* contains six introductory poems set in italic type, one standing at the beginning of each individual section and one placed at the very start of the book. The best actual introduction to the volume, however, may be found in the concluding stanza of the first "real" poem in the book, "Tuned in Late One Night":

> Now I am fading, with this ambition:
> to read with my brights full on,
> to write on a clear glass typewriter,
> to listen with sympathy,
> to speak like a child.

The passage recognizes the position of the writer—as an aging man, he is "fading," able to see his own death in the not so distant future—and indicates his desires as a poet: he wishes to confront the truth without blinking and to express it exactly as he sees it; he wishes to write beautifully, clearly; he will continue to approach the world with love, even when it errs; and he will not fear his own innocence.

James Wright once spoke of William Stafford as a natural poet, a man with a sensibility so lyrical that virtually his every utterance becomes poetry. One thing that makes writing such a spontaneous activity for Stafford is that he developed the characteristic form for his poems early in his career and has rarely strayed from it. Almost a sonnet, the typical Stafford poem is short and sounds chatty, the lines are neither precisely metered nor free; lyricism and relaxation balance one another on the page. The volume *Allegiances* does contain a few longish poems, but in general Stafford works in these short units. Indeed, his poems really do not form into sequences and, despite thematic clustering, his books remain collections of individual lyrics rather than becoming cohesive, unified structures. Because of

Review of *A Glass Face in the Rain,* from *Georgia Review* 36 (Winter 1982): 911–22.

the intimate, chatty voice in which they are spoken, Stafford's poems seem simple on a first reading; only closer attention shows the carefulness of their crafting.

A typically excellent Stafford poem, one which expresses the elegiac tone often found in the book, is "Survivor":

> Remember that party we had, the one
> we all said we'd always remember?
> No, not last year—longer ago.
> I was thinking of making a custom of going
> back there and saying the names. I'd stand
> under the streetlight; I'd imagine the rain
> that hollowed our town in an arch of silver.
> Joyce would be there, and the shadows around
> her face; a call down the street, and it would
> be all the rest at once. I would fall:
> rising out of my head like moths
> in the autumn dusk, everything we promised
> each other would whirl away. Every
> year I would do this, because I might
> forget sometime and we all be gone,
> who said that night we'd always remain.

The irony is delicate, growing out of the words *always* and *remember*. The speaker's desire is to give the party and those who attended it a kind of eternal life through the ritual he imagines. But it is clear that he has already forgotten for too long; mostly they are gone, and he is the lone survivor. The poem is beautifully lyrical, too playful to be sad, but hauntingly poignant and typically Stafford, as though written "on a clear glass typewriter."

Despite the presence of death in these poems, Stafford's gaze is not turned upon any world other than this one. His emphasis is on being, the process of life itself, as he says in "A Message from Space": "Everything that happens is the message: / you read an event and be one and wait, / like breasting a wave, all the while knowing / by living, though not knowing how to live." His outlook is, however, basically religious, morally and mystically. The moralistic appears in several poems which contemplate the apocalyptic end of the world, most likely through war (Stafford is a lifelong pacifist and was incarcerated in work camps as a conscientious objector during World War II). More prevalent is the mystical concern; many poems express a sense of something—a meaning, a sanctity—beyond and within the world we live in and see. What this is is never defined, only hinted at; the form it takes is of an instant which seems, by one avenue or another, to open into eternity, as when Stafford tells us "How to Get Back":

> By believing, you can get there—that edge
> the light-years leave behind, where no one
> living today survives. You can get there
> where the lake turns to stone and your boat
> rocks, once, then hangs tilted a long time:
> in that instant you don't want to leave,
> where talk finds truth, slides near
> and away; where music holds its moment
> forever, and then forever again.

Such epiphanic moments are common in the book and add a good deal of resonance to its thematic structure. But their truth is only a hint and a promise; Stafford never makes the mistake of trying to give solid definition to such hovering mystery.

Perhaps the weakest area of this book is called up by Stafford's desire to "speak like a child." When he discusses the creative process in interviews, Stafford customarily emphasizes how the poet must avoid becoming his own censor by cultivating too strong a critical sense of his own work. Surely this is good advice for the poet to follow as he writes, and it has obviously served Stafford well, judging from the great freedom of his own output. But one often wishes that the critical sense were stronger when it comes to the point of the poet's selecting poems to include in a book. Writing good lyrical poetry is a sophisticated undertaking; occasionally Stafford is so concerned to achieve a childlike tone that he seems to abandon poetry altogether and lapses into flatness and literality. Such is the case in a poem like "Friends," which begins: "How far friends are! They forget you, / most days. They have to, I know; but still, / it's lonely just being far and a friend." Similarly, the introductory poems to the sections in this book often have a childlike defensiveness to them, as Stafford both answers his critics and attempts to direct our reading of his work. For example, the opening lines of "A Tentative Welcome to Readers": "It is my hope that those who blame / these tentatives may find some other / reading and be supremely matched / by pieces worthy of them."

I will conclude these words on William Stafford by quoting a wonderful, though not entirely typical, poem. "Incident" has an apocalyptic tone to it, and that is familiar, but what makes it so appealing is its teasing inexplicability:

> They had this cloud they kept like a zeppelin
> tethered to a smokestack, and you couldn't see it
> but it sent out these strange little rays
> and after a while you felt funny. They had this
> man with a box. He pointed it at
> the zeppelin and it said, "Jesus!" The man
> hurried farther away and called out,
> "Hear ye, hear ye!" Then they coaxed
> the zeppelin down into the smokestack
> and they said, "We won't do that any more."
> For a long time the box kept shaking its head,
> but it finally said, "Ok, forget it." But, quietly,
> to us, it whispered, "Let's get out of here."

Some kind of allegory, I suppose, and much of the phrasing is biblical. The talking box reminds me of Stephen Crane; but as for what the whole thing may mean, I confess that I am as puzzled as John Berryman professed to be by John Crowe Ransom's "Captain Carpenter." Some poems work best this way.

MICHAEL McFEE

Just Being

Next year—Gods and Muses, Graces and Fates willing—William Stafford will quietly turn seventy. ("Quietly," for several reasons. First, writers do not always tiptoe across the threshold of a new decade: witness the Dickey-fest in Columbia this year, where "the once-wonderful Cracker poet," in Roy Blount, Jr.'s, phrase, turned sixty loudly. And then, Stafford seems to do everything— living, talking, writing—in a quiet manner. This may cost him the attention of those readers who, like scavenging crows, are attracted only by shiny or sensational things; however, as one of his poems ends, "'No harm in being quiet,' // My mother said: 'That's the sound that finally wins.'"") And it's about time to ask: is there a more exemplary poet among us?

Of the living, active poets born in the decade or so before World War I, Robert Penn Warren is probably considered king of the Parnassian hill. He certainly has a more varied bibliography than Stafford, if that counts as an example of anything. And he gets better press: people call him things like "America's dean of letters and, in all but name, poet laureate." For all I know, such talk may embarrass Mr. Warren, but his poetry encourages it. Or rather his Poetry, to give it its proper case. From the aerie of his nearly eighty years, Warren has been filling the twilight air with flocks of melodramatic poems, addressing Time and History and Eternity with bardic abandon. His performance has won many admirers, whether genuine or grudging: he can feather his nest with dozens of distinguished awards, and probably count scores of inferior imitators. It has also roused a few detractors. One of the latter, Donald Hall, characterizes Warren's recent style as "cliché and abstraction salted with violence."

Meanwhile, back at the rainy ranch in Oregon, far from East Coast litcrit popularity contests, William Stafford has produced a stream of steady lyrics. There is no stylish violence about them: they are calm, alert, ruminative poems, spoken sotto voce. They

Review of *A Glass Face in the Rain,* from *Carolina Quarterly* 35 (Spring 1983): 88–91.

may address so-called clichés and abstractions, like "love" or "truth," but in a self-effacing, unegotistical fashion: their method is exploratory, not declamatory. Stafford knows his place in the order of things, knows his "Vocation," in the title of an early poem, whose last line summarizes his entire enterprise: "Your job is to find out what the world is trying to be." Or to quote a more recent poem, "A Message from Space":

> Everything that happens is the message:
> you read an event and be one and wait,
> like breasting a wave, all the while knowing
> by living, though not knowing how to live.
>
> Or workers build an antenna—a dish
> aimed at stars—and they themselves are its message,
> crawling in and out, being worlds that loom,
> *dot-dash,* and sirens, and sustaining beams.
>
> And sometimes no one is calling but we turn up
> eye and ear—suddenly we fall into
> sound before it begins, the breathing
> so still it waits there under the breath—
>
> And then the green of leaves calls out, hills
> where they wait or turn, clouds in their frenzied
> stillness unfolding their careful words:
> "Everything counts. The message is the world."

The mind behind this poem is profoundly unpretentious and patient. (Describing a roadside flower, Stafford says, "It had what I always / admire—patience, and the one great / virtue, being only itself." And still elsewhere: "To be a world like this— you learn only / the one clear lesson, 'How It Is.'") Likewise, the style is unobtrusive, bending with the world and its message, plain yet evasive. Like most of Stafford's poems, "A Message from Space" is attentive, accepting, curious: it is easy, hearing such a level voice for the first time, to ignore the fine volume of such phrasing as "we turn up / eye and ear." These antennae don't miss much.

The space message is one of nearly a hundred in Stafford's latest book, *A Glass Face in the Rain.* Like his other volumes, the new one marks no surprising or gratuitous shift in direction for Stafford's poetry: it simply continues the conversation left off in

Stories That Could Be True: New and Collected Poems five years before. Stafford can be startling, but in ways indigenous to the poetry and the world, not by importing a sensational new mask to wear. Some people, regarding Stafford's single-minded if prolific lyricism, might find a redundant monotony where others see constancy and fidelity. And some people, with a glance toward Warren's generic diversity, might mark this characteristic as evidence of Stafford's limitations and file him under "minor poet." But Stafford, a man disdainful of literary posterity, would probably only shrug and point to "that one / open, great, real thing—the world's gift: day." Besides, there are stories enough in his imaginative treatment of fact, as in "Fiction":

> We would get a map of our farm as big
> as our farm, and unroll the heavy paper
> over the fields, with encouraging things
> written here and there—"tomatoes," "corn,"
> "creek." Then in the morning we would
> stick our heads through and sing, "Barn, be cleaned."
> "Plow, turn over the south forty!"
> But while our words were going out
> on the paper, here would come rumpling
> along under the map Old Barney,
> just on the ground—he couldn't even
> read—going out to slop the hogs.

The farm is probably that of his Kansas childhood, playfully translated. *A Glass Face in the Rain* contributes more details to the map of Stafford's midwestern poems, which are (by turns and all at once) comic, grieving, bitter, nostalgic, philosophic, and matter-of-fact. He has said that the voice he hears most clearly in his poems is his mother's, unassertive yet tenacious, "an attitude of not being impressed by the sort of stance or posture that most people take." (From an interview, "Dreams to Have," in a quite interesting book of prose pieces, *Writing the Australian Crawl: Views on the Writer's Vocation,* published by the University of Michigan Press in their Poets on Poetry series.) This points to an edge in Stafford's work—besides the technical edge: he began as a poet proficient in traditional form, and can still cut a subtle quatrain or sonnet in *A Glass Face in the Rain*—that many people miss. True, his poems are generally peaceful and welcoming to the world's influence; but the messages they send are not naively affirmative. There is a threatening darkness within him, surrounding him: throughout his work he returns to the verge of an abyss, sometimes apocalyptic, sometimes psychological, sometimes (and most awfully) only natural. "Suppose this happens," a poem ends: "The world looks / tame, but might go wild, any time."

And there is, not so far ahead, the shadow of death. But Stafford doesn't see the need to put on airs. "Friends, Farewell," he writes:

> After the chores are done I tune
> and strum. Nobody hears, nobody cares,
> and the stars go on.
>
> Now that I've told you this, maybe
> I've been all wrong—so faint a life,
> and so little done.
>
> But I want you to be easy after
> I'm gone: nobody hear, nobody care,
> and the stars go on.

"Now I am fading, with this ambition," he concludes the book's first poem: "to listen with sympathy, / to speak like a child." These are difficult qualities to achieve and appreciate. Stafford's childlike primal sympathy is embodied in the words precious to him: *friends, world, life, home, now.* His no-nonsensical mother survives in the bitter wind and the dark, in conditional words like *maybe* and *sometimes.* There is a subtle and fruitful tension here, one that has sustained a large body of work. As with any poet in the prolific mode—like his fellow surveyor of local color, A. R. Ammons, for example—there will be weak spots in the substantial harvest of poems. But for them, that risk is an essential part of the husbandry, part of their allegiance to the wor(l)d. All they can do is offer "Glimpses":

> A morning cloud throws a shadow but the sun
> says light. Our time goes on, a spider
> spins, the wind examines the ground
> for clues—just being is a big enough job,
> no time for anything else.

Is there a more exemplary poet among us? I don't think so. One doesn't have to choose between Stafford and Warren, of course: those are false alternatives. But they are useful extremes.

Warren, with his novelistic flair, constantly and self-consciously dramatizes the relationship between himself and the world. Stafford rocks back on his haunches and lets the world come to him, wrestling with it not for mastery but merely for understanding. Warren paints huge, operatic, highly charged Frederic Church landscapes; Stafford fills sketchbooks with hundreds of water-color studies, remarkable in their uninsistent vision, but never bothering to work them up into a sublime canvas. As at his readings, he interposes no apparent intellectual veils between himself and the poem, or between his poem and the reader or hearer: no time for those games, "just being is a big enough job," the one great virtue. That is the example of Stafford, that feeling of integration. It is the exception in our fragmented century, where disintegration has been exemplary, or at least fashionable; and so we may be uncomfortable with it, imagine it soft or somehow unsubstantial. But that prejudice is our fault, not his. Stafford tries to admit the problems as well as the possibilities, in his attempt to integrate "everything that happens," the harsh dark with the radiance:

WITH NEIGHBORS ONE AFTERNOON

Someone said, stirring their tea, "I would
come home any time just for this,
to look out the clear backyard air
and then into the cup."

You could see the tiniest pattern of bark on the trees
and every slight angle of color change
in the sunshine—millions of miles of gold light
lavished on people like us.

You could put out your hand and feel the rush of years
rounding your life into these days of ours.
From somewhere a leaf came gliding slowly down
and rested on the lawn.

Remember that scene?—inside it you folded the last
of your jealousy and hate, and all those deeds so hard
to forget. Absolution: swish!—you took
the past into your mouth,

And swallowed it, warm, thin, bitter, and good.

From *"News from the Glacier* and *A Glass Face in the Rain"*

Both Haines and Stafford are poets of minimums, men so astounded by the stuff of existence they want to strip it bare. What really matters? What is really bone? And how shall we bear the answers? They take nothing for granted, but start with their own long stares. No pretending that the *I* is a detached observer or persona. No need nor desire to shelter under historical or current fashions. Both believe that a poet's business is to finger truth and that a poem is his tool, his record, and his telegram. Both report their findings by means of understatement.

To achieve the effect of rhetoric while seeming not to use any is a risk, especially in an age when "communication" means a thick layer of lanolin: the comfort of hearing the expected in the expected way, even if the expected is a horror. Those who don't really want to be alerted and who are already numb to hyperbole and other conspicuous rhetoric don't always notice understatement. Perhaps the most difficult achievement common to *A Glass Face in the Rain* and *News from the Glacier* is that they both make us listen to apparent silence. These books represent their authors' mature work. Both Haines and Stafford are in their sixties and published their first books of poems in the 1960s. Both have written in the same distinctly individual voices in all their books, so that one does not look for experiments and departures in these new volumes, but for increasing ease and flexibility and further resolution of continuing concerns. We also look with dread for a falling off, a discovery that the pressure of public recognition may have forced a tired poet to write the same thing more weakly. But in the work of Haines and Stafford that hasn't happened. The new poems move in the same directions, but they move farther along and they strengthen.

Time now to differentiate, for these two poets report different visions and meet the risk of understatement in different ways.

Field 28 (Spring 1983): 69–76.

Haines is a solemn man—strong, alone, sometimes gentle, often bitter or sardonic, essentially sad. Stafford is simultaneously sober and playful, cynical and celebrative, angry and blissful, sure and hesitant. Haines makes his statement as directly as possible; Stafford is devious. Haines asserts; Stafford seems to assert, but really invites. . . .

Like Haines, Stafford accepts the bare, geological limits of existence. And when he stares at nuclear destruction or cosmic emptiness, he feels desolate, even despairing: "Someday your world won't last all day" ("Revelation"); "Maybe the end begins. / Maybe it has begun" ("Maybe");

> The corner never feels little enough,
> and I roll my head for the world, for its need
> and this wild, snuggling need and pain of my own.
>
> ("In a Corner")

But unlike Haines, Stafford takes great comfort in "the world" as it *is, now,* and spends his time exploring all the ambivalent relationships of any man with place, society, other individual human beings, and himself, as well as with ultimate extinction. The resulting tone is most often a simultaneous combination of wonder, joy, regret, concern, reproof, and quiet laughter. Haines's attitude is more familiar to us than Stafford's and more easily recognized. Stafford's ambivalence runs a greater risk of being misunderstood: when he makes a statement, he is sometimes accused of being sententious; when he expresses affection, of being sentimental; when he uses simple language, of being simplistic; and when he avoids ostentatious rhetoric, of being flat. The misunderstanding is caused by the fact that his chief device is a many-layered and disguised irony. Ironically, children and media-trained adults seldom recognize irony except in the form of loud sarcasm, and Stafford doesn't raise his voice.

Stafford has never shunned this risk; in *A Glass Face in the Rain* he flaunts it. In "Letting You Go" he talks to his body as if he had just died and left it—a routine matter. Night comes and then morning, he admits that he was too ambitious in life, trying to hold both moon and sun, but now he'll admit his insignificance, admit that he is "No one." This is not excessive modesty. It must be read, not as *nobody,* but *everybody.*

When you read "Yellow Cars" you may smile. A comforting trifle. You feel good. But why? That last line, "Hope lasts a long time if you're happy"? But look back at the first line: *all* the cars go by, even the yellow ones.

YELLOW CARS

Some of the cars are yellow, that go
by. Those you look at, so glimmering
when light glances at their passing. Think
of that hope: "Someone will
like me, maybe." The tan ones
don't care, the blue have made
a mistake, the white haven't tried.
But the yellow—you turn your head:
hope lasts a long time if you're happy.

"There Is Blindness" is especially tricky. In the first stanza, either blindness or vision can create victims; in the second, both those who give or receive anger deserve and don't deserve it; in the third, near and present pain is no more real than future pain, which looks, at a distance, like comfort; and in the last line, "the world" is offered as future comfort. "There's the world," but the line must also be read as saying that the world is already here, that the blindness that thinks it is vision and pities the blind is the world's permanent condition:

THERE IS BLINDNESS

There is blindness; there is
vision: accepting the symptoms
is not helping the victim.

Brought close and loud, faces
remind you—you deserve anger,
even their anger:

Pain is real.
But over their shoulders
there looms real home—

There's the world.

I'm afraid that the hasty reader will like or dislike this book strongly, but for the wrong reasons. Those who are willing to read the poems slowly and often and in different moods will find them much more mysterious, uncertain, and "dark" than they at first appear.

This use of often bitter ironies disguised as harmless, comforting platitudes has been Stafford's method since his first books. He just tightens it, I think, in this one. In the title poem of *Traveling Through the Dark,* when he pushes the dead doe into the ravine, he says, "I thought hard for us all, my only swerving," leaving open whether that means swerving toward or away from accepted notions of right. In the title poem of *Allegiances,* he says ostensibly that travel among strange ideas makes us come back "safe, quiet, grateful," realizing that we are "sturdy for common things," but the very "good" tone of those phrases and the excessive modesty of "we ordinary beings" and the fact that the strange beliefs "whine at the traveler's ears" suggest that this is the comfort of convention, perhaps even cowardice, and that Stafford is not wholly endorsing it. In "A Story That Could Be True" the "You" (one's self) has to believe he's a changeling, really a king, in order to face the world, and he wonders why others seem to go by calmly without that inner reassurance. Is he speaking of courage or cowardice, and who has which, the speaker or the others? Or do both have both?

The same understated irony pervades Stafford's forms. The poems tend to have the size and structure of sonnets. They set up a situation, scene, or bit of narrative, with firm concluding statements: "Your head and what you hit will sound the same" ("Revelation"); "Hope lasts a long time if you're happy" ("Yellow Cars"); "There is the World" ("There Is Blindness"); "And I say, 'No one'" ("Letting You Go"). Some of the poems are actual sonnets with slight variations: "In a Corner" is fourteen iambic pentameter lines, divided into two stanzas, the first of which introduces and the second of which resolves, though it lacks the sonnet rhyme scheme. "Letting You Go" is in four quatrains and a couplet, with an octave/sestet thought structure. "Our Kind" is three five-line stanzas with the conclusion in a closing couplet. "Torque" and "A Course in Creative Writing" are each three quatrains with a single-sentence, single-line conclusion. Many other poems have the same basic structure in fifteen lines or twelve. The rhythms are also sonnet-like. Many of the syntactical units are iambic pentameter lines disguised by appearing as parts of two consecutive lines: ". . . They accept each other / as they fly or crawl . . ." ("Not Very Loud"); ". . . Once we heard / someone stumbling and crying: . . ." ("Our Cave"). He sedulously avoids the appearance of metrics, the conscious expectation of regularity. A pentameter line will be followed by a tetrameter one. A line that could be read as if it were in one meter could as well be read in another, and the ends of sentences come as often in the middles of lines as at the ends. Stafford's sound repetitions have the same ghostly resemblance to conventional prosody: slant rhymes determined by emotional emphases, rather than schemes, and occurring between interior words and those at the ends of lines. Stafford has always appeared to be talking to his readers, reflectively but spontaneously. When I have heard him introduce poems during his readings, I could not tell without the book in my lap where the introductions ended and the poems began.

The same difference in temperament that makes Haines use understatement directly and Stafford ironically accounts for the fundamental difference between their "visions" which has pervaded all their books and intensifies in these. Haines examines the physical evidence, finds it conclusive, and braces himself. Stafford examines it too and finds it disturbing, comforting, and inconclusive. There is more that he can't get at or only in glimpses or blurred. Intuition, ecstasy, and hunch offer evidence that just may be more important than geology. As Haines, certain, braces himself on the edge, Stafford, cautious, crouching, inches off, sniff by sniff:

KNOWING

To know the other world you turn
your hand the way a bird finds angles
of the wind: what the wing feels
pours off your hand. Things invisible
come true, and you can tell. But are
there shy realities we cannot prove?
Your hand can make the sign—but begs for
more than can be told: even the world
can't dive fast enough to know that other world.

R. W. FLINT

From "Feeding the Hunger
for Stories"

"Hunger for Stories" is the title of the opening poem by William Stafford in *Segues,* an attractive "correspondence in poetry" he and Marvin Bell carried on for two years and fifty-two pages. A *segue* is defined in my dictionary as "an uninterrupted transition made between one musical section or composition and another" and "performed in the manner or style of the preceding section." The two poets met at the Midnight Sun Writers' Conference in Fairbanks, Alaska, in 1979 and decided, as Mr. Stafford puts it, on a game of "annie-over with poems. . . . Twenty-two poems apiece, loosely linked, growing out of each other."

It might have been a bust, but thanks to the senior partner's authority as man and artist it worked out extremely well. Mr. Stafford is not a poet to fool with or one to whom it is possible to condescend at close quarters. His justly famous simplicities of style and thought are not in the least deceptive or designed to hide coded messages for initiates. If any poet of the last three decades has meant exactly what he has said from line to line, it is he. In *Segues* the poem called "Losers" is an unabashed embrace of the whole category; in "Accepting What Comes," "Nothing Special," and "Hunting What Is," the same confident directness obtains. One could call it a supreme kind of honesty and not be wrong; still, the term seems slightly off the beat of his deeply considered, greatly coherent, accomplished, self-aware writing. Mr. Stafford is wilier than the wiliest fox, raccoon or other wild creature that makes tracks through his poems.

So plain an art may not be to every taste, but no art so plain has been less encumbered with mannerism or the rhetorical tricks that disfigured a lot of Western populism during the 1930s. With his powers intact, and assured of an abundant store of themes on which to play variations or from which, in the poet's

Review of *Segues,* from *New York Times Book Review,* 8 April 1984, 14. Copyright © 1984 by The New York Times Company. Reprinted by permission.

words, to "take off sideways," Mr. Stafford is our current king of the West. No brag or bluster, no cowboy crooning, no mountaintop metaphysicalities, just the absorbing actuality of many (mostly small) towns that somehow become one town, or of modest colleges and people whose lives are more real than any critic's surreptitious description could suggest.

JOSEPH PARISI

Segues: A Correspondence in Poetry

Many, and several of the finest, poems in the language are in answer to earlier poems; and like their forebears, contemporary poets continue to circulate manuscripts among their peers. Combining the two ancient and honorable customs, veteran practitioners Stafford and Bell have produced an alternating sequence of twenty-two poems apiece, which reflect, play off of, and pursue ideas, images, and individual preoccupations as the series progresses. Through the mail, the poets played "annie over," as Stafford says, anticipating and enjoying a correspondence that provoked each poet into further explorations. Like jazz improvisations, these poems delight with cunning combinations of the expected and unexpected, as the adaptable format provides continuity while allowing associations to work variations on both figures and forms. Reading the poets' mail, the reader can enjoy the byplay, while coming to appreciate the vagaries of the creative process. An unusual and intriguing experiment.

Booklist, 15 November 1983, 466.

From "The Poetry of Realism"

William Stafford is a lucky writer indeed. For more years than many of us have lived, he has, with relentless regularity, been turning out large numbers of surprisingly good poems. So many have there been, in fact, that he has found it necessary to keep not one but two segments of the book publishing industry busy at once. At the same time as Harper and Row has been issuing Stafford's major volumes, the ones he is best known for, a variety of small presses has been turning out limited editions composed entirely of poems not appearing in the more commercial books. The best of these poems have now been gathered into the selected volume *Smoke's Way*, issued by Graywolf Press. It is doubly appropriate that Graywolf should be the publisher of this selection; not only do they produce an unusually handsome book, but they are themselves tending away from the limited editions that have been their forte toward widely distributed books meant to compete with the products of the New York publishers.

In a typical poem, Stafford is likely to be moving in two directions at once—toward the particular, the minute, the concrete, on the one hand; toward the general, the suggestive, the abstract, on the other. Another tension is usually present, as well—that which exists when the folksy, almost the sentimental, impulse finds itself contending with something more searching and speculative. All of these elements are present in "Maybe Alone on My Bike," one of the best poems in this volume:

> I listen, and the mountain lakes
> hear snowflakes come on those winter wings
> only the owls are awake to see,
> their radar gaze and furred ears
> alert. In that stillness a meaning shakes;

Review of *Smoke's Way*, from *Poetry* 144, no. 4 (July 1984): 231–37.

And I have thought (maybe alone
on my bike, quaintly on a cold
evening pedaling home) think!—
the splendor of our life, its current unknown
as those mountains, the scene no one sees.

Oh citizens of our great amnesty:
we might have died. We live. Marvels
coast by, great veers and swoops of air
so bright the lamps waver in tears,
and I hear in the chain a chuckle I like to hear.

Because of the "aw shucks" tone of voice adopted by the speaker, this is a deceptive poem—when little Bill Stafford hears in his bike chain a sound seeming to prove the underlying goodness of the universe, we find ourselves on the verge of that folksy sentimentality which I mentioned above.

The rest of the poem, however, argues convincingly against this reductive reading of it. For one thing, the speaker turns out not to be a latter-day Huck Finn after all. In the first stanza, we note, it is he who listens but the lakes which hear; in the second stanza there is a similarly interesting separation established between seeker and object when the speaker says, "I have thought . . . think!" Through the agency of the poet's creative intelligence, the speaker is able to transcend his ordinary limitations and somehow perceive things from another level, able both to participate in the larger forces of nature and to see his bike-riding self as an object separate from himself.

Such a speaker does seem capable of knowing the "meaning" which "shakes" "In that stillness," though he cunningly will only hint its truth to us. As always in Stafford's best poems, a lot more is going on beneath the folksy surface than appears to us on a first glance. This is why, I think, a Stafford poem has to be lived with through several readings; one simply has to take the time necessary to begin to hear the deeper nuances of things. Before leaving this poem, I want to point to the skillfulness of the rest of the first stanza, how Stafford goes from the notion of hearing snowflakes, to the seeing of the owl, then to its ears, which takes us back to the level of sound; for it is through the agency of sound that the poem's ultimate truth eventually comes. This is a beautiful book in every way—the quality of the poems is perfectly complemented by the quality of the physical object, the book, which is a delight to hold in one's hands.

BERT ALMON

Roving across Fields and *Smoke's Way*

Anyone who has a shelf of little magazines could probably find
enough uncollected poems by William Stafford to fill a chap-
book. The books from Harper and Row, his major publisher,
represent him without really collecting him: there are poems in
the magazines and in pamphlets and chapbooks that we wouldn't
want to do without. Keats suggested that poetry should come as
easily as leaves to a tree, and this is the case with Stafford. Two
recent books have gathered some of the leaves.

Roving across Fields is a beautifully produced book. Thom
Tammaro has assembled nineteen fugitive poems from the last
forty years and prefaced them with an interview with Stafford
that he recorded in 1976. The interview is not one of Stafford's
best, though it has some good observations. The poems are not
among the best either, but as Tammaro points out, it is interest-
ing to see that Stafford's vision and tone have remained consis-
tent over forty years. The first poem, dated 1942, is a fable about
"The Country of Thin Mountains." The people in that country
have only false mountains painted on cardboard, and they don't
care, being caught up in profit and self-importance. But one of
their mountains is real, a joke on them that the poet shares with
us. This little story could come right out of *Someday, Maybe*. It
makes its point in a way typical of Stafford's voice: not insistent,
but persistent.

A more substantial collection is gathered in another beautiful
book, *Smoke's Way*. There are more poems, and some prelimi-
nary sorting has been done by the poet, since the contents first
appeared in fourteen limited editions—and not everything in
those has been reprinted. Stafford has provided helpful section
titles and the poems are in chronological order. Hence this is a
book rather than a miscellany. I am glad to have so many elusive
booklets brought together. I remember copying out *In the Clock
of Reason* for myself in a Rare Book Room, and ordering a copy

Western American Literature 19 (February 1985): 319–20.

of *Braided Apart* (an interesting book in collaboration with his son, Kim) from a small press distributor in New Mexico.

There are no surprises in the collection—we are in Stafford's familiar world of rain, wind, cold, and sunlight—but there are plenty of happy discoveries. It is a world the poet is definitely not alienated from; it sustains him, breath by breath. The chief sacrament in Stafford's religion is the simple act of breathing: count the poems in which that act is crucial. Dark things happen, but they can be accepted with a certain grace. Stafford learns patience not from Bruce's spider but from something equally common. Here is the conclusion of "Smoke":

> I saw Smoke, slow traveler, reluctant
> but sure. Hesitant sometimes, yes,
> because that's the way things are.
>
> Smoke never doubts, though:
> some move will appear.
> Wherever you are, there is another door.

Smoke may join wind, rain, and light as one of Stafford's key symbols. Wind reminds us of the freedom of natural process, rain of its impartiality. Light is impartial too, and has its revelations to make. Smoke shows us how to live with the process. Stafford is remarkably Taoist in spirit. His mountains are not the mountains of China, however. The poems abound with western place names: Missoula, the Platte, Eagle Creek, Glass Butte. And none of the mountains is painted on cardboard. *Smoke's Way* is a valuable addition to Stafford's canon.

A. PICCIONE

You Must Revise Your Life

Stafford's book is a new treasure that "talks along in its not quite
prose way" to readers and neighbors, and anyone else. It ranges
comfortably from poems, prose-rememberings, teaching, and
the unfolding journey toward an ethically consistent life. Rilke's
mandate is invoked in the substance of this volume as well as in
the title, and Stafford's own hard-earned clarity and generosity
of spirit exemplify such awakening. This revising of one's life
involves embracing—in bright present-tense awareness and con-
stant self-measurement—whatever happens, in things and in lan-
guage. In the process of poetry as in the introspective life, Staf-
ford reminds us, the task is to integrate, patiently, the conscious
and unconscious halves of self. In "Ask Me," a poem centering
on the connections between outward events and the inward
"mysterious river," Stafford knows: "What the river says, that is
what I say." This is how the book talks, calmly, among friends.

Choice, July–August 1987, 1697.

MICHAEL HELLER

From "Owls, Monkeys and Spiders in Space"

William Stafford has often been praised for the sincerity of his work. Recently, however, some critics, aligning themselves with the deconstructionists, have implied that Mr. Stafford has not been skeptical enough of the convention of naturalness which guides so much of his work. However, a close reading of *An Oregon Message* suggests that he is not a naive naturalist but a poet somewhat suspicious of his own utterances. He is often rather wry, codgerly, yet quite willing to play with the conventions of sincerity in much the way Wallace Stevens played with being philosophical.

True, some of his subjects lend themselves too easily to over-simplification, and he is weakest when he is being significant: "On earth it is like this, a strange / gift we hold, while we look around." But there are any number of comic and deflationary poems. In "Owls at the Shakespeare Festival," the night-birds are no Minervas; they screech "Darling, Darling" to one another. Knowledge is not a fact but an illusion, Mr. Stafford tells us:

> Each time the sun goes out a world
> comes true again, for owls:
> trees flame their best color—dark.

> At Shakespeare once, in Ashland,
> when Lear cried out, two owls
> flared past the floodlights:

> On my desk I keep a feather
> for those far places thought
> fluttered when I began to know.

The reference to Lear's howl of folly flushing the owls and the skillful ambiguity of "fluttered" show Mr. Stafford at his best.

The autobiographical poems in a section titled "St. Matthew and All" are particularly affecting. The subjects—family, friends, lovers—are close to hand and Mr. Stafford's careful rendering is just and sincere, as in "To the Children at the Family Album":

> Children, events can find any face,
> and many as leaves are, a little weight
> at last will make them fall. A hand
> that reaches with love can hurt
> any dear face in the world,
> as love raked across the Civil War
> and into the face of Grandmother Ingersoll.

VERNON SHETLEY

From "Short Reviews"

William Stafford's debut as a poet occurred unusually late in his life, even considering that belated commencements are common in American poetry. Stafford therefore appeared with a style already formed, a subject already chosen, and the course of his subsequent career has been one of development and elaboration rather than transformation. *An Oregon Message* shows Stafford working in a vein that his readers will find familiar—each poem is a brief bulletin from the imaginative life of its author, simple in diction and syntax, direct in effect, but with a deep core of mystery. One detects in Stafford's voice an odd combination of mentors, Robinson Jeffers and William Carlos Williams. The keen eye for image and the laconic exactitude of Stafford's phrasing derive from Williams, but Stafford rejects Williams's machine aesthetic and joins Jeffers in his concern for the unfathomable energies of the natural world and in his deep distrust of the supposed benefits that civilization has conferred on man. The energies of Stafford's style reside just in this unlikely combination of precise form and ineffable content; the poems present a deeply inward burden of feeling in a language devised to communicate immediacy of perception.

Stafford's poems inhabit a world very like our own, yet cleansed by a freshness of vision and, though orthodox religion nowhere obtrudes, saturated with a sense of spiritual potency, so that even such a banal activity as early morning jogging becomes a sort of quest through a demonized landscape. Nature, in Stafford's universe, figures as a vast otherness nevertheless magically connected to the human realm, and much of Stafford's effort is devoted to breaking through our modern alienation from the natural, pushing aside the fog of concepts to arrive at a receptivity attuned to the life of things. I instance the last section of "For People with Problems about How to Believe":

Review of *An Oregon Message,* from *Poetry* 152, no. 2 (May 1988): 98–112.

Sometimes you are walking: you begin
to know—even those things out of sight or hearing,
stones in the ground, flocks of birds
beyond the horizon. A little bit of snow
forms in the sky: you feel it furring
out there, ready; then it comes down.
A quality of attention has been given to you:
when you turn your head the whole world
leans forward. It waits there thirsting
after its names, and you speak it all out as it
comes to you; you go forward into forest leaves
holding out your hands, trusting all encounters,
telling every mile, "Take me home."

But for Stafford, as the quotation shows, the natural resides not merely in the world of nature, but also inheres within us, so that making contact with nature outside us is at the same time to make contact with that trusting and accepting element inside ourselves that is submerged in the normal course of life.

Childhood thus becomes for Stafford a privileged time; his poems of memory, clear-eyed and unsentimental but suffused with a sense of the peculiar vivacity of the world in a child's eyes, are among the best in the book. In the darker pockets of Stafford's vision dwells a Shelleyan idea of life as a pageant of damage done to the individual; in church the poet sees "Rows of children lift their faces of promise, / places where the scars will be." At times this gloomy view calls forth a demonology, a vision of unnamed manipulators whose business is that of stifling humanity. Thankfully, these forays into psychopolitics are few, and for the most part Stafford plays the role of a celebrant of recaptured innocence or remembered youth. The ballast of recollection seems a useful counterweight to Stafford's tendency to become overly elliptical or to assert rather than create mystery; poems like "Hearing the Song" and "Mother's Day" strike me as perfectly balanced in their combination of matter-of-fact reportage and an unspoken pregnancy of feeling. Though their ambitions are limited, such poems are as touching and fine as almost any on the poetic landscape today.

BEN HOWARD

From "Together and Apart"

Schools and movements come and go, but over the past three
decades the steady, demotic voice of William Stafford has deep-
ened rather than changed. It is today what it was in *West of Your
City* (1960)—a neighborly, confiding idiom, drawn from "the
big room where the plain world lives." If anything has changed
it is the temperature of Stafford's poems—their balance of hope
and fear, brightness and bleakness, richness and desolation. In his
recent collections (*A Glass Face in the Rain; An Oregon Message*),
Stafford's friendly manner has sometimes seemed incongruous
with his themes—loss, aging, mortality, survival—and with the
wintry severity of his vision. And in the present collection, Staf-
ford's ninth, that contrast is even more apparent. Thoughtful
and sometimes playful, these poems purport, through the power
of words, to "bring strangers together." Reflecting on his mid-
western boyhood, his high school classmates, and his "way of
writing," the poet offers "passwords" in the hope that they
might "link especially to some other person." But when his
thought turns to classmates who have died, to the terrors of the
nuclear age, and to "a man, / a self often shattered, and pieces /
put together again till the end," Stafford's casual tone seems
strangely at odds with his outlook. If the first evokes the warmth
of the church-basement supper, the second conjures an emo-
tional tundra.

"All I intended blew away," Stafford laments in "Young."
"The best of my roads went wrong. . . . " In "Some Words in
Place of a Wailing Wall," he finds similar outcomes in others'
lives:

> Agnes, our school beauty, sang in a rock
> band. She can't hear anymore.
> Doug, the class president, fought overseas.
> He was a hero and made lots of friends
> with money, and he got some. He's dead.

Review of *Passwords,* from *Poetry* 160, no. 1 (April 1992): 34–44.

Here, as often in these poems, Stafford places personal identities and triumphs in the long perspective, preserving their integrity but draining them of grandeur. Against the backdrop of a "sky that never made any promises anyway," a human life becomes a "stutter in the millions / of stars that pass, / a voice that lulled . . . ." Likewise the efforts of the writer, who brings "[his] little mind / to the edge of the ocean and [lets] it think," while feeling the immensity of the universe:

> When someone disturbs me I come back
> like Pascal from those infinite spaces,
> but I don't have his great reassurances
> of math following along with me; so somehow
> the world around me is even scarier.
>
> ("The Way I Write")

What fills the existential void is Stafford's evocation of the life-force and his belief in the interconnectedness of things. Countering the "great cold" is the recurrent image of breath, be it a breeze "breathing the fields / from their sleep," or the early morning breathing "a soft sound above the fire," or a mountain that "breathes / when I do, quiet, a friend beyond the world." In "Local Events," after enumerating slights, abrasions, and bad omens ("A mouth said a bad word. A foot / kicked me . . . / and a noise / came close and closer—a siren"), Stafford invokes the redemptive power of the life-force ("Air like the breath from our cellar lifted me / far where the sun was still shining"). In one of his most inveigling poems, a verse fable about discovery, the act of breathing integrates self and world:

> Long strokes of golden sunlight
> shifted over her feet and hands. She felt
> caught up and breathing in a great powerful embrace.
> A birdcall wandered forth at leisurely intervals
> from an opening on her right: "Come away, Come away."
> Never before had she let herself realize
> that she was part of the world and that it would follow
> wherever she went. She was part of its breath.
>
> ("The Day Millicent Found the World")

Elsewhere, the poet himself discovers that parts of the world— himself included—are deeply interconnected. "A candleflame in Tibet," he cryptically claims, "leans when I move."

Not everyone will be convinced by such bald assertions—or by Stafford's ingratiating style. At his least convincing, he can sound annoyingly chummy or archly naive ("Many people / are fighting each other, in the world. . . . / Birds are like that. People are like that"). For all his awareness of wildness and darkness, he can drift into a tone of cozy domesticity or amiable reassurance:

> But just when the worst bears down
> you find a pretty bubble in your soup at noon,
> and outside at work a bird says, "Hi!"
>
> ("It's All Right")

Designed to lift one's spirits, these lines have quite the opposite effect.

Yet such lapses are probably inevitable in a poet who has declared his willingness to accept "with trust and forgiveness" whatever occurs to him, and who views the act of writing as a kind of ambling exploration. Stafford's controversial "way of writing" has produced its share of ephemera, here as in his previous collections; but it has also allowed access to the "rich darkness" of the unknown and has strengthened a capacity, rare in contemporary poetry, for intuiting the miraculous. "There is a spirit abiding in everything," he suggests. And in the best of his new poems, a poet's sad wisdom fuses with a child's sense of wonder and a grown man's reverence for nature. "Willows," he reminds us, "never forget how it feels / to be young."

PART TWO   *General Essays*

JEFF GUNDY

Without Heroes, without Villains
Identity and Community in Down in
My Heart

Over William Stafford's long career, he has become well known
for an understated but persistent commitment to nonviolence in
both his life and work. Perhaps his least-known work is the early
Down in My Heart, a memoir of his days in Brethren conscien-
tious objector (CO) camps during World War II.[1] *Down in My
Heart* takes us deep into the challenges and conundrums of peace-
making, revealing both Stafford's particular philosophy of non-
violence in its formative stages and his debts to historic peace-
church philosophies and strategies. Starting from his sense of
membership in a marginalized but supportive alternative commu-
nity, Stafford explores some of the most crucial political—and
literary—questions of modern times through his treatment of
the styles, stances, risks, and rewards of efforts toward consis-
tent nonviolence.

His education slowed by the Depression, Stafford was in his
middle twenties but still a student at the University of Kansas
when World War II reached the United States. As he tells it,
"within two weeks, carrying a copy of *The Journal of John Woolman*
given me by my landlady, I was on my way to a camp for conscien-
tious objectors in Arkansas."[2] Somewhat older than the average
draftee, CO or not, he was in his early thirties by the time Breth-
ren Press published *Down in My Heart* in 1947. Although it served
as his master's thesis at the University of Kansas, and is written in
a laconic, impressionistic prose rather than the poetry for which
he became better known, the book is considerably more than
apprentice work. Unlike many first works, it is not an introspec-
tive bildungsroman; the narrative includes lightly fictionalized
versions of Stafford's own encounters, but the narrator serves
mainly as observer, only occasionally as participant. The narrative
more often focuses on group experience and its significance than
on merely personal feelings, and the overall design is to present, as

the introduction says, "a series of incidents, purposely planned to give the texture of *our* lives" (*DIMH*, 10; emphasis added).

Stafford depicts a group whose principles are constantly challenged on very human, immediate levels. Having declared themselves conscientiously opposed to fighting in a popular war, they must face the antagonism of neighbors and superiors, working with them while defusing the threat of personal hostilities that would be "a capitulation to the forces we held to be at the root of war" (*DIMH*, 9). Their stratagems vary:

> "When the mob comes," George would say, "I think we should try surprising them with a friendly reaction—take coffee and cookies out and meet them."
>
> "As for me," Larry would say, "I'll take a stout piece of stove wood, and stand behind the door, and deal out many a lumpy head—that's what they'd need."
>
> "Well, I don't know about you all," Dick would say, "but I intend to run right out of that back door and hide in the brush—'cause I don't want my death on any man's conscience." (*DIMH*, 13)

As these characters suggest, the men in the camps are hardly homogeneous and far from being saints. Each of these plans of action seems understandable and even defensible, though we might expect Larry's pacifism to go deeper than it evidently does. George's coffee-and-cookies hospitality looks forward to some aspects of the active nonviolent resistance of the civil rights and anti-Vietnam War movements to come. Yet he is also in a tradition of generous response to enemies that goes back at least to the Old Testament: "If your enemy is hungry, give him bread to eat; and if he is thirsty, give him water to drink; for you will heap coals of fire upon his head, and the Lord will reward you" (Proverbs 25:21–22, RSV). Dick's plan to hide, to avoid putting "my death on any man's conscience"—if we accept his reasoning—also involves more than the cowardice we may see at first glance. He is typical of traditional conscientious objectors of the religious, as distinct from the political, sort, whose aim has been not only to avoid doing harm to others but to stay as clear of systems and situations of violence as possible. It was, in the beginning, to avoid military service that large numbers of the historic peace churches (including Stafford's Brethren, as well as Quakers and Mennonites) migrated to the New World. Only after a considerable history of persecution, imprisonment, and struggle with civil authorities during American wars did the peace churches achieve full legal recognition of conscientious objector status and permission to do "alternative service" during World War II.[3]

Down in My Heart makes clear that such service—often in forestry service, sometimes in mental hospitals or other situations "of national importance"—was not merely an easy way out. Abruptly distanced from everything familiar, the men are not quite prisoners in the work camp but do hard physical labor in confined and penurious conditions, treated as traitors, cowards, or at best shirkers by many that they encounter. In the first chapter, several COs go to a small town near the camp on a Sunday afternoon and are drawn into a half-comical, half-threatening exchange with the townspeople. Ideas about cowardice, war, art, and poetry that rhymes or doesn't fly back and forth (the narrator has *Leaves of Grass* under his arm, and a companion has been writing a free-verse poem critical of the town). The COs manage to remain "quiet and respectful," mainly because they don't know what else to do, and the authorities finally arrive and send them back to camp, keeping their pictures, poems, and letters as "evidence." Stafford's narrator muses that "almost always the tormentor is at a loss unless he can provoke a belligerent reaction as an excuse for further pressure or violence" (*DIMH*, 20), but the chapter closes with a warning from the camp director about the difficulties their "little society within a society" faces:

> Don't think that our neighbors here in Arkansas are hicks just because they see you as spies and dangerous men. Just remember that our government is spending millions of dollars and hiring the smartest men in the country to devote themselves full time just to make everyone act that way. (*DIMH*, 22)

In the context of daily life, the task of the COs is not to "resist war" in some lofty, abstract sense. It is to work at being a distinct society within but not removed from the larger one, at living out their convictions in the face of both natural suspicion and all the propaganda resources of modern government, at building understanding and common human feeling between themselves and the officials, citizens, and others they encounter. This task—to be a witnessing, nonviolent community in but not of the world—is one that the Anabaptist ancestors of modern-day Brethren and Mennonites have been talking about since the sixteenth century, when they emerged in Switzerland and Holland as a sort of third wing of the Reformation. The first Anabaptists wanted to free Christianity from the worldly entanglements they saw in both the Catholic and Protestant churches of their day. They looked to the Sermon on the Mount, to the life of Jesus, and to the vision and practice of the early church, especially its sense of separation from earthly powers, as models of what their lives should be. And they saw the Emperor Constantine's transformation of Christianity into a state religion as having led to disastrous compromises of those models, particularly in the sanctioning of violence in the service of the state.[4]

In a peculiarly modern way, then, Anabaptists have long struggled with the questions of worldly involvement and withdrawal, of practical effectiveness versus ethical purity, that Stafford's COs encounter. His understated, subtle style itself models both the calm humility that Anabaptists have sought and the urge to find distance from the public world. The occasional passages of poetry especially model these qualities:

> Far up the canyon where the salmon leap
> and splintered sunlight nails the forest floor
> the people without houses put their feet.

> And often here below we drag a breath
> of something from the wind we missed, and steeply
> think: The place we built to live is too near death.

> (*DIMH*, 37)

The withdrawal from the world yearned for in this passage is seldom possible for the men; even their isolated camps provide no escape from the thinly veiled racism and nationalism that drove the war spirit of the time. Many episodes turn on the tensions and ironies created by unlikely conjunctions of people. On one firefighting trip, for example, three men sit at a campfire: a serviceman with a Purple Heart for killing Japanese, a Filipino prisoner sentenced to a life term for killing a Japanese man "out of season," and the narrator, "who's up because he refused to kill Japs" (*DIMH*, 53). The incident is simply recorded, in Stafford's typically laconic way. But here and elsewhere his irony serves a much different purpose than, for example, that of Robert Lowell's superficially similar poem "Memories of West Street and Lepke." Remembering his own World War II experience as "a fire-breathing Catholic CO.," Lowell recalls the jail in which he was thrown together with "a Negro boy with curlicues / of marijuana in his hair," the "fly-weight pacifist" Abramowitz, and Czar Lepke of Murder Incorporated.[5] The irony of Lowell's poem is that the murderer is the privileged one in the prison society, allowed a radio and crossed American flags on his dresser. But Lepke is merely glimpsed, described, and dismissed (in Lowell's typically caustic terms) as "flabby, bald, lobotomized"—a telling emblem of the murderous stupidity that Lowell sees suffusing American life, but an emblem only.

Stafford makes a far greater effort at sympathy for those outside his own circle; virtually every person in the book, including those most hostile to him and his position, is presented as capable of growing beyond stereotypical attitudes. Many years later he restated directly this Gandhian distinction between opponents and enemies:

> In a world like the one we face, we are an opposition; it has to be. Caught in a world center of power, we scramble for footing. But we are a loyal opposition, for our concern happens to be people, and there are no "enemies." Redemption comes with care. In our culture we can oppose but not subvert. Openness is part of our technique.[6]

Numerous incidents in *Down in My Heart* demonstrate such efforts at careful, open dealings with opposition. A small group, sent out on a trail crew with a hostile boss named Eric, runs into trouble with his abrasive, profane ways. Ken, the cook, bears the brunt of Eric's hostility and finally types out a list of conditions: he insists that Eric stop beating on plates, griping about the food, calling him "Chink," and so forth. When the other COs back Ken, Eric berates them for a while, then says he'll cook himself. The others do not accept this "settlement," however, and convince Eric to look carefully at Ken's statement, working at each part of it through "a reading, a pondering, a group decision" (*DIMH,* 35). By the district ranger's visit two days later, Eric reports that everything is "just fine": "He looked around at the society he lived in at Anapamu Creek. 'I was off my feed for a while, but going good again. . . . How's everything with you?'"

Not every situation in the book is so neatly resolved, and not only the Erics of this book find themselves changing. With a few exceptions, Stafford's COs have little of the smugness of those convinced of their own righteousness. Their intense study and discussion during the sparse time off work are repeatedly mentioned, as is their interest in the inner life and mystical experi-

ence: "Our thoughts in those wartimes were peculiarly suscepti-
ble to Ken's kind of [mystical] philosophy, for we met continual
frustration; and every magazine, newspaper, movie, or stranger
was a challenge to convictions that were our personal, inner
creations" (*DIMH*, 37). Spurred by this interest, some of the
men spend a week-long furlough at a retreat center in California
led by Gerald Heard. Heard, almost unknown today, was some-
thing of a mid-century forerunner of Alan Watts; Stafford de-
scribes him as a member of a "flourishing California group of
mystics" including Allan Hunter and Aldous Huxley. His many
books include meditations on the Lord's Prayer and the Beati-
tudes, mystery novels, and a number of works of the sort of *The
Human Venture*, an attempt to render "the inward story of man's
understanding and ordering of his own life" and to offer an
integrated understanding of life by drawing on Western, Chi-
nese, and Indian religions (xi).[7]

Heard serves as mentor for the group, and for the narrator in
particular, who remarks that his own attempts at meditation
were unremarkable but that he made up for it by jotting down
some of Heard's key phrases: "illumined spirit, inwardly profit-
able, the way of wonder, alert passivity, anonymous memories,
the love offensive, divine incarnation. . . . Suddenly everything
is lit with a terrifying heightening of significance" (*DIMH*, 45).
These phrases, I think, will sound familiar to anyone who
knows Stafford's work and suggest that a deeper investigation
of his links to Heard's thought than I can provide here would
be worthwhile.

A particularly crucial idea comes in response to a man who
asks how he might prove that he is not merely cowardly or
dumb for refusing to fight:

"Do not attempt to do so," said Gerald Heard. "We are each
of us fallible, cowardly, and dumb. We can say, as great men
have said before, 'Yes, it is true, I am a frail vessel in which to
transport the truth; but I cannot unsee what I see. . . . ' "
(*DIMH*, 45)

This simultaneous insistence on personal humility and steady re-
fusal to "unsee what I see" becomes a central theme of Stafford's
work. In practice its apparent simplicity demands a constant, sub-
tle process of negotiations and decisions: the commitment to rigor-
ous nonviolence leads toward just the sort of confrontations that
break relationships, while the commitment to maintaining dia-

logue can all too easily lead to compromise and mere accommodation. And in less political terms, it connects directly to Stafford's famed hospitality and generosity as a teacher, and his openness to a wide range of influences in his writing; when I interviewed him in 1988, he talked in almost the same breath of his unstinting admiration for both Nietzsche and Cardinal Newman.[8] For all this tolerance, and his oft-repeated willingness to accept whatever impulses or ideas occur in the process of writing, there is a countervailing steadiness running through all that he has written; I would suggest that one of the origins of that steadiness is here, in his experience at maintaining an unpopular position without surrendering to mere alienation.

In the last chapters of Down in My Heart, these issues are explored through the mounting tension between the narrator's efforts to pursue a middle course and the more radical and uncompromising position of the character named George. George is unmoved by the celebrations at war's end, unable to forget the injustice and oppression that remain. He asks, "How can we join in the celebration of the atomic bomb?" (DIMH, 81) and insists, "We've got to stay out to be consistent—no nationally advertised brands for us—of toothpaste, or soap, or salvation" (DIMH, 82).

The narrator feels the force of George's alienated vision, sees with him the hapless, materialistic citizens in their unreflective festivities. The men go back to camp after the celebration in a sort of limbo, still bound to their segregated camp, feeling "more foreigners than ever" (DIMH, 85). George soon leaves the camp illegally, having decided "You've got to draw the line against conscription—complete refusal to take orders" (DIMH, 90). We are told he "had found the exhilaration of making a complete decision that ended uncertainty and the need of making other decisions" (DIMH, 90). But while such absolutes also appeal to Stafford's narrator, he cannot accept George's once-for-all decision as either practical or right; as he says, "I want to change others, not alienate them." The book ends with the narrator visiting George as he lies, silent and unresponsive, in a prison hospital bed where he is on a hunger strike. "I'll keep on saying those things we learned," the narrator promises:

incidents without heroes and without villains, and with no more than a hint of that sound we heard during those war years, a memory of our country, a peace we looked for down in our hearts and all around us. (DIMH, 95)

What he and George have learned are quite different things. Yet while Stafford himself clearly has chosen the narrator's path, his narrator also grows restive at being kept in the camp rather than freed to begin the real work of peacemaking. He also feels his isolation from mainstream life, even while he is immersed in it, and the cost of the stance he has taken:

No one is watching you. You are the person beside the aisle. People who wave are waving at another person, someone behind you. On the street no one calls your name; but in spite of not talking to anyone you are learning everyone's language— more than ever before. You are going to a big school, with halls that go everywhere. It costs everything you have to attend it. Its books are all over the world. (*DIMH,* 87)

The narrator seems to become more isolated, less caught up in the group identity, as the book ends and the camp members go separate ways. Yet the promise to "keep on saying those things we learned" implies a continuing commitment to both the community of memory that the camp now forms and the outside community to whom the stories may be told. That commitment may be seen in Stafford's lifelong involvement with the Fellowship of Reconciliation, with other peace groups, in his teaching, and of course in his writing. The recent poem "Austere Hope, Daily Faith" contains a distant echo of those wartime days, and of the particular austerities our times continue to demand of those committed to renouncing the use of force. I do not think it an accident that the poem speaks in the plural:

> Even a villain sleeps—atrocities
> are intermittent. We assume few saints
> among us—and inattention or fatigue
> is what we like in our great leaders.
> Some days Hitler didn't kill anybody.[9]

This poem, it seems to me, travels the same razor's edge that Stafford begins to walk in *Down in My Heart.* The austerity, tough hope, and persistent faith required for true nonviolence have often been underestimated, dismissed as simply impractical, or seen as irrelevant to daily life. His memoir, and his example, form a valuable testament to the difficulty and the viability of such hope, faith, and practice.

NOTES

1. William Stafford, *Down in My Heart* (1947; reprint, Swarthmore, Pa.: Bench Press, 1985). Cited hereafter as *DIMH*.

2. William Stafford, *You Must Revise Your Life* (Ann Arbor: University of Michigan Press, 1986), 11.

3. For the history of American pacifism, see Peter Brock, *Pacifism in the United States from the Colonial Era to the First World War* (Princeton: Princeton University Press, 1968); and Robert Cooney and Helen Michalowski, *The Power of the People* (Philadelphia: New Society Publishers, 1987).

4. For an introduction to Anabaptist history, see J. Denny Weaver, *Becoming Anabaptist: The Origin and Significance of Sixteenth-Century Anabaptism* (Scottdale, Pa.: Herald Press, 1987). The seminal modern Anabaptist work on pacifism and social ethics is John Howard Yoder, *The Politics of Jesus* (Grand Rapids, Mich.: Eerdmans, 1972).

5. Robert Lowell, *Selected Poems* (New York: Farrar, Straus and Giroux, 1976), 91.

6. William Stafford, "Making Peace among the Words," *Festival Quarterly* 17, no. 1 (Spring 1990): 12.

7. Gerald Heard, *The Human Venture* (New York: Harper and Brothers, 1955), xi.

8. Jeff Gundy, "If Struck I Should Give Off a Clear Note: A Conversation with William Stafford," *Paintbrush* 17, nos. 33–34 (Spring–Autumn 1990): 48–49.

9. William Stafford, *An Oregon Message* (New York: Harper and Row, 1987), 129.

RICHARD HOWARD

William Stafford
" 'Tell Us What You Deserve,' the Whole World Said"

A poet—the Greeks had precisely that word for it, for the calling to which the poet William Stafford apprentices himself, which he masters and thereby chooses *over* himself (as anything which is mastered is a transcendence of the mastering power too, a submission of self for the sake of the song) in this terrible descrial:

> Remembering the wild places, bitter,
> where pale fields meet winter,
> he searches for some right song
> that could catch and then shake the world

—a poet is a maker, a *makar,* our old Scots word too for the man who sings "some right song," who fashions language into a contrivance that may not come apart but rather comprehend such disintegration:

> For all we have taken into our keeping
> and polished with our hands belongs to a truth
> greater than ours,

as Stafford says again, his emphasis rightly on the manual finish, the *handling* of utterance ("we open the book with care and hold our breath: begin—translating the vast versions of the wind"); congruently, a *scop,* the Anglo-Saxon poet, is a shaper, imparting form or *scape* to what he finds shapeless, whether it be the land:

Reprinted with the permission of Atheneum Publishers, an imprint of Macmillan Publishing Company, from *Alone with America: Essays on the Art of Poetry in the United States since 1950* by Richard Howard. Copyright © 1974 by Richard Howard.

calling for human help in the wide land, calling
into all that silence and *the judgment of the sky,*[1]

or the imperatives of life upon it:

> Right has a long and intricate name.
> And the saying of it is a lonely thing,

performing some gesture or ceremony of containment by means
of the word-hoard bequeathed to him. As it is said of the *scop* in
"Widsith," the oldest poem in English, or in Old English:

> his wierd [fate] is to be a wanderer:
> the poets of mankind go through many countries,
> speak their needs, say their thanks . . .

an errantry echoed by William Stafford, our Widsith of the Great
West, in his own effort to speak his needs, say his thanks, thirst-
ing for some act or emblem of ritual which might give *scape* to
the endless prospect, as in "Watching the Jet Planes Dive":

> We must go back and find a trail on the ground
> back of the forest and mountain on the slow land;
> we must begin to circle on the intricate sod.
> By such wild beginnings without help we may find
> the small trail on through the buffalo-bean vines.
>
> We must go back with noses and the palms of our hands,
> and climb over the map in far places, everywhere,
> and lie down whenever there is doubt and sleep there.
> If roads are unconnected we must make a path,
> no matter how far it is, or how lowly we arrive.
>
> We must find something forgotten by everyone alive,
> and make some fabulous gesture when the sun goes down
> as they do by custom in little Mexico towns
> where they crawl for some ritual up a rocky steep.
> The jet planes dive; we must travel on our knees.

If there are the shamanistic gestures here which preceded, even, a
poetry of the land—"we must begin to circle on the intricate
sod. . . . With noses and the palms of our hands, climb over the
map . . . and lie down where there is doubt and sleep there. . . .

We must make some fabulous gesture . . . as they do by cus-
tom . . . where they crawl for some ritual up a rocky steep"—
there are also the movements of making and shaping, the powers
of the *scop* mustered and mastered, for all his disinherited
status—". . . we must make a path, no matter . . . how lowly
we arrive . . . we must make some fabulous gesture"; and there
is also in this easily phrased, evasively rhymed meditation the
other action of the poet, the function of discovering the past, of
recovering, which reminds us that the poet is, as well as a *makar*
and a *scop,* a *trobatore,* a *trouvère,* a *trovatore*—all Mediterranean
words for the enterprise: presumably in the south it is more
frequent to find than to fashion—the poet is a *finder,* then, who
comes upon (literally, who *invents*) his matter, his treasure-*trove:*
"Your job is to find what the world is trying to be," Stafford
adjures himself, though in his case, the case of the alienated
scop—alienated from the community, the *kin* which might elect
him to celebrate itself and which, in the wrecked wilderness of
the American West, has departed from the land ("the jet planes
dive; we must travel on our knees")—it is distinctly a matter of
finders, weepers. And of *losers, keepers,* for Stafford continually
rehearses the maker's fortunate fall, his desolation which, like
Cleopatra's, does begin to make a better life:

> It is too late now for earlier ways;
> now there are only some other ways,
> and only one way to find them—fail.

Again and again, Stafford asserts his paradox: "reality demands
abjection . . . you prove you're real by failing," he remarks in a
note on Richard Eberhart; and in his poems, acknowledging
that, sacerdotally, "we are somehow vowed to poverty," Staf-
ford exults: "a perfect flower blooms from all failure."

It is pleasing and profound, this identity or rather this conver-
gence of the poet's vocation, which in each instance, Attic, Ro-
mance, and Germanic, suggests that a man accountable to other
men for the way life is or has been framed—

> our molten bodies remembering some easier form,
> we feel the bones assert the rites of yesterday
> and the flow of angular events becoming destiny—

engages by definition in an undertaking ("meanings in search of a
world") which concerns something more than himself, rather a

transaction with something *out there,* whether landscape, love, or war, which can in part be learned, mastered, come into, as by apprenticeship or indenture, "some little trap to manage events, / some kind of edge against the expected act." But what is truly unified can never be uniform, and the *nuances* of the calling, too, the partings of the poet's ways as the various cultures distinguish them—"maintaining the worth of local things," Stafford calls it—are precious; such distinctions may help us out, may help us on to the recognition by their variance, by their chosen emphasis, of one poet or another—which is all we may ask of general terms, that they may aid us in the recognition of specific cases. There are, we notice, different kinds of poets, nor shall we expect the same performance, the same obligations of an open man, a man isolated in space, as of a closed one, a man isolated in society:

> It is all right to be simply the way you have to be,
> among contradictory ridges in some crescendo of knowing—

that is Stafford giving himself permission to exist in his *paysage moralisé,* and it is so particular a voice, with such particular claims upon the soil, that we do well to remember Hawthorne's warning: "We must not always talk in the marketplace of what happens to us in the forest"; for from the start of American experience there have been discrepant dialects for the seacoast and the plain, the woods and the mountains, not always understood to each other.

Thus I find it a matter of expedience, when I cannot make it a matter of ecstasy, to identify, to exalt one of our poets, the William Stafford who calls it his *duty* (just as he calls his duty a certain "high kind of waiting—the art of not knowing" and confesses "our need reaches for duty"):

> to find a place
> that grows from his part of the world—
>   . . . an imagined place
> where finally the way the world feels
> really means how things are,

as a *scop.* In a society of the great Inlands, where Stafford's poetry has since 1960 been launched:

> *West of your city*[2] outside your lives
> in the ultimate wind, the whole land's wave,

and sometimes lodged (his second book, *Traveling Through the Dark,* was given a National Book Award in 1962) and sometimes merely left around (so that the poet gathered up the leavings, some fifteen pieces from that first book, and included them in his third, *The Rescued Year,* in 1966, without any sense, either reported by the poet or registered by his public, that there might be some division, some cleavage between his early utterance and his late), the *scop* discovers his function—to bring together, to bridge, to braid into the one strand the double vision:

> Love is of the earth only,
> the surface . . .
>
> Not so the legend under,
> fixed, inexorable . . .
>
> So, the world happens twice—
> once what we see it as;
> second it legends itself
> deep, the way it is.

By a fidelity to failure, a submission to his own exile, he will "lease a place to live with my white breath," and ultimately, a favorite word of Stafford's, by an attention so urgently bestowed as to become *intention,*

> by listening with the same bowed head that sings,
> draw all into one song . . .
> the rage without met by the wings
> within that guide you anywhere the wind blows.

By means of a one-man anabasis from Liberal, Kansas, and environs to Portland, Oregon, with intervals of teaching and degree-taking in Indiana and California and Iowa—

> I found so misty a trail
> that all not-you cried, "You!"
> like a wedding bell—

the poet discovers himself, as the quotation affirms, identified by precisely what he is not, by what I have called *the missing parts of the contexts,* and the identification is a nuptial occasion: by his alienation from the land, the *scop* becomes one with it. "The

Hero Learning to Leave Home" is the title of one Stafford poem, and "Truth Is the Only Way Home" of another; and both leaving and returning are accommodated by the union longed for and finally attained:

> My self will be the plain,
> wise as winter is gray,
> pure as cold posts go
> pacing toward what I know.

I spoke just now of the society of the great Inlands, the space so cruelly open to interpretation ("beyond this place is many another place / called *Everywhere*"); barely a society ("where I come from withdrawal / is easy to forgive") and barely indeed a landscape ("a continent without much on it"), the West of Stafford's poetry is nonetheless, or all the more, a focus of judgment ("I'd speak for all the converging days . . ."); the *scop* is the sentenced keeper of the traditions, guardian of the word-hoard, celebrant of the rites—meager, harsh, necessary:

> We weren't left religion exactly . . .
> but a certain tall element,
> a pulse beat still in the stilled rock
> and in the buried sound along the buried mouth of the creek—

which hold the *kin* or tribe together, just as the ruler of the kin, the *king,* is the keeper of that other hoard of gold which is the kin's only possession and defense. The older a sword, the older a word, the more it is valued by the *kin.* In such a society, such a landscape, *because* of their very minimal realizations, all language has a religious, literally a *binding* significance. That is why the language of the *scops* is so profoundly conservative, conventional, *given,* and that is why William Stafford's words and verses, why his *art,* accommodates so many simplicities of repetition and so many echoes, so many correspondences between early and late, between poem and poem—the diction is unchanging because the task is unchanging, it is all one poem by which the labor of recuperation is performed:

> I plow and belong, send breath
> to be part of the day, and where it arrives
> I spend on and on, fainter and fainter
> toward ultimate identification, joining the air
> a few breaths at a time.

But suppose the king dies or withdraws his favor—then the kin is dissolved, the *scop* is alienated, as we should say, literally exiled, "traveling through the dark," as our own *scop* calls it. Born in 1914, Stafford was drafted in 1940, and served as a conscientious objector throughout the war (forestry, soil conservation in Arkansas and California); in 1948, Stafford published his master's thesis, a book about conscientious objectors, *Down in My Heart* (whose title collides meaningfully with that of his first book, *West of Your City*), and it was not until he was forty-six that that first book of poems was ready. For the king *had* died, the kin *was* dissolved, and justice, judgment, sentence could be sought, could come only from the severed land ("we were judged; our shadows knew our height") or from the severe weather of the place:

> the final strategy of right, the snow
> like justice over stones . . .

The *scop* cannot look to his community or even to his communication with himself ("to sigh is a stern act—we are judged by this air") for the sanctions of conduct, the meting-out of verdicts in the actual sense of the word, *truth-tellings:*

> Where are the wrongs men have done?
> He holds out calloused hands
> toward that landscape of justice.

And he wanders through the empty, forbidding land, past the kind of trees "that act out whatever has happened to them," in mountains where every rock "denied all the rest of the world," apart, dry, but not dumb, "catching at things left here that are ours," seeking a vindication, a judgment, a rank:

> And so I appeal to a voice, to something shadowy,
> a remote important region in all who talk.

For if it is the *scop* who assigns meaning, value, significances to the world of his disgraced kin ("we live in an occupied country, misunderstood; / justice will take us millions of intricate moves"), it is just that world which in turn justifies his own being, allows his existence to work out the salvation for which Stafford craves; when he says, in his third book, "our lives are an amnesty given us," we are reminded of Aquinas's proposition that the Creation was an act of generosity, not of justice, and when the poet, in a poem to Willa Cather in his first book, says that "the land required some gesture: conciliation," we recognize that longing for sacrifice, for submission which will bring this *scop* home to himself by identifying him with "one tree, one well, a landscape / that proclaims a universe." Accusing himself of holding the land away with "gracious gestures," Stafford seeks the kind of wound, the infliction of pain which will, as in the poem "Ceremony," wed him to the source of judgment, even by a muskrat bite:

> The mangled hand made the water red.
>
> That was something the ocean would remember:
> I saw me in the current flowing through the land,
> rolling, touching roots, the world incarnadined,
> and the river richer by a kind of marriage . . .
>
> Under the bank a muskrat was trembling
> with meaning my hand would wear forever.
>
> In that river my blood flowed on.

Only by such submission to earth ("the little clods come to judge us again"), by an imploration of the "promise of the land," as in this little prayer:

> Yew tree, make me steadfast in my
> weakness: teach me the sacred blur

can the disinherited *scop* regain his authority, his hope of authorship. No longer from the center of a society, Stafford speaks from the verge, the brink, the margin where his desolation is informed by an alien knowledge:

> It is people at the edge who say
> things at the edge: winter is toward knowing.

No longer imparting shape, no longer daring to impart it, to the land ("if we purify the pond, the lilies die"), the *scop*, by a radical reversal, by choosing other, outer claims over his own, allows the land to shape *him,* and from that submission, that surrender of privilege, "while earth whirled on its forgotten center," as well as from that mastery, that rehearsal of celebration ("while meager justice applauds up through the grass"), achieves, earns his heroism. There is a poem, central to Stafford's central book, in which the poet I have preferred to see as an outcast *scop* is able, by this very vision where the land prevails and speaks *through* him—

> there is a reward
> here: maybe the mountains, maybe only the sense
> that after what is must come something else, always—

to recognize his *authority*, to *find* himself for once with the great Mediterranean, the great Classical figures (also fugitive, also disinherited) he had seemed to be forever sequestered from; at the end of "In Medias Res," having seen on the Main Street of his own bleak town, "one night when they sounded the chimes," his father walking ahead of him in shadow, his son behind coming into the streetlight, and on each side a brother and sister, and his wife "following into the shades calling back," Stafford realizes in a great explosion of identity who he is, who he might be ("not able to know / anything but a kind of Now"), for all the black hills and blocked heavens:

> as overhead
> the chimes went arching for the perfect sound . . .
> I had not thought to know the hero quite so well.
> "Aeneas!" I cried, "just man, defender!"
> And our town burned and burned.

NOTES

1. Emphasis mine. The notion of a judgment passed by what is not included in some human assessment, of a sentencing by the missing parts of the contexts from which we draw our delegated efficiency, is crucial to Stafford, and I shall return to it, though its appearance, so immediately, in a quotation is characteristic.

2. The title of his first book: the lines in which it occurs suggest something of the arrogant otherness of Stafford's persona, the separateness, the exclusion in which his voice is raised, and yet the assurance— almost, the complacency—that he has got hold of an eschatological argument: "the *ultimate* wind," "the *whole* land."

RICHARD HUGO

Problems with Landscapes
in Early Stafford Poems

William Stafford is more than just a landscape poet, but as a
landscape poet he is one of the very best. By landscape poet I
mean a poet who uses places and experiences in those places as
starting points for poems. For such a poet, as several critics have
noted, there are two landscapes, one external and one internal.
The external one is simply "used"—indeed, usually sacrificed—
to get to the internal landscape where the poem is. The differ-
ence in the two scapes is probably arbitrary and in reality nonexis-
tent. However, some immediate problems are evident. What to
leave out of the real picture? What to add? How to lie about the
world in *your* way in order to get at truths about yourself?

Then there is the major problem of possession, of being "at
home" in the external scape used, of putting yourself in the
scene. This is difficult. Willing a persona is usually too feeble for
the purpose. The poem cannot merely happen because the poet
saw the nice farm in the sunset and would "like to write a poem
about it." First he must steal the farm. He must emotionally own
the external landscape because selfishness precedes sharing. Most
bad landscape poems are bad not because, as we usually pre-
sume, they were written by a sentimental old lady or are filled
with the clichés of youth, but because, before the poem was
started, the poet had generously presumed that the external land-
scape belonged to others as well as himself and that attitudes
toward the external were shared or communal. Such generosity
and warmth may be commendable in life but seldom find their
way into good poems. (All this assumes is that to be good a
poem should have some depth of personal commitment. Actu-
ally, I suppose all a good poem need do is to be interesting.)

I'll limit myself here to two external landscapes in William
Stafford's poems, the Midwest and the Far West, specially the
Pacific Northwest, and of Stafford's relative success in each area.

Kansas Quarterly 2 (Spring 1970): 33–38.

His first book, *West of Your City,* brought much critical acclaim and called enough attention to Stafford to help his second book win the National Book Award. As astute a critic as Louis Simpson praised the true originality at work in the early poems. The first poem, after an introductory piece, is called "One Home," and the poem opens "Mine was a midwest home—you can keep your world." This could mean: what was mine is mine and you can have yours. That would indicate that Stafford selfishly owns his material, his external scape. It could also imply: you can keep your world because there's no danger of my stealing it as long as I'm obsessed with mine. Either way, the rest of the poem works out. Stafford's world was limited by forces long dead: "Indians pulled the West over the edge of the sky." Throughout the poem, Stafford's landscape, his external one, is working poetically for him, helping him and us to his internal scape where the poem is. The sun is "like a blade" that is always over man, threatening. And to escape the drabness of a world where "plain black hats rode the thoughts that made our code," where "we sang hymns in the house; the roof was near God," the oppression of a God and a sun always too close, the loneliness where "To anyone who looked at us we said 'My Friend,'" "we ran toward storms." In other words, anything to get away, even running toward danger to find the escape of excitement. This theme is developed in a later, profoundly touching poem called "Thinking for Berky." But there is no getting away: "Wherever we looked the land would hold us up." Of course, the land also held them up the way a child is held up to see a parade. The world is psychologically restricted, but the vision is vast.

In such a world one dreams, gropes, tries to make his way like a catfish with "feelers noncommittal and black" ("In the Deep Channel"), and one's deepest feelings, "the deep current," fights the desire to grow or perhaps to break away: "tugged at the tree roots below the river." Nor is any amount of questioning helpful. In "At the Salt Marsh," Stafford's questioning of the world in which he finds himself becomes as morally inconsequential as the firing of a shotgun. Nothing will tell him what's right or wrong and only reality, here the head of a dead duck, remains. In "Hail Mary" the shadows of cedars in graveyards become obsequious in the face of a threat of detection and yet are lonely enough to bow "to the wind that noticed them." What we can do is listen, and whatever can touch us will seldom come from the drab and barren world of Stafford's childhood (except of course that we are touched constantly in the poems) but from "that other place."

On page 19 of Stafford's first book is this poem:

THE FARM ON THE GREAT PLAINS

A telephone line goes cold;
birds tread it wherever it goes.
A farm back of a great plain
tugs an end of the line.

I call that farm every year,
ringing it, listening, still;
no one is home at the farm,
the line gives only a hum.

Some year I will ring the line
on a night at last the right one,
and with an eye tapered for braille
from the phone on the wall

I will see the tenant who waits—
the last one left at the place;
through the dark my braille eye
will lovingly touch his face.

"Hello, is Mother at home?"
No one is home today.
"But Father—he should be there."
No one—no one is here.

"But you—are you the one . . . ?"
Then the line will be gone
because both ends will be home:
no space, no birds, no farm.

My self will be the plain,
wise as winter is gray,
pure as cold posts go
pacing toward what I know.

People have frequently remarked that Stafford, like many good poets, has little personal taste about his own work. It is said he doesn't know his good poems from his bad ones. It's not for me to discuss his bad poems ("The Gun of Billy the Kid" and "B.C." are hopelessly awful), but I have noticed that his best poems seem to appear in the best (often highest-paying) magazines, and the above poem is placed at the end of the first section of the first book, a conspicuous position. It also appears next to last in the first section of his third book, *The Rescued Year,* and is followed by "Listening," another fine poem from his first volume; together they make a strong ending for the first section of his third volume. Of course, editing could account for all this, but I suspect Stafford is a shrewder judge of his work than some people, including myself, used to give him credit for. At any rate, he'd have to be really dense not to know that the above poem is the one we are all looking for.

If a poet can find out how he feels and then have the courage to state it, he has done almost all he can. This sounds simple, and maybe it is. It is anything but easy. This poem is so simple and direct, so emotionally honest that it goes beyond its affecting impact and begins to haunt the reader. At least it haunts me, and has for years. By naming things this way Stafford resolves many of the problems he has been trying to solve in the first section (called "Midwest") of his first book. Much of the poetic energy has gone into illuminating, demonstrating, and, in the weaker moments, talking about problems imposed by environment, problems of outer and inner landscapes affecting each other, being at odds with each other, complementing and supplementing each other. He has been finding ways to cope, discovering escapes, developing strategies (Stafford's word).

"The Farm on the Great Plains," on one level, is the poet's battle against and victory over regression. The poem is central to an understanding of Stafford as landscape poet. Home tries to reclaim him first, the telephone line is cold yet the farm (the past) tugs it. He calls every year but no one is home until on the right night he finds someone, who is of course himself and who is obliged to tell him what he already knows—no one is home. It is Stafford's peculiar kind of courage that he can admit to playing the childish games we all play, asking himself over and over the question to which he already knows the answer, taking strange comfort in his desperation. Finally, the cycle of regressive dependence on the past is broken when his final question, weakened perhaps by repetition and certainly by his preceding firmness with self, trails off to nothing. He hangs up on himself. The phone line (umbilical cord if you want to be smartass) is severed for good. The last self left at home dissolves, and the poet is left with only those selves of the past he took with him. Everything, including death, can be faced. He is home anywhere with his plain, gray sensibility, once he has accepted what he is.

Once a poem as excellent as "The Farm on the Great Plains" has given license for freedom, the poet might be presumed free to write in any landscape. But poets always have troubles. If not, they create them. And we find in the second section (entitled "Far West") that the poet is not as at home as he might have hoped. It is one thing to say both ends of the line will be home and another to know it's true. Some of the reasons for Stafford's poetic difficulties in the second section become apparent. Stafford's original external landscape, and (since he is an honest poet) his internal one as well, is Kansas. Flat vistas, a harsh cruel weather but one that comes from far off, can be predicted, even spotted early, and consequently prepared for (strategy?): drab customs, at least in Stafford's day, drab towns, repressive social codes. This is the Kansas represented in the poems.

The west, especially the Pacific Northwest, is another matter. In western Washington and Oregon, vistas are usually limited. Trees are tall and thick, and in your way. Hills and mountains are in your way. The deep, long, uninterrupted gaze is rarely possible. Air is often hazy. Clouds are heavy and frequently low—something is oppressive no matter where you are. The scenery is dramatic and sudden, the weather mild, and the moral and social codes, what there are of them, are at best diffuse, free of a single rigid influence. Most of all, it is an area of surprise. You need not run toward storms to get your kicks. Just innocently drive around the next curve and a grand snow-covered mountain you never expected will bang your eyes.

In the first poem in the section, "Walking West," Stafford is forced to more regular rhythms than we've come to expect in his best work. He goes to externally half-rhymed quatrains, and while "The Farm on the Great Plains" is in quatrains, there one feels the poem found the form. Here, the form seems superimposed. Standard form is one resort of a poet in trouble. "Walking West" is not a bad poem but anyone might have written it. Certainly this is not Stafford at his best. At his best he is subtly rhythmic in an exciting way or can grope morally about, planning his strategies.

In other pieces you can sense he is not at home. In his town

"To anyone who looked at us we said 'My Friend.'" But in "The Research Team in the Mountains," which appears in his second volume, *Traveling Through the Dark,*

> If your policy is to be friends in the mountains
> a rock falls on you: the only real friends—
> you can't help it.

I suppose that's true, if one can generalize that people in the Far West are not as friendly as people in the Midwest, though who in hell knows? The point here is that although nature in the Midwest is far less hospitable to man than in the Far West, Stafford finds it more so, at least in the poems. But the real danger in the Far West, I suspect, is neither the threat of falling rocks nor of unfriendly people but rather the danger of not writing his own poems. (He would write poems—and good ones—anywhere.) Here, external and internal landscapes are at unpoetic odds.

Going back to the first volume, in "A Survey" Stafford is once again reduced to being "poetic" to bring off the poem. And nowhere does Stafford seem more uncreatively foreign than in "In the Oregon Country." Here he can do little more than pile up names of places and tribes and in an effort to mold the poem, he fails to escape the "tyranny of narration." He seems dazzled by the relatively rich history, topography, and myths. The Northwest is rich and Stafford has always been Kansas dirt poor. The external Northwest landscape bears no relation to his internal one, at least none strong enough to get to the poem. They do not supplement or complement each other, and there is no *mutual* alienation.

Stafford's early poetic failures to conquer the Northwest are the result of his abandoning his capacity for ruthlessness. He does not own the places he tries to use for poems, and so he can only *try* to use them. The obsessive quality of emotional ownership is missing. It is essential; the external must be possessed, not just observed. Anyone can snap a camera. (I should qualify what I'm saying by emphasizing that all early poems growing out of the Far West are not bad poems. Far from it. Some are very good. What I'm saying is that the real poem, the one growing out of the inner landscape and revealing previously unknown personal relationships with the world, is often missed. Good or bad, it was seldom missed back home.) This failure to reach out and make the "new world" his, to treat the pines, gulls, mountains, and streams as if he were the first man to see them, leads

Stafford to resolve early Far West poems with overly public "poetic" statements: "So many Chinook souls, so many Silverside." But of course he succeeds. He was always too much the poet not to:

TRAVELING THROUGH THE DARK

Traveling through the dark I found a deer
dead on the edge of the Wilson River road.
It is usually best to roll them into the canyon:
that road is narrow; to swerve might make more dead.

By glow of the tail-light I stumbled back of the car
and stood by the heap, a doe, a recent killing;
she had stiffened already, almost cold.
I dragged her off; she was large in the belly.

My fingers touching her side brought me the reason—
her side was warm; her fawn lay there waiting,
alive, still, never to be born.
Beside that mountain road I hesitated.

The car aimed ahead its lowered parking lights;
under the hood purred the steady engine.
I stood in the glare of the warm exhaust turning red;
around our group I could hear the wilderness listen.

I thought hard for us all—my only swerving—,
then pushed her over the edge into the river.

This poem seems a great favorite of Stafford readers; it appears everywhere. I happen not to care for it much, but for irresponsible reasons which I'll state later. Let's say the world is right, I'm wrong, and the poem is a success. If so, one reason is that it transcends the difficulties he had with the earlier Far West poems. The elements of the Pacific Northwest are there: the night-dark limit on vision contrasted to the unlimited views of bright, open Kansas plains (sometimes the Midwest is brighter at night than the Northwest during day), the surprise you can't plan for because you can't see it coming from far off (what road ever curved in Kansas or ran straight in western Oregon?), the dead deer suddenly there, the canyon, the narrow road, and Stafford honestly awkward in the scene: "I stumbled back of the car." His magic is gone.

> In scenery I like flat country.
> In life I don't like much to happen.

he says in "Passing Remark," and so the situation on the Wilson River road is definitely not his kind. What strategy will handle this? He takes some strength from the car, the indifferently relentless headlights and from the steady purr of the engine, etc., before he finds a way out.

Now for my sour digression, my irrelevant reasons for not liking the poem—this may be my only chance. Simply put, it jars my Northwest soul. I could argue aesthetically that a poem cannot afford time to wait for a decision, only time for the decision to be rendered or better, named. But I can't defend this. Besides, it's probably wrong. Being from the Northwest, however, I have no doubt what the decision should be, and at least I can understand my impatient urge to say: stop thinking hard for us all, Bill, and get that damned deer off the road before somebody kills himself.

Why he uses this as the first and title poem of his second book is probably the more important question. I think he realized that he had "used" that foreign external landscape and managed to write a sound poem (I'm sure one he likes much) out of himself. Stafford's world may not be large, but his poems are big enough. Here, I think he knew he had literally traveled through the dark and now both ends of the Kansas line are home. He carries his world within him for good, and no matter how foreign the external landscape, he will travel through its darks and find his poem. Of course, he had already demonstrated this in other poems before writing this one, but this time he has convinced himself he can do it. The real sacrifice is not the deer but the external world, and the real salvation is not the life of the next motorist but the poem itself. If this was a moment he told himself as poet he would go on writing his poems anywhere, it must have been one of the best moments in a career that has had more good ones than most.

WILLIAM HEYEN

William Stafford's Allegiances

I.

Intentionally or not, several of the poems in William Stafford's *Allegiances* (1970) are parables of the poet in action, suggestions of where a Stafford poem comes from, how it gets its life, what its beliefs are, how it develops and turns in on itself as it moves out toward the reader's life. In "The Preacher at the Corner" Stafford—I sense less of a need in Stafford's later work to talk in terms of his masks—says:

> the way I found him is the way I like:
> to wander because I know the road,
> and find stray things, wherever they come from.

There's a lot going on here. Stafford believes in staying "loose in the harness," as Robert Frost phrased it, and we know that Frost didn't believe anyone should or even could play tennis with the net down. (This idea of the poet as athlete and the poem as an athletic performance goes a long way. When we see a Jerry West drive, we witness a combination of muscle memory and inspiration.) And Richard Wilbur has argued that the genie gets his power precisely because he is confined in a bottle. (Better lamp, the outer form plus the idea of light, lux, and the rubbing and wishing and ordering.) The compression principle. Piston and gas. Stafford, I think, would agree, but he'd say that if you dig in the corners of the old farms in the Midwest and West, excavate those mounds built up like the layers of Troy with decades of garbage, or maybe come across other dumps, overgrown, whose patrons are long since dead, you'll find the damnedest bottles, all shapes and sizes, bitters and snakebite and patent medicine and mineral water bottles, some bent by the heat of old fires, but still unbroken, some stained by the earth or by their long tenure in the sun, some even fused together (for analogy's sake). The bottles

Modern Poetry Studies 1 (1970): 307–18.

are stray things but some of them may be as important as Keats's urn or Stevens's Tennessee jar, at once artifacts and mementos of our culture. And all sorts of smells, mildew, and rot and the perfume of lingering traces of honeysuckle flow around in the air inside those bottles. The wind will sound like an owl as it blows over the bottle's neck, or like no bird we have any name for.

Loose in the harness. Freedom within a form. You know those dog runs, a wire stretched between two trees where the leashed dog can get plenty of action. Or, the wind whipping a poplar just so far, to just so much of an arc, and no further, no more. After a while, says Stafford (no brag, just fact), you know the road because you've committed yourself to the integrity of a poem; you wouldn't dream of allowing it (if you can help it) to offend itself. At the same time, failures will prove you are human. But you will allow your poem to find the shape it wants, the shape it needs in order to say just what it has to say. You know the road, so it's all right to walk down the middle for a while, and then to scuffle up the dust and gravel at the edges, even to lean way out for some huckleberries ripening past the shoulders. Hell, even jump all the way off, but not for long because, and here's where the figure breaks down, this road can't get where it's going without you. After all, it's a road of words, and all the words we know can't exist all at once in any single utterance, and someone has to say the ones that want to be said and in the order they want to be heard. Stafford is fond of using what he calls "an organized form cavalierly treated." The room to follow impulse within outer strictness. The second line of Thomas Gray's "Elegy Written in a Country Churchyard": "The lowing herd winds slowly o'er the lea." "Winds," the sense of a path, not necessarily the shortest, straightest line to the stable, but still a path within infinite possibilities of paths. The cattle of the imagination graze all over the place but, finally, the path winding homeward.

Stafford once told a group of us at dinner that he always has about fifty poems off in the mail. This kind of production has always been suspect to me, but Stafford is a natural. As James Dickey once said, Stafford turns out so much verse "not because he is glib and empty, but because he is a real poet, a born poet, and communicating in lines and images is not only the best way for him to get things said; it is the easiest." The thing is that Stafford is beginning to know and feel what a Stafford poem sounds like. There isn't that intense struggle for a voice, that hither and thither of angles and tones that cause us to label many a poet "promising." But Stafford doesn't just shoot from the hip and, to change the image from cowboy to circus, it's surprising how tight a tightrope so many of William Stafford's lines walk. The rope actually vibrates in the wind of the breath. Let me talk about this for a minute.

Certainly, sounds make meanings beyond the ability of criticism to get at them. Sound patterns give us the feeling of ritual, as John Crowe Ransom says somewhere, and the logical meanings of the sounds either are lost way back (as, I understand, is true of frequent passages in the Noh) or, perhaps, as the language changes, are just beginning to assert themselves, just becoming apparent in the clusters they make, the tints of feeling they give groups of related words. So, I can't say anything about the added meanings the sound control in a Stafford poem gives it any more than I can pinpoint the meaning of, say, the repeated use of a hard *g* sound. But in an essay, "Finding the Language," Stafford describes his own faith in "certain reinforcing patterns of sound which the language, as if by chance, has taken up into itself. That is, all syllables tend to slide by inherent quality toward certain meanings, either because of varying demands on the throat in utterance, or because of relations among clusters of syllables which have become loaded with associated meanings, and so on." What I am trying to say here is that I cannot say anything specific about the added meanings the sound control in these ten lines (picked almost at random from ten poems in *Allegiances*) adds, but what is apparent and important is Stafford's need to ride range (back to the cowboy) on his choices and on the upwelling of the unconscious:

> according to any of us; but after the others
> the tone of his voice roamed, had more to find,
> he comprehends by fistfuls with both hands.
> One aims a single-shot and hears the muffled past
> the old saints, who battered their hearts,
> When winter strikes, that camp sinks
> altering space by the way they wait
> In the yard I pray birds,
> teach me; for, somewhere inside, the clods are
> the world, wide, unbearably bright,

Stafford is a poet who allows the world's language to move in on him, nuances and suggestions, intimations; a poet who wants to keep himself ready for "those nudges of experience," as he calls them. And: "it's like fishing—the person who keeps his line wet catches a fish." But as the world does move in on him, he gathers it together, for his poem's sake, line by line, whole poem by whole poem. Notice the internal rhymes, the natural break at one sound and the locking-in of that sound at line's end, road's end. The art of successful repetition. Sort of a refrain. Lovely, really, the echoes in the lines, and the pacing (for there are in the end only two sounds, silence and nonsilence), the pauses and then the poem going on. Resonance. The poem coming off the page, toward our bodies. Louis Zukofsky quoting Chapman's "the unspeakable good liquor there" and saying: "Obviously, the man who wrote that knew what it was to gargle something down his throat." Sounds connected with things and actions.

And I would think that Stafford, more than nine out of ten American poets, would *sound* like a poet to someone who couldn't understand English. The full rhymes are infrequent, pyrotechnics are at a minimum, but the lines are held together by a sort of unstudied point-counterpoint. It is apparent that they were said in a lot of diferent ways before just the right combination of sounds and silences declared themselves inseparable forever.

Well, anyway, I am an admirer of William Stafford's poetry. First, for the craft that does not call attention to itself—Stafford admits that he almost flaunts nonsophistication in his work—but which is always there, being necessary and important just by being there; second, though this is never distinct from the craft, for the downright power of what he has to say. Writing of "The Farm on the Great Plains" Stafford said: "plains, farm, home, winter, . . . these command my allegiance in a way that is beyond my power to analyze at the moment." Yes, and his world commands my allegiance. I am caught up in his sense of space and time and of the American Dream, his sense of loss, his sense of joy in the here and now, his feeling for the land and the seasons, his belief (manifested in the poems themselves) that the smallest events in our lives and the smallest feelings that travel our spines are miracles—a puff of air, an extension of muscle and memory as we reach out to turn on a light. In his best work I come away with a sense of myth, and of prophecy, that I had better not try to define here. In any case, there are four or five poems in *Allegiances* that do for me what Stafford wants them to: "I would not like to assert these poems; they would climb toward the reader without my proclaiming anything. But sometimes for every reader a poem would arrive: it would go out for him, and find his life." This is the dream of a real man, wanting his poems to be gifts, wanting, essentially, to leave the earth a little better place than it was when he began to draw breath.

"Montana Eclogue" is one poem that is moving out after me, is beginning to touch me, many of its lines not wanting to be forgotten. When I first read it I wrote in the margin of my book: "½ lousy." I went back and now its roughnesses glitter, its risks raise it up. It's a deep poem and finds that comfort cognizant of but beyond darkness that the best poems find. "Montana Eclogue" is about winter and the world most of us do not have to face but "tell our lies with all the beautiful grace / an animal has when it runs." In this poem winter, as it gathers itself to storm the high places, becomes Winter, the culmination of all wild elements of other Stafford poems, becomes the head winter as Ben in Faulkner's *The Bear* is the head bear and Lion the head dog. Winter is the immediate, the apocalyptic, the postatomic: "We glimpse that last storm when the wolves / get the mountain back." And juxtaposed against wilderness, bearing the brunt of this winter for all of us is Logue, who closes down the Montana camp as thunderheads gather. Logue, the chosen one, the appointed one. "And Logue, by being there, suddenly / carries for us everything that we can load on him." What Stafford manages to do is to give winter the stature of some great force apprehended as though for the first time, beyond habit, something awful, full of awe. Because he accomplishes this I can take real emotional comfort in the thought that against what nature is I can be free. My part becomes "too small to count, / if winter can come." This is the poem's end:

> Logue brings us all that. Earth took
> the old saints, who battered their hearts,
> met arrows, or died by the germs God sent;
> but Logue, by being alone and occurring to us,
> carries us forward a little,
> and on his way out for the year will
> stand by the shore and see winter in,
> the great repeated lesson every year.
>
> A storm bends by that shore and
> one flake at a time teaches grace,
> even to stone.

This is from a true poem. Logue is both a man and a spirit, the spirit or nature-genius of the old pastoral. "Montana Eclogue." A true poem and I don't want to let go of it. There's a stanza that opens its second part during which Stafford, incredible as it may seem, enraptured by his subject, calls on the ghost of Gerard Manley Hopkins to help him:

> Far from where we are, air owns those ranches
> our trees hardly hear of, open places
> braced against cold hills. Mornings, that
> news hits the leaves like rain, and we
> stop everything time brings, and freeze that one,
> open, great, real thing—the world's gift: day.

But perhaps no other poet evokes the sheer grandeur of nature as does Hopkins, and he is not as alien a ghost to Stafford as we would at first think. In any case, the rhythmic variety and rightness of "Montana Eclogue" are remarkable. To quote a line from this poem is to note the sheer excellence of its particulars. To read it entire is to be left without words. Luckily, I don't have to prefer "The blackbird whistling / Or just after."

"A Sound from the Earth," "Space Country," "Believing What I Know," and "Earth Dweller" are other poems in *Allegiances* that are reaching out for me. These are poems, firmly rooted in the earth, that "curve"—a favorite Stafford word: the horizon, the edge, the verge of knowing and feeling, the out there—into the momentary truths that are poems. Their language is sure. Stafford's speech is sincere, his imagination a very wide net indeed.

II.

But I have reservations. I don't think there is as much fine work in *Allegiances* as there is in any one of Stafford's first three books. *Traveling Through the Dark* (1962) is one of the best books of the decade. At least the fourteen poems from *West of Your City* (1960), Stafford's first book, reprinted in *The Rescued Year* (1966), his third, remain authentic: the haunting "The Farm on the Great Plains" and "One Home" are classics; "In the Deep Channel" and "The Fish Counter at Bonneville" display Stafford's gift for mystery, for reaching out and touching the outer limits of thought; "At the Bomb Testing Site" is as frightening a poem as I can imagine. And so on. And *The Rescued Year* as a whole rivals *Traveling Through the Dark*. *Allegiances* is more hit and miss, less sure of itself, sketchier. One thing, or some related things, especially bother me. I think I can best get to these by first quoting the initial stanza of "Montana Eclogue":

> After the fall drive, the last
> horseman humps down the trail south;
> High Valley turns into a remote, still cathedral.
> Stone Creek in its low bank turns calmly
> through the trampled meadow. The one scouting
> thunderhead above Long Top hangs to watch,
> ready for its reinforcement due in October.

Here Stafford's aesthetic is working. As he said in a statement for *The Distinctive Voice* (1966), "When you make a poem you merely speak or write the language of every day, capturing as many bonuses as possible and economizing on losses; that is, you come awake to what always goes on in language, and you use it to the limit of your ability and your power of attention at the moment." In "Montana Eclogue" the lines move into one another inevitably, the poet is obviously at full attention, his perception precise and his language perfect. There is that sense of ease, probably after much labor, that Yeats talks about in "Adam's Curse." The conversational tone here is engaging. There are the small surprises we've come to expect from Stafford, the verb *humps,* the use of *cathedral,* the playful but ominous image of the earliest thunderhead as scout. Stafford is at his best here, flowing forward, natural. This is the conclusion of "Space Country," again natural, perfectly modulated:

> The world had passed something in space
> and was alone again. Sunset came on.
> People lay down, and the birds forgot
> as they sleepily clucked and slept, close
> on boughs, as well hidden as could be
> in the air again clear, sharp, and cold.

But what of this from "In Sublette's Barn," a poem that for me never gets off the ground:

> Like a badger by that stream—so strong the trap that
> grabbed his feet was bent, with his teeth grooved on everything
> he bit, and miles ringed all around, so target was the place,
> where—now—the sky kept saying out and out because

> its color would never be at all but what it was—he took
> his paw back from the steel, and watched the trap.

I can only conclude that here the poet's taste failed him, that his
ear let him down. The words never manage to control their
ideas. I keep rushing forward trying to get to the sense of this,
and *target* doesn't help or the sky "saying out and out." And the
rhythms are crotchety. Ezra Pound once said that poetry ought
to be at least as well written as good prose. I don't think this is.

Nor is "Behind the Falls," which is a typical example of what
happens when a Stafford poem goes bad, falls flat. What Stafford
does, and he has explained this in an essay on "Traveling
Through the Dark," is to trust his story (or whatever the motiva-
tion for the poem is) to tell itself. He has experienced something
that has affected him deeply, and he has the faith that what he has
to do is to talk along in his not-quite-prose way, bringing in the
details that insist on being brought in, trusting the language to
rise naturally to depth, trusting the language to evoke the way it
was. There is no doubt that "Traveling Through the Dark" is a
successful poem, a triumph of the method (too mathematical a
word) that brought it into being. More: it's a powerful reading
experience time after time. The ease of its speech plays against
the starkness of its theme. Its narrative, finding just the right
words, the right details, "helped to produce a kind of redoubling
of experience," as Stafford mentions in an interview in *Prairie
Schooner* (1970). "Behind the Falls," on the other hand, though
its story line has a great deal of potential, remains dull. The "we"
of the poem, a cigarette lighter their only light, explored a cave
behind falls. When the lighter dimmed:

> We stopped, afraid—lost
> if ever that flame went out—
> and surfaced in each other's eyes,
> two real people suddenly
> more immediate in the dark
> than in the sun we'd ever be.

It seems to me that this, by any standards I can imagine, is bad
writing. Again, the rhythms are awkward. There is too much
saying and not enough showing. Interest dies. The inversion in
the sixth line and the "suddenly"-"be" rhymes here are terrible.
And the poem's last four lines are even worse, descending into
the dreariest kind of preaching:

When men and women meet that way
the curtain of the earth descends, and they
find how faint the light has been, how far
mere honesty or justice is from all they need.

Then there is the problem exemplified by the beginning of "A Gesture toward an Unfound Renaissance," the problem of abstraction and of speech so pictureless and low-key that it remains boring. In Stafford's best work there is a sense of studied artlessness; in his worst, just a sense of artlessness that does not reach out, does not intrigue:

There was the slow girl in art class,
less able to say where our lessons led: we
learned so fast she could not follow us.
But at the door each day I looked back
at her rich distress, knowing almost enough
to find a better art inside the lesson.

This is pretty dry stuff. And here, trying to reach this poem and to talk about it, I feel that I'm walking on thin ice indeed, because after the imposing title and with the last couple of lines above, the poem must (at least to Stafford's mind) be moving toward some concern that I just can't fathom. But I don't know what Stafford thinks of this slow girl and can't move into the poem's symbolic concern, or even surface concern, because his language is not sharp enough, precise enough, or its contexts are not deep enough, or something!—Marius Bewley, in an article on James Fenimore Cooper and William Cullen Bryant, does his best to enumerate the reasons most of Bryant's work went awry and just doesn't talk to us today, but finally throws up his hands in frustration and simply says: "Something went wrong somewhere." Anyway, there is no sense of urgency or color in a bad Stafford poem. And I don't think Richard Howard is right when he says that Stafford's diction is unchanging from early to late work. In general, Stafford's diction has become a bit more flaccid, diffident, unexciting in more poems.

It may well be, given his allegiances, that William Stafford has to write two or three bad poems for every good one, and that his fourth book in ten years after a very late start is making this clear. It may be, on the other hand, that Stafford has come to trust his way just a little too much. "To me," says Stafford, "poetry is talk that is enhanced a little bit." To me poetry is talk that is enhanced quite a bit. What a poem tries to do as it moves along is to track down the implications of what it has just said. Maybe more of the impulses that surface are to be distrusted than Stafford thinks: maybe there *are* such things as irrelevance and poppycock and random impulse and words and ideas of second or third intensity that rise as we write and against which we have to be constantly on guard. When you spread a net across falls you're as likely to catch driftwood as salmon and to catch nothing as often as you catch driftwood. When you leave a sheet of sensitized metal on the moon to be bombarded by cosmic rays or dust later to be measured your research can be messed up by stray meteors that beat the sheet to smithereens. Maybe the poet is less of an instrument, less of a receiver, and more of a shaper than Stafford believes him to be. Maybe just a little bit more critical consciousness, consciousness coming out of the cortex, would go a long way. Maybe the line between poetry and everyday language is a little thicker than Stafford would concede. Maybe Stafford is just a little too worried that a bit more heightening of his speech, a bit more flash and gold, would result in an effect of artificiality. And maybe Stafford takes the democracy of poetry and poets a few shades too far.

But beyond my few reservations and questions and because of the undeniable grace and force of so many of his poems, he deserves the last word. Our differences, to be sure, are only differences of degree, not of commitment. The following is from the *Prairie Schooner* interview:

We already have the skills for poetry when we learn to talk. What we need is the faith to carry right through with it. Besides the language, and all the opportunities in it—the language we all know so well—there is also that other dimension, those patterns that may lead if we can follow right. I might put it in William Blake's lines that go something like: "I give you the end of a golden string, just roll it into a ball and it will lead you into the gate built in Jerusalem's wall." I have this same feeling about writing. If we can start where we are, with the impulses that come to us, it's like taking hold of the end of that golden string. And we must follow along. The justification for whatever occurs to us is simply that it does occur to us. As a writer, if I know that I'm writing important things, then I know that I'm not writing original things. That's the way I can identify the value of my work rather quickly. It's already established. But if I can start with any tiny impulse that I may have—most of the time it remains small and it doesn't amount to anything—that's the only way out from where I live to some kind of cumulative effect which, if you want to use a grandiose term, might be called the creative effort.

ALBERTA TURNER

William Stafford and the Surprise Cliché

To say that a poet uses cliché is enough to warn off editors of little magazines, prevent readings on prestigious campuses, and turn foundation awards in the direction of more bold and risk-taking writers. William Stafford has suffered none of these reversals, yet a close reading of his poems shows that one of the most frequent devices which creates his special originality, or voice, is a skillful handling of cliché.

Stafford's method is to draw attention to the cliché *as* cliché— to make the reader recognize the familiar phrase by using exactly the expected words or enough of them so that the reader knows what specific substitution has been made. The surprise is created by using the familiar phrase (1) in an unusual context, (2) in an expected context but in such a way that the meaning becomes ironic, or (3) by changing the phrase just enough so that the expected words become even more applicable than they would have been before the change.

All three methods can be illustrated from the poem "Glimpse between Buildings":

GLIMPSE BETWEEN BUILDINGS

Now that the moon is out of a job
it has an easy climb, these nights,
finds an empty farm where a family could live,
slides wide over the forest—all those
million still violins before they are
carved—and follows those paths only air
ever uses. I feel my breath follow
those aisles and stumble on the moon
deep in forest pools. . . .

South Carolina Review 7 (April 1975): 28–33.

Moon, you old unsinkable submarine,
leaf admirer, be partly mine,
guide me tonight along city streets.
Help me do right.

At least eight phrases in the poem are familiar enough to appear
in a cliché dictionary:

    1. out of a job
    2. an easy climb
    3. follow those paths
    4. stumble on
    5. you old [so and so]
    6. be mine
    7. guide me tonight
    8. help me do right

All but two (nos. 5 and 6) are used in their expected forms. The
first exception, *be mine,* contains the insertion *partly,* which alters
but does not disguise the poetic lover's usual proposal to his lady.
The second altered cliché, *you old so and so,* substitutes *unsinkable
submarine* for *so and so,* a change which, again, does not disguise
the fact that Stafford is using the familiar phrase in its familiar
affectionate, slightly amused tone. Of the remainder, phrases
nos. 3, 7, and 8 are clichés of the hymnal, and nos. 1, 2, and 4 are
colloquial, everyday expressions. Their occurrence in a poem
whose last four lines are an address to the moon and whose last
line is a familiar address to God suggests that Stafford is being
either tritely sentimental or ironic. The way that he mixes these
clichés of the love and religious traditions with the colloquial and
mundane ones leaves sentiment intact but gives an ironic twist
which prevents sentimentality. The moon is not Diana; it is an
old man out of a job (the moon's job as inciter of love and poetic
madness has been abolished, the moon-man thrown out, and his
moonscape taken over by a research laboratory). The old man is
not only unemployed but a vagrant and a dreamer: he uses his
older mythic occupations just for fun. Instead of haunting empty
houses, he examines them as possible family homes; instead of
inspiring moonlight sonatas, he admires the forests as still,
uncarved violins; instead of laying moon paths that bewitch and
lead lovers astray, he follows paths that are nameless and to no

mortal or lunar purpose; where once he lit pools for lovers and dryads, he now takes his own midnight dip and submerges for his own pleasure. But the speaker still prays to him in the clichés of the lover and the religious believer. "Be mine," "guide me tonight," "help me do right." By changing "be mine" to "be partly mine" and adding "along city streets" to "guide me tonight" Stafford alerts his reader to the fact that the clichés must not be taken in their usual senses. In this context the unchanged phrase from a hundred Christian prayers, "Help me do right," becomes "Help me realize that the so-called easy climb may be the hard one, that the traditional job may be easier than a discriminating and truly fulfilling vagrancy, and that the glimpse of the moon as vagrant, from between buildings, may be just the perspective on regimentation which makes human civilization bearable." Without the clichés, phrased as they are, there would be no tension between the expected and the unexpected. There would be only a flat prose statement.

Cliché as Stafford has used it in this poem acquires the strength of historical or literary allusion. We follow its expectedness just short of complacence, then by addition of a word, or by placing it in an unexpected context, he makes the old phrase tilt us in a new direction.

A second poem in which Stafford uses cliché in the same way is "Sophocles Says":

SOPHOCLES SAYS

History is a story God is telling,
by means of hidden meanings written closely
inside the skins of things. Far over the sun
lonesome curves are meeting, and in the clouds
birds bend the wind. Hunting a rendezvous,
soft as snowflakes ride through a storm their pattern down,
men hesitate a step, touched by home.

A man passes among strangers; he never smiles;
the way a flame goes begging among the trees
he goes, and he suffers, himself, the kind of dark
that anything sent from God experiences,
until he finds through trees the lights of a town—
a street, the houses blinded in the rain—
and he hesitates a step, shocked—at home.

For God will take a man, no matter where,
and make some scene a part of what goes on:
there will be a flame; there will be a snowflake form;
and riding with the birds, wherever they are,
bending the wind, finding a rendezvous
beyond the sun or under the earth—that man
will hesitate a step—and meet his home.

In this poem few of the clichés are used in their usual forms,
though modifications clearly imply those forms:

Clichés	In Stafford's Forms
Simon says	Sophocles says
The heavens are telling the glory of God	History is a story God is telling
lonesome people are meeting	lonesome curves are meeting
birds are blown by the wind	birds bend the wind
keeping a rendezvous	hunting a rendezvous
at home	touched by home
	meet his home
a man goes begging	a flame goes begging
suffers indignity, shame, injustice	suffers the kind of dark that anything sent from God experiences
eyes blinded by rain	houses blinded in the rain
hesitates a moment	hesitates a step

The especially heavy concentration of clichés in this poem can
be attributed to the poem's central point—a modification of the
popular understanding of what Sophocles said about fate: that it
comes to men as a surprise, that they cannot forestall it, that it is
grim and tragic, but that its very tragedy can leave a heroic man
wiser and resigned. Stafford says the same thing, but changes the
tone of Sophocles' statement. *Fate* becomes *home*. To the denota-
tion of justice and inevitability and surprise, he adds the connota-
tion of comfort, of personal completeness. A cliché situation is
twisted just enough to make it a new situation. Each cliché
strengthens this effect: "Simon says" is a child's game, and Staf-
ford is about to take the threat out of Sophocles: astronomical
curves are humanized by being called lonesome; the wind be-
comes less threatening because birds bend it; a rendezvous with

destiny is not imposed, but sought; flame does not scar or blind or beckon, it begs; man does not suffer a unique and impersonal cosmic punishment, but the kind of warm darkness that anything sent from God knows. Conversely, the clichés of absolute comfort have been made less comforting: the houses that offer welcome and security to travelers lost in the woods in the stock fairytale situation are blinded by rain. Most important, the word *home* goes through a gradual change which makes the reader aware that it both *is* and *is more than* the cliché concept of stove, wife, and security blanket: the seeker is *touched by home* (surprised); shocked to find he is already *at home,* and finally made (as Sophocles' heroes were) aware enough of the nature of home to meet it. Home is security only in the sense that it is fate. Sophocles says that fate will surprise, fit, determine, enlighten, and Stafford says he should have added that fate will also comfort us.

The two poems I have selected work the device of surprise cliché harder than many of Stafford's poems do. But the device occurs often enough in other poems to show that it is one of Stafford's most powerful tools for suggesting mystery in a mundane situation. For example, in "At the Fair" (*The Rescued Year,* 44) the lines "What more could anyone ask / We had our money's worth" come just after the list of usual sideshow attractions and just before an incident which is both less than and much more than any of these: "And then besides, outside the gate, / for nothing, we met one of those lithe women— / The whirling girl, laughing with a crooked old man." In "The Well Rising" (*West of Your City,* 50) the substitution of *brimming* for *cutting* in the expression "plowshare brimming through deep ground" occurs while Stafford is taking the usually unnoticed commonplaces of the field and interpreting them as actions of "thunderous" intent; he ends with the lines, ". . . I place my feet / with care in such a world." In "At the Bomb Testing Site" (*West of Your City,* 31) he substitutes "at the flute end of consequences" for the usual "at the tail end," in order to say that a lizard waiting for an important change, its hands gripping the desert, is waiting for a beginning rather than merely for the final explosion which the rest of us have been taught to expect. In "Aunt Mable" (*The Rescued Year,* 17) he writes, "shaken by intermittent trust, / stricken with friendliness" where custom would lead us to expect "shaken by intermittent pain, stricken by fear." Again the modification is organically necessary to the thrust of the poem, which is saying that we are so accustomed to being shaken by mistrust and fear that we are numb to it, that the only thing which can really shake us is trust and friendliness. And I could cite dozens more.

To use this device entails great risk, for the poetic "decorum" of the 1970s forbids the too-familiar phrase in the expected context, whether that phrase be allusion, pathetic fallacy, or everyday colloquialism. Yet Stafford has found it a risk worth taking because it insures that the reader will go at least partway with the poet on the strength of his old awareness before he is jerked into or flooded with new awareness, that he will come close for a look and so give the poet a chance to surprise him. If everything in a poem is entirely original, the reader may not get a firm enough grasp on it to permit it to take him anywhere. Stafford does invite a quick or cursory reader to see the familiar signs, think he's been there already, and turn back too soon. But more often than not he succeeds in surprising his reader into going farther than he thought he could go. When his method succeeds, the reader can agree with him that

> Walking along in this not quite prose way
> we both know it is not quite prose we speak.
> ("Near," *The Rescued Year,* 77)

ROBERT COLES

William Stafford's Long Walk

The United States of America is William Stafford's country; it is
Richard Nixon's country too, no doubt about that. Allen Gins-
berg, from the Eastern Seaboard, is right: there is plenty of
greed, envy, and murderous competitiveness abroad in the land.
But there are also other sides to our people. The Nixons came
from the Midwest, ended up near the Pacific, and soon enough
confronted us with much of what we have become—and one has
in mind not just the thirty-seventh president but his two ever so
adroit and vigorous brothers. No arrangement is too complex
for them, and if there is any sanction needed, there is always that
marvelous, smiling, dynamic Billy Graham around, who doubt-
less appeases any anxieties he has with the utterly compelling
truth: a minister must not flinch from a sinner, and we are all
sinners.

But William Stafford also comes from the Midwest, and he
too found his way to the Pacific. And though his eyes are as
sharp as Ginsberg's and his ears as attentive, one meets quite
another America in his poems. For ideologues the apparent con-
tradiction is easily resolved—it is a matter of the superficial as
against the deep. Everything is rotten in the state of Denmark, or
else the nation is in fine shape, despite a few problems—and
they, of course, are exaggerated for various reasons by various
individuals. For Stafford, this is a land of compelling opposites, a
nation that has indeed brutalized generations of Indians (toward
whose habits, beliefs, and customs he is drawn) but a nation
blessed with a marvelously varied natural landscape, at once
subtle, striking, awesome, and for him, impossible to overlook.
And too, a nation whose people can be generous, kind, and
thoughtful; a nation of which his beloved parents and brother are
citizens, and his son Kit, and the dying Bess, a librarian of tact

American Poetry Review 4, no. 4 (July–August 1975): 27–28. Reprinted from *That
Red Wheelbarrow: Selected Literary Essays* by Robert Coles by permission of the
University of Iowa Press. Copyright © 1988 by the University of Iowa Press.

and grace, and Althea, and the nameless girl whose boyfriend lied, and on and on. From those people, moments of whose lives Stafford evokes in his poems, one obtains a particular vision of America—not Whitman's lyrical urging, really, but not a voice of despair either, and certainly no inclination to disgust or self-righteous condemnation.

Stafford is wondrously attentive to the land, sky, water, and foliage of our Midwest and West. He presents us with territory many of his readers will, perhaps, know not at all:

> At the border of October
> where Montana meets Alberta
> that white grass that worshipped wind
> climbed from summer to the sky,
> which began to change.

He presents us with "the firred mountains of Oregon," the "hay towns beyond Salt Lake." He presents us with "cornfield farms," with "a town by the track in Colorado," with a "prairie town," and the prairie dogs he used to gaze at for long stretches. Born in Kansas, he "lived in Indiana once," we learn, and while there "put these hands into those lakes / of counties near Fort Wayne." He knows a tornado—knows it the way someone watching the weather map on the *Today* show over coffee in Boston or New York cannot: "first the soul of our house left, up the chimney / and part of the front window went outward— pursued / whatever tore at the chest." There are people, he knows, connected to the land he wants to bring before us, and in his own quiet, indirect, unauthoritative, yet telling manner he introduces them to us. In a few lines he can offer more than a shelfful of sociological, anthropological, and psychological studies (with their "worldviews" and the "psychosocial" this or that of these or those):

> At the end of their ragged field
> a new field began:
> miles told the sunset that Kansas
> would hardly ever end,
> and that beyond the Cimarron crossing
> and after the row-crop land
> a lake would surprise the country
> and sag with a million birds.

You couldn't analyze those people—
a no-pattern had happened to them:
their field opened and opened,
level, and more, then forever,
never crossed. Their world went everywhere.

So does his world it seems, in America at least—everywhere a
lot of us tend to think of as nowhere. Who else brings us Elko,
Nevada, or Sharon Springs, Kansas? More important, he has his
very own way of bringing to bear nature on man, the willful and
self-conscious one who threatens the planet with extinction. "At
the Bomb Testing Site" goes like this:

At noon in the desert a panting lizard
waited for history, its elbows tense,
watching the curve of a particular road
as if something might happen.

It was looking for something farther off
than people could see, an important scene
acted in stone for little selves
at the flute end of consequences.

There was just a continent without much on it
under a sky that never cared less.
Ready for a change, the elbows waited.
The hands gripped hard on the desert.

History interests Stafford, both the land's and our people's.
He can't help noticing what people do and leave behind as they
move about, fit into valleys, come close to rivers, trek the desert,
and accommodate themselves to mountains, to the seasons, to
the ocean's final no: not a step beyond. The Indians, more than
any other Americans, know and treasure the Western land, and
of course, they made a beginning of our history long before
"we" were here, so full of ourselves and so determined to bend
history to our purposes. A section of *Someday, Maybe* is titled
"Wind World" and contains poems that in one way or another
address themselves to Indians, to their experience on this conti-
nent and their way of looking at life. The poems turn out to be
quite brief—"Indian Caves in the Dry Country": "These are
some canyons / we might use again / sometime."—or only a
little longer—"People of the South Wind" or "Origins." The
latter offers a finely wrought piece of Indian lore every bit wor-

thy of what one hears Indian parents telling their children in the Southwest. No boasting and vainglory; no effort to prove one's superiority; no ethnic pride; but rather an almost casual effort to link one's ancestors with the concreteness of life's "every-dayness," to draw upon a word both Kierkegaard and Heidegger have used in an attempt to fight off the demons of the abstract, so tempting to those two men, among others. "So long ago that we weren't people then," one is told, "our hands came upon this warm place on a rack / inside a high cave in the North, in the wilderness." A Hopi mother recently told me that when her children ask her about where they all came from, she tells them: "It was too long ago for you or me or anyone to know. The stars know, though. They have watched, and they remember. They will not tell us, but that does not mean we have no history. In the world there is knowledge of us, even if we don't possess it." Such children may at first get restless: tell us more, make us more satisfied. So she goes on: "There must have been a moment when a man and a woman stopped and began to dig into the earth. They spent the night nearby, and in the morning they felt the wind upon their skin, and heard the wind's message: stay. They did, and now we are here."

At times Stafford emphasizes the rootlessness of some Americans; he himself knows what it is to drive, drive, drive on Route 40, to enter and leave those towns, so many of them ghosts of their former selves yet by no means dead and gone—simply holding on proudly and bravely for dear life. But there is a sense of continuity, a faith in the ways of nature and at least a certain kind of man (themselves) that Indians unselfconsciously have as a psychological possession and as elements in their cultural tradition. These are not often to be taken for granted by the rest of us, even those Mr. Stafford knows, likes, and is moved to portray. Somehow we have lost touch with the world around us and ourselves, and the two developments surely go together, at least in Stafford's gentle but tough vision of America. "It is the time for all the heroes to go home," he begins the poem whose title, "Allegiances," he has given to his most recent volume of poems. Then he adds one of his elliptical asides ("if they have any") and goes on: "time for all of us common ones / to locate ourselves by the real things / we live by." The rest of the poem goes like this—and it is not at all a long-winded pronouncement or a self-important philosophical credo but simply a way of calling upon "heaven and earth," as those Palestinian nomads and prophets of several thousand years ago would put it:

Far to the north, or indeed in any direction,
strange mountains and creatures have always lurked—
elves, goblins, trolls, and spiders:—we
encounter them in dread and wonder.

But once we have tasted far streams, touched the gold,
found some limit beyond the waterfall,
a season changes, and we come back, changed
but safe, quiet, grateful.

Suppose an insane wind holds all the hills
while strange beliefs whine at the traveler's ears,
we ordinary beings can cling to the earth and love
where we are, sturdy for common things.

Stafford is just that, one of the "common" ones, and he is indeed
"sturdy for common things":

The writer's home he salvages from little pieces
along the roads, from distinctions he remembers,
from what by chance he sees—his grabbed heritage;
and from people fading from his road, from history.
He reaches out far, being a desperate man;
he comprehends by fistfuls with both hands.

Stafford will not let up; he will not be, he knows not how to be,
immodest. In such a confessional poem there is no hidden
agenda—that ironic self-congratulatory line or stanza that will
serve to punch any literal-minded doubter in the nose and let
him know that pity is not what the poem really wants—but
rather the kind of awe that may creep up but eventually obtains
complete control. No, the next lines establish Stafford's know-
ing, touching, lyrical voice as utterly and convincingly diffident
and unassuming: "But what can bring in enough to save the
tame / or be home for them who even with roofs are shel-
terless?" It is, he is telling us, for others to criticize, berate, and
condemn, "them," all those near and far away who are fellow
citizens of this nation. He knows their sadness, the virtual hope-
lessness they must sense if not recognize, even as he knows how
it has gone for Sitting Bull and his descendants. And knowing,
he still wants to sing—because as anyone who lives in a small
town, however isolated, out West knows, you never can tell
who will appear on the horizon, slowly work his way near, and
reveal himself to have receptive ears and responsive eyes.

FRED CHAPPELL

Two Views of the Lone Man

The difference between solitude and loneliness? The mystic hermit knows. He has entered his cave in the desert to find solitude, he has sought it out. We feebler mortals inherit loneliness. Here we stand, and Time and Change are working to bereave us of our dearest.

It is no crime for the poet not to be a mystic hermit, he commits no artistic gaffe if he stands closer to the main huddle of humanity than does Jeremiah. They mistake him who look upon William Stafford as a rather-more-formal Robert Bly, for there is more Frost in him than Zen. It is true that the lone man in Stafford's poems has found out things, but he has lost more than he has found. "Losing a Friend" begins:

> Open the rain and go in,
> close the gray door. Look
> around. The whole world
> is falling, and you are, and
> all else outside the world falls.

Often enough this poet uses the word *world*—along with *wind* and *storm*—as a trope for loss, for the slipping-away of connections. "You Night Men" ends with the line "Funneled out, lost in the storm of the world." In speaking of an old family homestead, he addresses this loss personally, "Listen, World, you did it wrong;" and he vows never to forget, as the world has forgotten.

This attitude is at the opposite end of the universe from the one embodied by Bly's "Hermit":

> There is a man whose body is perfectly whole.
> He stands, the storm behind him,
> And the grass blades are leaping in the wind.
> Darkness is gathered in folds
> About his feet,

Small Farm 9–10 (Spring–Fall 1979): 52–54.

He is no one. When we see
Him, we grow calm,
And sail on into the tunnels of joyful death.

Opposed attitudes, and I can't help feeling that Stafford's is the truer, as it is the more humane. Attempting to depict an emblematic figure outside the range of our experience, Bly necessarily creates a "literary" figure which smells of the lamp and the book ("folds / About his feet."). Finally it is all unconvincing, and I for one begin to suspect that a grossly mundane sensibility is trying to wrack itself into mysticism. Here is the strategy of the poet who not only desires unlimited credit but expects by God to receive it. There is a fat and tipplesome Goliard streak in Bly's monkishness, and though he has forsworn it, yet shall it betray him at the last. Why not give it rein?

Stafford's lone man seems more genuinely lone than Bly's. Storm-thinned, wind-emaciated, he stands stark in a drifting Western space. He stands the starker too because once he did possess family, friends, and homeplace—but now no more.

I was to return,
still selfish, but kind. Now nobody's here.

Another flake, and another—and nobody's here.

In Stafford, there is more Art of Fiction, as in Bly there is more Art of Fable. Stafford's lonesome westerner, weather-beaten and befuddled, is close kin to the figures in Wright Morris's novels, to the absent figures in his photographs. Stafford's figure might easily live in Morris's Lone Tree, he might be the protagonist of *A Life*.

In his detail also Stafford displays more Fiction. Here, in "Love in the Country," is a weather observed:

In the rain yesterday, puddles
on the walk to the barn sounded their
quick little drinks.

It has been made into poetry, true enough, but first it has been observed. It is not visually improbable, as in Bly's "the backbones of the sea," or overgeneralized like his "The vast waters / The cry of seagulls," or simply iconographic like his "The blind horse among the cherry trees."

Perhaps I am saying no more—I should certainly like to say no more—than that these two poets are aiming at different ends. It is comforting to know that poets are different from one another; it is *necessary* to know it. Yet I have observed that some of my friends often confuse the poems of Stafford and Bly, even at times attributing remembered lines incorrectly. But this confusion results from an accidental similarity in diction between the two. There is a rhetorical likeness between these lines from Stafford's "Waking at 3 A.M."

> You look upon all that the darkness
> ripples across. More than has ever
> been found comforts you. You open your
> eyes in a vault that unlocks as fast
> and as far as your thought can run.

and these lines from Bly's "A Journey with Women"

> At dawn we are still transparent, pulling
> In the starlight;
> We are still falling like a room
> Full of moonlight through the air. . . .

But with verbal strategy the likeness stops. The sensibilities of the two poets are dissimilar; they are both extremely interior; but Bly's is the more delicate interiority, and delicate in spite of the fact (perhaps because of the fact) that it is more deliberately and carefully self-willed. I have the impression from his poems that Bly has gone actively to seek out not solitude but loneliness, while a more commonplace but more purely tragic loneliness has gathered itself into Stafford. He has learned how not to live without it, he has even learned to value it sorely, but he had had to sacrifice a more carefree part of himself in order to accommodate such a valuation. His poem "Rescue" is something of a spiritual diary which records this process, and this is the way that poem ends:

> From now on in my life there would be a place
> like a scene in a paperweight. One figure in the storm
> would be reaching out with my hand for those
> who had died. It would always be still in that scene,
> no matter what happened. I could come back to it,
> carefully, any time, to be saved, and go on.

How forcibly I am reminded in Stafford of the figures of the sculptor Giacometti! Those spindly, elongated, rubble-textured figures, are they not men and women whose lives have crumbled away, been bitten away? And what is left to them? A strong purity of outline, a singleness of identity, a sense of personal destiny. They stand pure in the impure weathers that have so harshly shaped them, and stride alone through the vast echoless spaces that their presences make more lonely.

Yet for all the independence this lone figure exhibits, the poet is drawn to it. He feels admiration and love, though both feelings are tempered by foreknowledge. If there were some way to escape foreknowledge, or to forget it, then perhaps Stafford's poems *would* be a bit like Bly's. But the bitter wisdom is in him, and he will not deny it. Here is his "Friend":

> For anyone, for anyone,
> the years are a sufficient storm:
> over horizons in channels of wind
> they blow, steady and long.
>
> When I was young, when I was young,
> I ran that storm—I walk it now.
> And those who then companioned me,
> save one, are gone.
>
> They are nothing. They are nothing.
> Forget them. What the sky can hold,
> it holds, by day by day. But they—
> they're lost, even on my inner sky.
>
> From human loss, from gravel, from stone,
> after years, one holds what one can.
> I look out—that boy: undeterred,
> he runs on through the withering world.

DONALD HALL

William Stafford

Eight Notions

1. One needn't write about *Stories That Could Be True* as if it were cast in bronze. One can pick it up and read in it for an hour or two, as one expects to do with prose. Few good poets are subject to the accusation of readability. To admirers of poetry at its most ambiguous and enigmatic, "readability" may imply triviality or minority: Eliot is wonderful, but neither he nor Hopkins is "readable." Anyone whose preconceptions exclude Stafford on account of his accessibility loses too much.

2. Stafford is a poet of ordinary life. His collected poems are the journal of a man recording daily concerns. That is why his daily method of writing is relevant to his life's work. You could say that his poetry is truly quotidian: he writes it every day; it comes out of every day. And the poet of the quotidian did not find it necessary to become *maudit,* to follow Hart Crane to the waterfront or Baudelaire to the whorehouse or even Lowell to McLean's. He got up at six in the morning in a suburb of Portland and drained the sump.

3. If we attend to chronology, William Stafford is a member of the tragic generation of American poets. Stafford was born in 1914, the same year as Weldon Kees and Randall Jarrell and John Berryman, three suicides; Delmore Schwartz was born in 1913, and Robert Lowell in 1917. How wonderfully the survivor contrasts. What makes him so different? Like Lowell, Stafford was a C.O. [conscientious objector] during the Second War. Like Berryman and Kees he came from the Midwest. But Stafford is a low-church Christian far from the rhetorical Catholicism that Lowell and Berryman entertained. I suspect that his survival is related not merely to his Christianity but to his membership in a small, embattled, pacifist sect.

Small Farm 9–10 (Spring–Fall 1979): 50–51. Also published in *The Weather for Poetry: Essays, Reviews, and Notes on Poetry, 1977–81* (Ann Arbor: University of Michigan Press, 1982), 172–74.

4. The poetic surface is often ordinary (not always: Stafford salutes a lost Cree inside a knife . . .) with famous dead deer in roads, with remembered loves, with fancies about wind and weather. This ordinariness doth tease us out of thought; while we are thoughtless, the second language of poetry speaks to us. Stafford has referred to an unspoken tongue that lives underneath the words of poetry. This second language is beyond the poet's control, but we can define a poet as someone who speaks it. English teachers afflicted with students who lack control over their own language—ignorant, illiterate, wordless—often assume that the best language is the most controlled and the most conscious. Not so, or not always so: poets are literate, poets control, poets command syntax and lexicon—but the best poets *also* write without knowing everything that they are up to, trusting in the second language's continual present hum of implication.

5. For years, Stafford has built a reputation for modesty, while accumulating 263 pages of poems. This "modesty" is steel plate twelve inches thick which allows penetration into enemy territory (I pick this analogy for a pacifist), there to plant not mines but tough flowers that endure.

6. Looking at photographs of poets, printed on jackets and in magazines, one continually discovers that the photographer of the best portraits is William Stafford: close-ups, characteristic in expression, inward and meditative. Is it far-fetched to find the poet in the photographer, the photographer in the poet? These photographs allow no fantasy; they are inquiries into reality directed by intelligent, watchful, patient *attention*. Most photographs make a glossy surface. Stafford's speak from a level of the second language.

7. English poets and critics have a hard time judging American poetry, as Americans do with English. Sometimes mistakes illuminate. It is a mistake to place Stafford, as I have seen English critics do, with the Black Mountain inheritors of William Carlos Williams. Yet it is an observant mistake, because Stafford writes a plain American which from a distance looks like any other endeavor at plain America. Stafford differs because the rhythm of his characteristic speech makes a noise wholly at odds with the noises common to Black Mountain; it is slower, less nervous, more metaphoric and contemplative, just as idiomatic but less concerned to represent or embody idiom. Still, this long distance English view helps to isolate Stafford from other Americans, for instance from the rhetoricians of his tragic generation.

8. I mentioned his Christianity earlier, to begin to name a

quality. It need not follow, but Stafford's poems show forth goodness and compassion. These qualities together with affection and shrewd reticence make him unusual in the great zoo of contemporary American poetry. Torture, pain, cruelty, egotism, and selfishness, madness, and lust are common to human existence. Much poetry will—must—represent cruelty, pain, torture, lust, madness, egotism, and selfishness. But there is an unexamined and neurotic notion that only these qualities equal seriousness; Stafford gives the lie to this currency.

BOB PERELMAN

From "The First Person"

In his essay on Pasternak, O'Hara quotes Zhivago: "You in others—this is your soul. This is what you are." It's true for O'Hara. What's personal in his poems doesn't come from a pre-existing Frank O'Hara. He never "found his voice." It's not a recording of the self, the self is *listening*.

You could almost call his I a persona. Let me read you some work where there definitely is a persona, and it's used, I think, to less advantage. This is from the second Canto. And you can see Pound being very impressed with Browning's dramatic monologues:

> And by the beach-run, Tyro,
>   Twisted arms of the sea-god,
> Lithe sinews of water, gripping her, cross-hold,
> And the blue-gray glass of the wave tents them,
> Glare azure of water, cold-welter, close cover.
> Quiet sun-tawny sand-stretch,
> The gulls broad out their wings,
>   nipping between the splay feathers . . .

Then, skipping a little:

> God-sleight then, god-sleight:
>   Ship stock fast in sea-swirl,
> Ivy upon the oars, King Pentheus,
>   grapes with no seed but sea-foam,
> Ivy in the scupper-hole.
> Aye, I, Acoetes, stood there,
>   and the god stood by me,
> Water cutting under the keel.

My take on this is that the really fantastic writing occurs when Pound is on his subject, which is the sexual divinity of the sea.

Hills 6–7 (Spring 1980): 147–65.

But then, he puts in this character. I think that's a terrible line, "Aye, I, Acoetes, stood there." It's incredibly clunky. It makes that whole last part sound phony, made up. After the early Cantos, he drops personas, and then I is always a historical person. It's almost never Pound himself. He's backstage. . . .

Looking at Olson, *The Maximus Poems,* in terms of persona is interesting. The beginning is the same story as with Pound: when Olson is trying hard to create a persona, the writing falls off. Especially the first poem, which is the weakest of the series by a long shot:

> Off-shore, by islands hidden in the blood
> jewels & miracles, I, Maximus
> a metal hot from boiling water, tell you
> what is a lance, who obeys the figures of
> the present dance

I just don't believe that at all.

> The nest, I say, to you, I Maximus, say
> under the hand, as I see it, over the waters
> from this place where I am, where I hear . . .

It's just rhetorical frosting. If he wants to say where he is, he does it in the other poems, very beautifully quite often.

Compare that persona with the end, which is:

> my wife   my car   my color   and   myself

There's no way you can say that's Maximus. That's Charles Olson: his wife is dead, his car is gone, and in fact, he's just about dead. My color—he's dying of cancer—and myself. Even the verb or verbs are gone.

Just to nail this down a little further than it needs, I want to read part of a poem by William Stafford, which I think is all persona in the worst sense. It's the persona of the real life self speaking normally:

TRAVELING THROUGH THE DARK

> Traveling through the dark I found a deer
> dead on the edge of the Wilson River road.
> It is usually best to roll them into the canyon:
> that road is narrow; to swerve might make more dead. . . .

The car aimed ahead its lowered parking lights;
under the hood purred the steady engine.
I stood in the glare of the warm exhaust turning red;
around our group I could hear the wilderness listen.

I thought hard for us all—my only swerving—
then pushed her over the edge into the river.

So, this is a "voice" poem. William Stafford has "found his voice." It's all realistic, but all it leads up to is the pathetic fallacy of "I could hear the wilderness listen." A typical neo-academic dirge for nature. The poet is firmly in the driver's seat, "*I* could hear the wilderness," and firmly in control of all the meaning, "*I* thought hard for us all." All the other work I've read insists on the reader participating, which is reasonable, seeing that language is as much in the reader's head as the writer's. But here, the I is in a privileged position, unaffected by the words.★

Robert Grenier: I don't think it's fair to dump on the emotional self as commodity. What is there of interest that draws people to that poem?

Perelman: The Stafford poem? I don't know. It's a question of how people read and the circuits that have been opened in readers' minds. The way poetry is being taught now there's less sense of possibility and the mass of people who do read poetry, which isn't very big, have read poems like this, and it's a reassuring, soothing sense of self.

Grenier: That you don't often have in your daily life.

Perelman: Yes.

Grenier: And that you can project yourself onto and identify with as a kind of locus of sensibility that you'd like to be possessed of, at least while reading the page, to give the world a center of feeling it might not have in the flux of shifting phenomena. . . .

Ron Silliman: O'Hara's work so often is calling attention to its devices, constantly defusing what Allan [Tinker] calls the myth of unity.

Perelman: Except that he means it, too.

★What follows are excerpts from the discussion prompted by the original presentation of the paper.—Ed.

Silliman: But, in the Stafford poem, all the language is subservient to this umbrella structure, which only surfaces in the poem at the word *I*. What makes the poem work is that same sense of agreement you get in bad didactic writing, whether it's talking about the individualized subjective I or the People or Logos. We've seen a lot of umbrella terms used badly in poetry. And Stafford simply represents one form of that, where all the language dissolves as you're reading it. When you hear language being used "poetically," like the car purring, it comes across in a really smarmy way.

Jeanne Lance: I'm not sure whether the Stafford poem works because of the I or not. I didn't feel that. I felt the I was a convention, and not particularly apt. But the clarity and simplicity of the poem are why people like it. It doesn't have much to do with I.

Perelman: It seems to me the climax of the poem is "I thought hard for us all."

Lance: But that's the line, the whole line. It's not the use of the I.

Perelman: But the focus of the line is on the I thinking, isn't it?

Tom Mandel: He pushes the deer for all of us. It's not bad enough that he does it. We have to do it, too. People like that poem because it makes them feel shitty. [*laughter*]

DICK BARNES

The Absence of the Artist

I'd like to talk about the desire or attempt of some artists in this century to be completely absent from their works. Going back in time, we could think of Pound or Browning hidden by a mask to speak through, or of Stephen Dedalus's achieved Dramatic artist indifferent to his works and (somewhat vulgarly, I always thought, as if Joyce were signaling that he wasn't Stephen Dedalus) paring his fingernails; coming closer I think of Samuel Beckett's character exasperated by his own voice as it proceeds from one book to the next, longing for nothing but his own absence, speaking only to find the last word and say it and then be silent in the last dust; or John Cage with his many ingenious schemes for rescuing his works from his own intentions and the intentions of whatever performers may be involved, with the intention of involving everybody in an art that can imitate Nature according to Nature's own mode of operation. I am opinionated about all of these authors and would gladly share my opinions but wish for now only to invoke their presence in our thoughts while examining the issues raised not long ago when a keen critic attacked a good poet. The poet is William Stafford and the critic Bob Perelman. The attack occurs in a talk entitled "The First Person," published in the spring 1980 number of *Hills,* that comes at this same question ("Who's writing it") from the angle of language, or "Language." Perelman has been talking about how the poetry of Pound and Olson loses energy when they "try hard to create a persona" when he goes on:

> Just to nail this down a little further than it needs, I want to read a part of a poem by William Stafford, which I think is all persona in the worst sense. It's the persona of the real life self speaking normally:

Field 28 (Spring 1983): 27–34.

Traveling through the dark I found a deer
dead on the edge of the Wilson River road.
It is usually best to roll them into the canyon:
that road is narrow; to swerve might make more dead . . .

[here Perelman skips two stanzas, but I think I'll include them]

By glow of the tail-light I stumbled back of the car
and stood by the heap, a doe, a recent killing;
she had stiffened already, almost cold.
I dragged her off; she was large in the belly.

My fingers touching her side brought me the reason—
her side was warm; her fawn lay there waiting,
alive, still, never to be born.
Beside that mountain road I hesitated.

[here Perelman resumes]

The car aimed ahead its lowered parking lights;
under the hood purred the steady engine.
I stood in the glare of the warm exhaust turning red;
around our group I could hear the wilderness listen.

I thought hard for us all—my only swerving—
then pushed her over the edge into the river.

So [Perelman continues], this is a "voice" poem. William Stafford has "found his voice." It's all realistic, but all it leads up to is the pathetic fallacy of "I could hear the wilderness listen." A typical neo-academic dirge for nature. The poet is firmly in the driver's seat, "*I* could hear the wilderness," and firmly in control of all meaning, "*I* thought hard for us all." All the other work I've read [that's to say William Burroughs, Robert Creeley, Gertrude Stein, Catullus, Frank O'Hara, Olson, and Pound] insists on the reader participating, which is reasonable, seeing that language is as much in the reader's head as in the writer's. But here, the I is in a privileged position, unaffected by the words.

Now, this gives me my assignment. There are some things I want to say about "the persona of the real life self," the "voice" poem, the "pathetic fallacy," and William Stafford that will put me in a position to say something about the absence of the artist.

The pathetic fallacy first, in hopes it can be dealt with most briefly. Maybe it isn't a pathetic fallacy when he says, "I could hear the wilderness listen." If something unusual happens in the wilderness, such as a car stopping by a highway, the ordinary little noises that go on all the time are suddenly quiet because the wild things hold still and listen; and if you knew the wilderness and were standing there by the dead doe behind your car, you could hear that. But there are, elsewhere in Stafford's works, plenty of examples of something that might be called the pathetic fallacy. Think of the wind, or Wind World as he's called, that Stafford heard about one day from a Joshua tree near Mojave:

> Wind World always made friends with
> the Indians, who wore feathers for him.
> Even today when he finds an arrowhead
> in the dust or sand
> he just leaves it there.

Or think of the dandelion cavalry, surrounding a church:

> After the service they depart singly
> to mention in the world their dandelion faith:
> "God is not big; He is right."

Or think of the grass, the morning someone's heart stopped

> and all became still. A girl said, "Forever?"
> And the grass: "Yes. Forever." While the sky—

Think of the sky. For William Stafford there are no inanimate objects:

> It's alive, the whole world is alive.
> Breathe on its mirror again,
> tease it along over the fern
> lean with it toward the light.

And so, for him, the attribution of feelings to objects can't be fallacious, and the pathetic fallacy becomes quite impertinent as a critical term. Actually, the idea of the pathetic fallacy belongs to a brief if mischievous period that sought to perceive in terms of alienation and control—what seemed for a while the scientific mode, though I'm told science itself has now outgrown it—instead of by identification and humility, which is the perceptive mode of all true poets. This benighted period began perhaps with Bacon and Descartes and ended with Blake (though not everybody noticed when it ended). Stafford's way of perceiving resembles the animism of an earlier age, when Sir Philip Sidney, for instance, could imagine that in the springtime, when the snow melted and the warm breezes blew across a meadow, that meadow might start feeling sexy and want to put on a new coat embroidered all over with flowers. Doctor Johnson argued that such a comparison is incorrect: it might be proper to say an embroidered coat is like a flowery meadow, but you can't say a meadow is like embroidery because (if I remember his argument) the coat is dignified by being compared to Nature but the meadow degraded by being compared to Art. A Cartesian distinction has done its work on Dr. Johnson. Suffice it for now to go back to Beckett and Cage: Beckett because the intolerable fix his characters are in is precisely where you would be if you applied the ideas of Descartes (and Geulinx) with rigor; Cage because he once said, "In the Renaissance we opted for clarity and got it. But now we are in another historical period."

Next, the "voice" poem. Bob Perelman says sarcastically, "William Stafford has 'found his voice.'" What he means can be clarified by something he had said earlier in his talk, that "what's personal in Frank O'Hara's poems doesn't come from a preexisting Frank O'Hara. He never 'found his voice.' It's not a recording of the self, the self is *listening*." Now this seems to me quite true of O'Hara, and profound. The only profound thing I know about poetry is that it's talking and listening at the same time, and I believe that's what Frank O'Hara does; but it seems to me equally true of Stafford, as I know both from things he has said and from his other poems. In poems he likes to say things not for their truth value but to hear how they sound: "Maybe I'm a king." He likes to tell the reader to do things he knows the reader can't do: "Be like the sun." (Then he can listen to how it sounds after he's said that.) In one poem he climbs a dune with his child to look at the far cold waves, and the child asks,

"How far could you swim, Daddy,
in such a storm?"

"As far as was needed," I said,
and as I talked, I swam.

So to me the line "I thought hard for us all—my only swerving"
has a redeeming tremor of uncertainty and life about it, the self
listening, while for Bob Perelman it merely represents the poet
"firmly in control of all meaning." And I'd say in this case I am
correct and Perelman mistaken, but in a way that opens up a
difficult problem. Because while I agree with him that what's
both personal and valid doesn't come from a preexisting person-
ality of the poet, I claim that I can listen better than he can to this
particular poem precisely because of a familiarity with the poet
that does preexist in *my* own mind. The idea goes back nicely
into Perelman's essay: he quotes Frank O'Hara quoting Paster-
nak, "You in others—that is your soul. That is what you are."
But this soul-in-others, this William Stafford of my mind who
enables me to hear that the poet is listening, is a dangerous
character to Stafford if Stafford finds out about him:

> You have to watch out, or a follower will
> praise you, and the stumbles you need for your life
> will be harder to take.

Is it all right for us readers if this William Stafford preexists in
our minds when we're reading, but crippling for the poet if he
preexists in his mind when he's writing? That may well be. And
this mental William Stafford is, I believe, precisely the self that
the poet desires be absent from his works. It's in us, not in the
works? But we have learned about it only from the works?
That's hard, but may be true. In my experience, poets don't talk
much about their careers or what they have done to advance
them, maybe because there's no money in it anyway; I've found
visual artists, who can hope to produce salable artifacts, to be
much more up front in talking about their careers. (When they
get together they also like to talk about real estate: you can see
why that would be.) So it was John Mason, a sculptor, who put
it succinctly when he and I were talking about this recognizable
personality one's works create, a mysterious and powerful cre-
ation who can confer intelligibility on poets and salability on
sculptors: "Yes you do have to have him and that's okay so long
as he doesn't look over your shoulder when you're trying to
work." The personality prison or trap self, who would have
made Marx a Marxist or Descartes a Cartesian if he could, must

be absent in us if our personality-that-belongs-to-others is to flourish. In a recent ceramic sculpture show at the Whitney Museum it was remarkable that Robert Arneson's macroheroic self-portraits (while wonderful) seemed like what they are, visual representations of the artist in various guises, while John Mason's pieces, abstracts that didn't look like anybody at all, had a presence that made each one of them seem like John himself, standing there exercising his usual taciturnity.

In the same way, what John Cage does really works. He uses chance operations, indeterminacy, various means of assuring local unpredictability, because he wants to get himself out of the way; then whatever is there can be seen and heard to operate according to its own nature—and he does, and it does. But precisely when his self is gone his presence is there: this John-Cage-who-belongs-to-others; and it does affect our appreciation of 4'33" of our own concerthall silence, or whatever else he brings to our attention, by whatever means. He hasn't escaped from that and doesn't need to because it's a listening, liberating presence.

The Cartesian object-of-its-own-perception self, in Beckett, is a prison inescapable in its own terms; Beckett allows us to experience palpably what it is like, how absolutely intolerable an impasse it is, until in an explosion of recognition and exasperation we are liberated, by miracle,—or anyway that's what happens to me when I read Beckett. Beckett himself would never acknowledge such a possibility because if he did, that possibility would merely become incorporated as another cell block of the prison. To be possible, liberation must be impossible. Which doesn't explain, but illuminates, Beckett's inexhaustible and humane anger.

As for William Stafford, freedom seems to come more easily to him, to be something skillfully accepted rather than anything achieved:

> Thus freedom always came nibbling my thought,
> just as—often, in light, on the open hills—
> you can pass an antelope and not know
> and look back, and then—even before you see—
> there is something wrong about the grass.
> And then you see.

> That's the way everything in the world is waiting.

—or anyway that's the kind of thing he likes to say, just to hear how it sounds.

This brings us to "the persona of the real life self speaking normally," which Bob Perelman says is the worst kind. I'm not sure I agree with him there. "Speaking normally": for normal-sounding speech to work in a poem the kind of art that hides art is needed, which is a rare kind but not the less to be valued for that. And it oughtn't be necessary to talk funny all the time just to signal that what you're saying is a poem. As John Cage says, everything is there already. The "real life self": we've already said enough about the trap self and the self in others to be ready for that, but I want to bring up another consideration.

It's customary now for a poet to bring his poetry to other people by standing up in front of them and reading it out loud. Some poets even regard what they write as scores for performance, and any poet now is more aware of his body as an instrument than poets had to be during the time when their work almost exclusively took the form of printed books. So when a poet writes "I" in a poem he's as aware as Chaucer was that people will first suppose it means either him, the poet standing there in front of them, or else someone the poet is impersonating. Mouth, breath, voice, chest: the origin of the poem in the poet's body became a matter of theory as well as practice at the hands of Charles Olson and Robert Creeley (though I claim it's been the true practice all along). In these circumstances the "persona of the real life self" is not just a fiction or lie, though it may be both: it's an act.

That we see too many sloppy acts at poetry readings is beside the point—the abuse is never an argument against the use—and if a poet has an act that becomes entertainment instead of art that's up to him, and his audience, and what they both want. The act becomes entertainment when the persona of the real life self becomes fixed and familiar, objectified, and therefore subject to judgment whether that judgment turn out to be admiration, derision, a warm chummy acceptance, or whatever. The artist is colder and as artist quite indifferent to judgment, like Cunizza in Dante's *Paradiso* remembering her sins on earth. The entertainer speaks in company, for the company, and listens (if he listens) in the self, over against the company, to see if he's getting over. The artist speaks from utter solitude, a solitude that others (and maybe the artist himself when not occupied with his art) can scarcely dare imagine, where the self is dead and the soul opens inward upon eternity. What makes his act complete is that, speaking that way, he listens at the same time, and in listening joins any others who may be hearing in a kind of casual communion. I know this sounds rather exalted, and to me it is in fact as holy as anything else, but at the same time entirely common and everyday, involving the kind of wisdom we all must have had when we noticed what it took to be "popular" in high school. We were wiser than we knew, then, even in the words we used, because the name for the one sin that would keep anyone from being popular no matter how accomplished or admirable in any other way was to be "conceited." I'm arguing now that the conceit, or concept of oneself, is the very thing that makes the self a prison, when in our true and inner nature we suffer no such limitation, being beyond any predication, and so, free. Yet to become aware of this freedom we must acquire, painfully, a thorough and exact awareness of the conceit that afflicts us. Every man, says the author of the *Book of Privy Counseling,* is his own cross. To know the conceit in that deep kind of knowing is to be free of it and as poet to be blessedly absent from one's own works. Somebody seems to be there, as in Frank O'Hara, to do this, to do that, to be

> the
> center of all beauty!
> writing these poems!
> Imagine!

or in Stafford,

> liking the cut of a thought, we could say "Hello."

But the poet is out here with us, listening, imagining too.

It was some time after reading Perelman's essay that I came across another Stafford poem that like "Traveling Through the Dark" had to do with driving along in a car at night; this one, "The Dialectic of the Mountains," is about driving home from teaching a night class on literature, meditating in the car about eloquence and the act of reading. Part of it seemed to allude to Perelman's contention that in "Traveling Through the Dark" "the poet is firmly in the driver's seat, '*I* could hear the wilderness,' and firmly in control of all meaning, '*I* thought hard for us all'": the poem says

Teachers live by trying, have to drive and go carefully past
the trumpet writers and beware the trumpet critics and go around
Saddle Mountain, and sometimes not even reply to challenges; not
    say anything
where there is nothing in the car for the wise to say, steering.

You need large eyes at night, throat for carefully saying,
luck on the road, teaching State Extension Division Lit 109.

So when he visited our campus last year I asked William Stafford
if that was a reply to Perelman (or a nonreply). He said he hadn't
heard of the article but would like to read it: "I might agree." I
showed it to him and he read it eagerly: "Yes, I do agree," said
he, abandoning a difficult pose quicker than gravity pulls or
gunners pretend: "I was thinking about something like that my-
self. That's why I put together a book of poems called *Things
That Happen Where There Aren't Any People*." A brief glance at
that book will bring us to a conclusion.

First, one has to admit that amidst all its emptinesses and
lonesome wind, snowflake and juniper and fern under changes
of light, there are all these souls, his own and ours, if maybe
without our conceits—no people, only us. In "Notice What This
Poem Is Not Doing" there are

> A house, a house, a barn, the old
> quarry, where the river shrugs,

but the people are gone;

> the light
> along the hills has come, has found you.

> Notice what this poem has not done.

—That is, I guess, it hasn't included anybody in the picture
except the unpictured but noticing "you," who didn't find the
light but were found by it. In "Crossing the Desert" we're the
ones who are driving along invisible behind our headlights:

> Pardon! Pardon!—
> the ditch at night is a church
> where eyes burn their candles
> mile after silent mile
> to meet whatever comes, whatever comes.

But maybe in the next incarnation (if that's what "the next time this world is ours" means) we won't be in a car:

> we'll cry out from the ditch
> to find our cousins there safe
> offering us their paws and letting
> the light we bring return from their eyes
> to shine forth, part of our own.

Identification and humility, not alienation and control, are how we know, and knowing that way is all the safety we have. That's why we're glad in "Dawn on the Warm Springs Reservation" that we can't "give away, or buy, / or sell, or assign these hills" that hold spirits the same way we've noticed junipers, in the fog, holding daylight,

> And it's the same all over the world—
> any tree, any rock, any hill.

That's how we know the water, in "What It Is," because we're like it:

> It
> has forgotten as soon as there is
> anything to forget. It likes everything
> but never notices itself. When still,
> it says the sky.

That's why, when the "Hinge in the Wind" says "Nobody home, nobody home," and when we get to be more like "Nobody" so

> when trains go by the engineer
> no longer answers our wave,

and when we learn of the "End of the Man Experiment,"

> the whole world
> one storm,

we aren't afraid. Or are we? We need poems like this to feel what our fear is, how it comes from our conceit, and how it vanishes whenever our conceit is vanquished, time after time; and how sweet it can be, sometimes, when that happens, as in "Learning Your Place":

They have other studies in their eyes
than anyone, the wolves that pace their bars,
priorities afar, and bonuses
no zoo-goer comprehends. "Invest a paw
and get a world," their shoulder says when they
turn. They own you once when you arrive,
then give you away for good: no elaborate
trial—a glance—you don't exist.

PETER STITT

William Stafford's Wilderness Quest

When William Stafford talks or writes about his poems—as he has done in many interviews and in the prose pieces collected in *Writing the Australian Crawl* (1978)—he almost never views them as finished, analyzable objects of art, preferring instead to concentrate on the process of composition that brought them about. To use a type of analogy Stafford himself often uses, we might view him as an eternal analysand in the psychoanalytic process, one who resolutely refuses to act the role of analyst to any meaningful degree. This cast of mind may seem typical, but in fact the degree to which Stafford insists on it does set him apart from his fellow writers. In the creative process as followed by most poets, there seems to come a time when the writer emphatically wants to understand, dominate, and shape his materials intellectually. The overall process may begin organically, with the poet simply accepting the signals that arrive, but by the time it is finished, the poet knows what is going on and asserts his control in order to be sure things turn out right. Not so with Stafford, one of whose "cherished" beliefs is "that a writer is not trying for a product, but accepting sequential signals toward an always-arriving present."[1]

In psychoanalysis, the analysand receives only one, apparently simple, instruction, intended to help him achieve free association: Say whatever occurs to you at a given moment. That something very like this is William Stafford's procedure when he composes his poems is apparent whenever he discusses how he does his writing:

> When I write, I like to have an interval before me when I am not likely to be interrupted. For me, this means usually the early morning, before others are awake. I get a pen and paper, take a glance out of the window (often it is dark out there), and wait. It is like fishing. But I do not wait very long, for

From *The World's Hieroglyphic Beauty: Five American Poets* by Peter Stitt (Athens: University of Georgia Press, 1985), 57–87. Copyright © 1985 by the University of Georgia Press.

there is always a nibble. . . . To get started I will accept anything that occurs to me. Something always occurs, of course, to any of us. We can't keep from thinking. Maybe I have to settle for an immediate impression: it's cold, or hot, or dark, or bright, or in between! Or—well, the possibilities are endless. If I put down something, that thing will help the next thing come, and I'm off. If I let the process go on, things will occur to me that were not at all in my mind when I started. These things, odd or trivial as they may be, are somehow connected. And if I let them string out, surprising things will happen.[2]

So committed is Stafford to this free-associative way of writing, "This"—as he calls it—"process-rather-than-substance view of writing," that he would prefer not even to think about meaning and content while he writes: "I cannot . . . insist on high standards. . . . By 'standards' I do not mean correctness. . . . I am thinking about such matters as social significance, positive values, consistency, etc. I resolutely disregard these. Something better, greater, is happening! I am following a process that leads so wildly and originally into new territory that no judgment can at the moment be made about values, significance, and so on."[3] Clearly what Stafford is trying to avoid is having his poetry controlled by the reflective, rational, intellectual, analytical portion of the mind. Occasionally, however, this side will gain the upper hand, and when it does, Stafford yields, though only briefly and with great distrust: "At times, without my insisting on it, my writings become coherent; the successive elements that occur to me are clearly related. They lead by themselves to new connections. Sometimes the language, even the syllables that happen along, may start a trend. Sometimes the materials alert me to something waiting in my mind, ready for sustained attention. At such times I allow myself to be eloquent, or intentional, or for great swoops (Treacherous! Not to be trusted!) reasonable. But I do not insist on any of that, for I know that back of my activity there will be the coherence of my self, and that indulgence of my impulses will bring recurrent patterns and meanings again."[4] Even in the psychoanalytic process there are many times when free association stops so that the analysand can participate with the analyst in an examination of what has been said. For the poet, this would mean thinking critically, intellectually, about his own work—a function that William Stafford is most reluctant to perform. And it is in this fact that both his greatest strength and his greatest weakness as a poet may be found.

The strength lies in his spontaneous creativity, the ease with which he writes. It is for this reason that Stafford is widely recognized, by critics and fellow poets alike, as a natural writer. James Dickey, for example, began his review of Stafford's first book, *West of Your City* (1960), with this observation: "There are poets who pour out rivers of ink, all on good poems. William Stafford is one of these. He has been called America's most prolific poet, and I have no doubt that he is. He turns out so much verse not because he is glib or empty, but because he is a real poet, a born poet, and communicating in lines and images is not only the best way for him to get things said; it is the easiest."[5] Stafford has published a great many poems, and there is no denying that most of them are of high quality, as pleasurable to read as they were effortless to write. The problem with all this is that William Stafford's conception of his poetry is really not any larger than the scope of the individual poem, as seen—reductively, the critic has to feel— from inside the creative process.

That Stafford is himself aware of this limitation is apparent from a statement he has made in an interview. He suggested that contemporary "poetry is trapped trying to do little adventitious piddling jobs. . . . It is interesting, but it isn't overwhelming the way Pascal is overwhelming, or the way some writer like Alfred North Whitehead, who turns his first-class mind to a sustained communication project, is overwhelming. I think there are many prose projects now that are calling forth more of the talents and the serious and sustained attention of writers than the kind of crochet work many of us are doing in poetry. You can write a poem rather quickly, close it out, and publish it in a magazine. Then you put together a collection of these fragments—but it is not the same thing as a book. There may be someone who writes a collection of poems as a whole book, but I've never done it. Mine always come in pieces. My feeling is that the most interesting parts of those collections of poems are the spaces not written out between the poems. Maybe we're trying to do the wrong thing."[6] Although this observation is stated as though it were generally true of contemporary poetry, the poet who most perfectly fits the pattern is, of course, William Stafford himself. Other of today's poets may not have written *Paradise Lost,* but they have written such coherent efforts as *The Dream Songs* (John Berryman, 1969), *The Book of Nightmares* (Galway Kinnell, 1971), and *Kicking the Leaves* (Donald Hall, 1978). Indeed, even most of the more loosely constructed books of lyrics by other poets considered in [*The World's Hieroglyphic Beauty*] are more carefully structured than the tightest of Stafford's volumes. As James Wright has said, echoing Robert Frost: "If you have a book of twenty-four poems, the book itself should be the twenty-fifth."[7] About the most that Stafford is willing to do structurally is "cluster" similar poems together in a given area of a given book: "I try to choose poems that will make a chord—that would be one way to put it—with the other notes that are in this part of the book." (See "Interview with William Stafford.")*

Whatever coherence, whatever thematic depth, there is within the body of Stafford's poetry has to be given its pattern by the critic (or the "analyst," if you will) to a much greater degree than is the case with most other poets. The problem is compounded by the complicated publishing history of Stafford's work. Nearly all of his published poems have appeared in magazines. Many, though not all, of them have subsequently been collected into books—some issued by small presses and some by his major publisher, Harper & Row. Because Stafford admits to having saved his best and most characteristic work for the Harper & Row volumes and because these are the volumes most readily available to readers, the present essay is based almost entirely upon those collections.[8] Finally, because of the un-planned, occasional nature of Stafford's poems, they will not be discussed in chronological order; instead, the poems will be presented here according to the thematic pattern that I see running through them.[9]

Generally speaking, William Stafford must be grouped with the other "optimistic" poets being studied in this volume—Richard Wilbur and Robert Penn Warren. If the dominant mood of American poetry from the 1950s into the 1970s is the pessimistic, even despairing one we find in the confessional writers and others, then these three poets are among the exceptions to the rule. As will soon be demonstrated, Stafford's poetic terrain is the village and the country; he believes in the small-town virtues and is even able to feel the presence of a vague sacredness within nature—most of which sets him apart from more pessimistic writers. And yet—although some readers have chosen to view him this way—Stafford is no Pollyanna; he is, in fact, considerably more doubting in his beliefs than is either Wilbur or Warren.

---

*In *The World's Hieroglyphic Beauty.*—Ed.

Thus, the first stanza of "An Introduction to Some Poems," which opens the volume *Someday, Maybe,* turns out to be less surprising than it seems on first reading:

> Look: no one ever promised for sure
> that we would sing. We have decided
> to moan. In a strange dance that
> we don't understand till we do it, we
> have to carry on.[10]

Obviously Stafford is speaking less directly for himself than for what he perceives to be the dominant attitude of the poetic age; and yet this attitude must be recognized as a component of his own thinking as well.

During an interview conducted by Sanford Pinsker, Stafford indicated something of what might make him "moan" in some poems: "Loneliness is something you'll have plenty of without trying to induce it. You can count on it. As a matter of fact, you don't have to be a neurotic to discover that the world can be a frightening place."[11] This powerful sense of loneliness has two causes in Stafford's work: one is the hard fact of death, and the other is the absence of God. Among Stafford's best and most affecting poems are several that deal with the double kind of loss that results from an awareness both of death and of the passage of time—for example, "Stereopticon." The title of this poem refers to a double-lensed slide projector that allows one photograph to fade out while another is fading in. The title is not so specific in its usage; we are to understand simply that the act of looking at photographs of old scenes can reanimate those scenes in our minds:

> This can happen. They can bring the leaves back
> to the cottonwood trees, those great big rooms
> where our street—as long as summer—led
> to the river. From a rusty nail in the alley
> someone can die, but the street go on again.
>
> Hitler and others, those pipsqueak voices,
> can twitter from speakers. I can look back
> from hills beyond town, and every person
> and all the alleys, and even the buildings
> except the church be hidden in leaves.

This can happen, my parents laughing
because they have already won. And I can
study and grow up and look back and call "Wait!"
and run after their old green car
and be lost again.[12]

The manipulation of time in this poem is very careful—it is the
perspective of yesterday that reanimates things like "Hitler and
others," while the perspective of today, knowledge of Hitler's
ultimate defeat, robs them of fearful sting, reducing them to
"those pipsqueak voices." Conversely, it is today's knowledge
that makes the appearance of the speaker's parents doubly upset-
ting by projecting a more recent, fearful knowledge back upon
the memory drawn from childhood: then they failed to see him
because their eyes were on the road ahead; now they fail to see
him because they are dead. In either case he is left behind, alone.

The second cause of the loneliness that Stafford finds to be so
pervasive and frightening a force in the world derives from his
religious beliefs. What matters most in this regard is not the fact
that Stafford is a Christian, but the fact that he has been a pacifist
for his entire life. During World War II he declared himself to be
a conscientious objector and was incarcerated in work camps for
four years. On the occasion when he and I met to finish the
interview in this volume, Stafford handed me a pamphlet enti-
tled "That Men May Live: Statement of Purpose of the Fellow-
ship of Reconciliation," with the words, "This explains pretty
much what I believe." The organization was founded on a reli-
gious base, "with its roots in the ethic of love as found preemi-
nently in Jesus Christ," but since has shifted to a more humanis-
tic orientation, now welcoming the "community of Judaism" as
well as those who simply "affirm their faith in man and in the
unity and interdependence of the human race." In fact, it is not
the religious dimension that is primary here; rather, the most
important tenet of belief of this group (and, one has to assume,
of William Stafford as well) is that found in the opening sentence
of the pamphlet: "The Fellowship of Reconciliation is composed
of men and women who recognize the essential unity of man-
kind and have joined together to explore the power of love and
truth for resolving human conflict." The aim of all pacifist orga-
nizations is to find a positive solution to a pervasive negative
threat within the world—that of war and death. It is especially
important from the perspective of Stafford's poetry that the fel-

lowship does not call upon God to intercede in the affairs of man, but upon mankind to change its own ways.

When Stafford speaks of God in his poems, as he does occasionally, the allusions are generally more convenient and predictable than suffused with a heartfelt belief. What is far more convincing than any of this are the many poems that express a sense of the absence of God, a longing for his presence—for example, "A Walk in the Country" (*STCBT,* 197–98). As is often the case in Stafford, this poem has a parablelike quality; that is, it tells a vague story—in which neither setting nor event is quite specific enough for solid, literal grounding—that seems intended primarily to deliver a generalized point. The opening stanza presents a kind of thesis by asking a question:

> To walk anywhere in the world, to live
> now, to speak, to breathe a harmless
> breath: what snowflake, even, may try
> today so calm a life,
> so mild a death?

The calm "walk"—metaphorical for "life"—is presented as a natural ideal, unfortunately thwarted somehow by factors of today. Most often in Stafford, such negative factors have to do with society, technological progress, the dangers of human conflict, but here the context is metaphysical, referring to the gradual loss of religious faith, the death of God. Thus, when the speaker of the poem goes out to walk in "the hollow night," he somehow is caused to carry the empty burden of moonlight:

> a terrible thing had happened:
> the world, wide, unbearably bright,
> had leaped on me. I carried mountains.

Mountains are later identified metaphorically as "my fear and pain." Daylight, more comforting and cheerful than night, temporarily returns a semblance of faith to the speaker's world— "God had come back there / to carry the world again"—but knowledge of his loss remains ineradicable for the speaker, and the poem ends plaintively:

> Since then, while over the world
> the wind appeals events,
> and people contend like fools,

like a stubborn tumbleweed I hold,
hold where I live, and look into every face:

Oh friends, where can one find a partner
for the long dance over the fields?

By identifying his speaker with a rooted, a stationary tumble-
weed—whose natural function ought to be to roam freely wher-
ever the wind blows, "To walk anywhere in the world," to
"dance over the fields"—Stafford is expressing the paralyzing
effect that the speaker's loss of faith has had upon him. The
religious hunger, the longing for "a partner" is a powerful, but
all too often unrequited, desire in the modern world of Staf-
ford's poems.

A poem with a similar message—though a somewhat differ-
ent method—is "Late at Night." Here the action is concrete and
specific rather than vaguely metaphorical, though an interpreta-
tion of the events is suggested at the end of the poem (which is
quoted in its entirety).

Falling separate into the dark
the hailstone yelps of geese pattered
through our roof; startled we listened.

Those V's of direction swept by unseen
so orderly that we paused. But then
faltering back through their circle they came.

Were they lost up there in the night?
They always knew the way, we thought.
You looked at me across the room:—

We live in a terrible season.

(*STCBT,* 86)

The poem represents almost a twentieth-century reversal of Wil-
liam Cullen Bryant's "To a Waterfowl," in which the instinctive
sense of direction possessed by a duck, which invariably leads it
to its destination, is seen by the poet as proof of the existence of a
guiding, paternalistic God:

There is a Power whose care
Teaches thy way along that pathless coast,—

The desert and illimitable air,—
Lone wandering, but not lost.

Stafford's poem, by contrast, suggests not just the death of God but also the failure of natural, instinctive processes—processes that one might expect would supply guidance (and thereby a measure of assurance and comfort) in a godless world. Furthermore, we must note that all this is an interpretation by Stafford and his speaker—migrating geese regularly break formation and circle in the process of landing for a rest. So uneasy is the twentieth-century sensibility portrayed in this poem, however, that it is apparently unable even to consider this explanation. The position of mankind generally in the modern world in Stafford's poems is probably best expressed by the title of one of his books—we are *Traveling Through the Dark,* alone and unguided, perpetually and ignorantly "In Medias Res" (as one section of that book is subtitled).

Nature serves many functions in Stafford's poetry, appears in many guises, some of which also go to show (like death, time, the absence of God) "that the world can be a frightening place." Stafford is always aware that nature has at its disposal forces far greater than any that man could summon—earthquakes, hurricanes, tornadoes, even so simple a thing as winter, which he often uses as a metaphor for the coming of death or for the death state itself.[13] Probably the best expression of this metaphor is to be found in the poem "Kinds of Winter," which tells a parablelike story of hunting:

> It was a big one. We followed it over
> the snow. Even if it made no mistakes, we
> would have it. That's what The World means—
> there are kinds of winter that you meet.
> And that big one had met us, its big winter.
>
> But there was a hill, and when we rounded
> it the tracks were gone. We had used up
> the daylight. The wind had come and
> emptied our trail, back of us, ahead of us.
> We looked at each other. Our winter had come.[14]

Winter in this poem represents the primal destructiveness Stafford always feels as a potential within nature.

However, it is also true that Stafford consistently locates whatever god or godliness may remain in the universe within nature, within the created world, within God's original physical manifestation of himself. The theology that results from this perception is not always a comforting one—as is evident in another poem, "Walking the Wilderness." Here, God is associated explicitly with nature and winter's destructiveness; Stafford speaks of "His / eye that freezes people, His zero breath / their death" (*STCBT*, 138). The poem concludes on lines that describe the ending to man's presumptuous "walk in the wilderness":

> Warm human representatives may vote and
> manage man; but last the blizzard will dignify
> the walker, the storm hack trees to cyclone
> groves, he catch the snow, his brave eye
> become command, the whole night howl against
> his ear, till found by dawn he
> reach out to God no trembling hand.

The lesson administered to man's pride here is extreme, the result not just of nature's wintry cold, but of God's volition as well, which uses nature's power to this destructive end. And that the poem is another following the parablelike pattern generalizes the lesson—this is what lies in store for all mankind.

All of which does seem to place William Stafford convincingly within the camp of the twentieth-century pessimistic poets, despite his failure to flirt poetically with mental illness, alcoholism, and suicide. But again a distinction must be made—the poets I am labeling pessimists (in [*The World's Hieroglyphic Beauty*], primarily James Wright, though others, such as John Berryman and Robert Lowell, could be mentioned) tend to derive that attitude from contact with, immersion within, society and the city. As was said earlier in this essay, William Stafford is a poet, not of the city, but of the small town and the countryside. In fact, a case could be made for considering him to be a modern pastoralist, even though his work does not exhibit most of the conventional, external trappings of traditional pastoral poetry. Indeed, we would not expect to find in the work of any twentieth-century poet such elements as "The unhappy shepherd, the fair shepherdess, the wandering flock, the daisies and violets, the greensward dance, the flowery wreath and oaten pipe [that] represent a cluster of motifs which can be traced in the tradition from Theocritus to Pope and beyond into the nineteenth century,"[15] and none of these characteristics is found in Stafford's pastoral poetry—nor in that of Robert Frost, one of his few twentieth-century predecessors in the mode. One could argue that yet another of the traditional elements does appear in the work of both writers. I refer to the rural swain, who appears as farmer or roving handyman in Frost and as the Indian in Stafford. What is most centrally relevant to both poets, however, is none of this surface detailing but rather the moral vision that gives significance to the pastoral tradition.

At the heart of pastoralism is a contrast between two locales, two different ways of life. As John F. Lynen has pointed out, "Pastoral comes to life whenever the poet is able to adopt its special point of view—whenever he casts himself in the role of the country dweller and writes about life in terms of the contrast between the rural world, with its rustic scenery and naive, humble folk, and the great outer world of the powerful, the wealthy, and the sophisticated."[16] The moral distinction is implicit within this social or geographical contrast: "Behind all this, of course, lies the idea of innocence. Pastoral tends to merge with the myth of the golden age, because it assumes that in the rural world life retains its pristine purity. The swain, untainted by the evils of civilization, is a sort of ideal man, like the noble savage—not that he can escape from evil or is completely free from it himself, but he has not been exposed to the subtle corruptions of a complex society."[17]

Despite his preference for the natural world over the world of the city, William Stafford is not a traditional nature poet, one whose chief goal is to describe and venerate nature. He is instead a wisdom poet who uses the world of nature as a means to an end—he is in pursuit of a truth higher than those customarily perceived by ordinary men leading ordinary lives. Thus, in those poems mentioned above wherein nature's power to destroy is emphasized, the lesson is one of humility for mankind—in the face of tornadoes, earthquakes, erupting volcanoes, the numbing cold of winter, even the strongest of man's devices pale to a powerless insignificance. This truism is very much in line with the general pastoral vision, which locates delusion in man's works and cities, while the real, the elemental, the essential and true, is to be found in the less-peopled places of earth. Stafford is concerned to draw this basic contrast in many of his poems. In "Evening News," for example, he portrays the apparent power and significance of television—with its ability to show how "a war happens, / only an eighth of an inch thick"—as shallow and unimportant when contrasted to the quiet depth of nature:

In the yard I pray birds,
wind, unscheduled grass,
that they please help to make
everything go deep again.

(*STCBT,* 183–84)

An apparent irony in the work of so prolific a poet as Stafford is his association of a shallow volubility, talkiness, with society and of a profound silence or carefully measured speech with nature. It is possible to trace several stages in this subtheme or motif, three of them especially relevant here. The poem "Representing Far Places" (*STCBT,* 96–97) is actually concerned with the empty talkiness of society, although its first stanza dwells entirely on the silence of nature, describing the actions of fish "In the canoe wilderness":

Up through water at the dip of a falling leaf
to the sky's drop of light or the smell of another star
fish in the lake leap arcs of realization,
hard fins prying out from the dark below.

By contrast to this, the second stanza shows the generic Stafford protagonist at a party, wisely struck dumb amid the hubbub:

Often in society when the talk turns witty
you think of that place, and can't polarize at all:
it would be a kind of treason. The land fans in your head
canyon by canyon; steep roads diverge.
Representing far places you stand in the room,
all that you know merely a weight in the weather.

Although this nature-oriented man may look like a fool when keeping such witty, dialectical company, the familiar prejudices of pastoralism make clear that we are meant to see him (however difficult this may be) as a wise man surrounded by fools.[18]

What truly meaningful verbal communication might be is revealed in another poem contrasting the social and pastoral realms. At first glance, the title—"I Was in the City All Day"— appears irrelevant to the poem itself. Stafford's method, however, is one of stark contrast; the title shows how a day can be wasted, while the poem itself tells how time might best be spent:

Into the desert, trading people for horses,
the leader rode toward a responsible act:

the having one person at the last campfire,
telling just the next thing to that one person,
with all around only the waiting night waiting,
in the shadows horses eating wild hay—
and then the last word without distraction,
one meaning like a bird slipping out into the dark.

(STCBT, 79)

Language here is significant, instructional; wisdom is being passed on to a lone young acolyte by a knowledgeable old man—a Sam Fathers sort of figure.

At a further extreme from the empty noise of society is the seeming silence of nature itself, which embodies what may be the greatest wisdom of all. In "From the Gradual Grass," Stafford again begins with the emptiness, the hollow sound and fury, found in so much of society's noise (the effect of which is only to draw attention to itself) and moves to the more resonant sounds of nature:

Imagine a voice calling,
"There is a voice now calling,"
or maybe a blasting cry:
"Walls are falling!"
as it makes walls be falling.

Then from the gradual grass,
too serious to be only noise—
whatever it is grass makes,
making words, a voice:
"Destruction is ending; this voice

"Is promising quiet: silence
by lasting forever grows to sound
endlessly from the world's end
promising, calling."
Imagine. *That voice is calling.*

(STCBT, 98)

Such a "sound" is always an inherent possibility, Stafford suggests, for those with enough imagination to listen beyond the world's insistent cacophony. The person who would hear this call, this promise, has to seek it actively by pushing first beyond noise to silence and then beyond silence to an actually unheard, but convincingly imagined, wisdom.

Of course it is likely to be the poet—whose primary tool of trade is the imagination, which creates wise sound from silence—who can best make such wonders available to the rest of us. And there is a poet at the heart of Stafford's poems, most of which are spoken from the first-person point of view by a character or characters who seem to resemble closely the poet himself. It would be a naive mistake, however, to assume that this speaking character *is* William Stafford, that all details of its life belong to Stafford's as well, that all of his opinions are also Stafford's. In fact, among these details, facts, and opinions, there are subtle shifts and inconsistencies, leading one to conclude that Stafford, in order to achieve his larger goals, is willing to sacrifice a purely surface consistency. Stafford has himself commented on this procedure: "I feel like such an unreliable character in a poem that I can say something . . . and then drop it, just leave it, because I don't mean that for the rest of my life at all, I just mean that's a remark to make in order to get along to the next remark."[19] The conclusion reached by Jonathan Holden on this issue is both accurate and reasonable: "Generally, in a Stafford poem biographical content is placed wholly in the service of imagination, as material for fiction."[20]

It is curious that statements such as these carry us virtually to the borderline between an essentially traditional poetry—in which the poet's ultimate commitment is to telling the truth, in small matters as in large—and that minority movement known as postmodernism—where the spirits of play and parody are preeminent and in which the poet's commitment is to the logic of the poem's world rather than to the external truth of the world that surrounds him. Rightly understood, the term *postmodernism* describes, not a historical literary age, but this still rather specialized approach to the possibilities of literature. Despite his basic devotion to telling what he perceives as the truth, William Stafford does also have an interest in the possibilities of a freer kind of invention, wherein poetry makes its own rules and its own truth. In a short series of aphorisms collected under the title "Writing and Literature: Some Opinions" in *Writing the Australian Crawl,* Stafford says, laying the groundwork for this spirit in his poetry: "Literature is not a picture of life, but is a separate experience with its own kind of flow and enchantment."[21] Going even farther in a recent interview ("Interview with William Stafford"), Stafford chose to compare himself to John Ashbery—postmodernist par excellence—rather than to more sincere kinds of poets: "I feel a lot more harmony with someone like Ashbery and his assumptions about poetry . . . than I do with many other poets: . . . those people who seem to feel that they are corraling ultimate truth. . . . I think poetry is ultimately playful, no matter what anyone says. And Ashbery is explicit about this."[22]

Such a statement should not be applied too literally to Stafford's poetry. His words accurately indicate, however, the rich vein of playfulness that can occasionally be found in his work. His newest book, *A Glass Face in the Rain,* provides several examples. In "We Interrupt to Bring You," for instance, the speaker leaves his television set to go to the bathroom; while he is away, a meteor is discovered speeding towards earth, everyone is evacuated into

> those new domes on the ocean
> floor . . . and the domes
> collapse, and I'm the only one left.
>
> (*GFR,* 74)

The speaker returns to his TV and is mildly unhappy because he, the last man on earth, cannot find his favorite show, "Perry Mason." Another poem, "Incident," tells a similarly apocalyptic, fanciful story:

> They had this cloud they kept like a zeppelin
> tethered to a smokestack, and you couldn't see it
> but it sent out these strange little rays
> and after a while you felt funny. They had this
> man with a box. He pointed it at
> the zeppelin and it said, "Jesus!" The man
> hurried farther away and called out,
> "Hear ye, hear ye!" Then they coaxed
> the zeppelin down into the smokestack
> and they said, "We won't do that any more."
> For a long time the box kept shaking its head,
> but it finally said, "Ok, forget it." But, quietly,
> to us, it whispered, "Let's get out of here."
>
> (*GFR,* 67)

As is so often the case, Stafford invites his reader to find sequestered meanings by casting his statement in the form of a parable or an allegory. In this case the poem obviously expresses further disenchantment with the age of industrialism and technology. It doesn't matter how much antipollution equipment a factory installs, the speaker seems to be saying; the situation is still going to be dangerous to my health. In contrast to this rather solemn message, the story the poem tells is amusing. Stafford is toying with the tools of his trade in an almost mock-heroic manner, and the ultimate effect is enticingly close to self-parody.

Such playfulness is certainly a component of Stafford's work—and yet we must not lose sight of the fact that he is a serious poet committed to telling his version of the truth. In line with this, he is more interested in achieving an overall authenticity of vision than he is in harmonizing the specific details presented in separate poems. Sincerity (a surface truthfulness) is a poem-by-poem matter in Stafford's work—each individual poem is honest unto itself and internally consistent, but similar poems placed side by side may well reveal contradictory details. For example, amid several poems in which Stafford's speaking character talks of his father as a kind and gentle man, there are a few poems that portray him as cold, indifferent, cruel. We must recognize that different poems may demand different fathers, just as they demand slightly different versions of the same basic central character.

It is, in fact, this central, basic character, this more or less singular speaking voice, that lends the greatest unity to Stafford's poems when they are studied as a whole. It is important that we investigate this character in order to understand something of his personality, his way of living and thinking in the world. We might begin with what he seems to have learned from his parents, proceed to a consideration of the kind of faith that seems to sustain him, and then investigate how, in several poems about poetry, he says he wants to embody this faith in verse.

Just as Stafford has accounted for his own early commitment to poetry by pointing to his parents and the storytelling atmosphere they created for him as a child ("Interview with William Stafford"), so the speaking character in the poems often points to *his* parents to illustrate the attitudes and character traits that have guided and determined his life. To the mother figure of these poems is ascribed the source of the pastoral desire to be separate from the dominant aims and values of the larger society—as in "Our Kind," which provides a wry definition of success:

> Our mother knew our worth—
> not much. To her, success
> was not being noticed at all.

> (*GFR*, 69)

The pastoral attitude is especially evident in the ironic conclusion of the poem:

> She sent us forth equipped
> for our kind of world, a world of
> our betters, in a nation so strong
> its greatest claim is no boast,
> its leaders telling us all, "Be proud"—
>
> But over their shoulders, God and
> our mother, signaling: "Ridiculous."

The speaker prefers his apparently lowly position because it is morally superior—humility may not walk off with the prize today, but it will be triumphant in eternity. Even in their battle against the War Department, the most effective technique available to the pacifists is patience, as the speaker is advised in "My Mother Was a Soldier":

> Tapping on my wrist, she talked: "Patience
> is the doctor; it says try; it says
> they think we're nice, we quiet ones, we die
> so well: that's how we win, imagining things
> before they happen." "No harm in being quiet,"
>
> My mother said: "that's the sound that finally wins."
>
> (GFR, 75)

The gaze of the mother in Stafford's poems is from a pastoral world toward society; she is defined in terms of her power of opposition. The father, contrastingly, turns his eyes toward the more mysterious, elusive world of nature, where the stories are. It is from him that the figure of the poet learns to look into things—and learns to tell his own stories. The poem "Listening" defines the character of the father well:

> My father could hear a little animal step,
> or a moth in the dark against the screen,
> and every far sound called the listening out
> into places where the rest of us had never been.

More spoke to him from the soft wild night
than came to our porch for us on the wind;
we would watch him look up and his face go keen
till the walls of the world flared, widened.

My father heard so much that we still stand
inviting the quiet by turning the face,
waiting for a time when something in the night
will touch us too from that other place.

(*STCBT,* 33)

The father is, in fact, a kind of nature mystic who listens, even beyond hearing, not to the other world of religion but to something implicit within this world, nature. From him the son learns a desire to hear the same sounds, see the same signs, and this desire becomes the major quest enunciated in Stafford's poems. In "A Thanksgiving for My Father," the son indicates the strength of this inheritance by speaking his obligation almost as a lament:

Oh father, why
did you ever set your son such being!

Your life was a miracle
and could build out of shadows
anything: your restless thought
has made the world haunted.

(*STCBT,* 135)

The role of the father in Stafford's poems has been accurately described by George S. Lensing and Ronald Moran, who see him as "the high priest of the wilderness. Like Sam Fathers to Isaac McCaslin or Natty Bumppo to the neophytes of the frontier, Stafford's father is initiator and instructor to the son, not only in relation to the wilderness itself, but in the moral values which inhere within it. Again like Fathers and Leatherstocking, he is imbued with certain mystical, almost superhuman, powers."[23] From the mother in these poems comes an attitude of opposition to the false values of society, a tough pacifism; from the father comes a sense of the mystery inherent in nature, a love for the stories that might unlock it. Given the importance of narrative and storytelling in these poems, it appears that most of the poetry comes from the father.[24]

There is, however, one important area in which the father's approach to and view of the world is significantly different from that of the speaker. The attention of the father is so concentrated upon particulars that he often fails to perceive the larger flow of reality. As the poem "Parentage" explains, this makes him uneasy, an insecure and uncomfortable citizen of the world:

> My father didn't really belong in history.
> He kept looking over his shoulder at some mistake.
> He was a stranger to me, for I belong.
>
> There never was a particular he couldn't understand,
> but there were too many in too long a row,
> and like many another he was overwhelmed.
>
> (STCBT, 67)

Essentially, the father attempts to know and understand the world by trying to control it, subject it to his own categorizing mind. Underlying such a method is an inevitable attitude of competition, opposition—the father sets himself against the continuum of history and is eventually overwhelmed by the volume of its never-ending flow. Rather than frustrate himself in this way, Stafford's poet chooses instead to become part of the world's process, its being and flow. At the end of "Parentage," he describes what this means:

> I want to be as afraid as the teeth are big,
> I want to be as dumb as the wise are wrong:
> I'd just as soon be pushed by events to where I belong.

The ultimate source of wisdom for any pastoral poet is of course nature, the earth itself, and at the end of another poem, "In Response to a Question," Stafford attributes this go-with-the-flow method for gaining wisdom to the earth (the unstated question of the title is, "What does the earth say?"):

> join
> the sparrow on the lawn, and row that easy
> way, the rage without met by the wings
> within that guide you anywhere the wind blows.
>
> Listening, I think that's what the earth says.
>
> (STCBT, 76)

What has just been defined is essentially the faith of the poet in William Stafford's poems. He may not know just where he is going or what he will find when he gets there, but he does know how to travel down the path he thinks will lead him there. In the many ars poeticas that Stafford has written over the years, poetry is similarly defined, not as an end result, a goal or product, but as a process, an ongoing method that itself ought inevitably to lead to—or toward—the truth sought by this wisdom poet. In the first stanza of "With My Crowbar Key," for example, Stafford gives a basic definition of his method:

> I do tricks in order to know:
> careless I dance,
> then turn to see
> the mark to turn God left for me.
>
> (*STCBT*, 65)

What is described here is quite similar to the free-associative system discussed at the beginning of this chapter. Stafford insists that he does not know his thematic destination when he begins a poem. Rather, he allows some more instinctive or unconscious process to guide him and has faith that, once the poem is finished, he will be able to look back and see *how* he got where he was going; the guideposts appear after the journey, not before.

The image implicit in "With My Crowbar Key" is of a path down which the poet dances; in "An Introduction to Some Poems" (a more extensive and suggestive poem on the same topic), the image is of a "line" that holds seemingly disparate things together. The final four stanzas constitute what is probably Stafford's most crucial poetic statement on his own art; he speaks for poets generally, using the first-person plural:

> Just as in sleep you have to dream
> the exact dream to round out your life,
> so we have to live that dream into stories
> and hold them close at you, close at the
> edge we share, to be right.
>
> We find it an awful thing to meet people,
> serious or not, who have turned into vacant
> effective people, so far lost that they
> won't believe their own feelings
> enough to follow them out.

The authentic is a line from one thing
along to the next; it interests us.
Strangely, it relates to what works,
but is not quite the same. It never
swerves for revenge,

Or profit, or fame: it holds
together something more than the world,
this line. And we are your wavery
efforts at following it. Are you coming?
Good: now it is time.

(*STCBT,* 201)

Because of its surface discursiveness, the poem is itself an inter-
esting example of the doctrine enunciated within it. The
"authentic"—metaphorically described as the "line" that unites
seemingly different things—is here possessed in common by
dreams, by unlocked feelings, and by poems. Poetry as a process
is similar to these other things because it functions as they do—
each allows entry to the subconscious portion of the mind,
where the authentic, untrammeled personality (the glue that
holds together all that man is and does) can be found. The key
that opens this level is that free-associative process central to
both dreams (in the area of the personal) and poems (in the area
of art).

Implicit within these poems on the poet's faith and on his
methods as a writer is the idea of a path, a road, a direction;
movement; by extension a quest or a searching.[25] All these
things in their turn imply an end point or goal; because he is a
wisdom poet, one of the things that Stafford is pursuing in his
poetry is some ultimate sense of truth, some kind of final knowl-
edge. However, Stafford also has serious doubts about the ade-
quacy of human knowledge. He has expressed this many times,
but most succinctly in the essay "Some Arguments against Good
Diction": "I saw inscribed in gold on a pillar in the Library of
Congress this saying: 'The inquiry, knowledge and belief of
truth is the sovereign good of human nature.' To me, such a
saying is hollow; I see it as demonstrating man's pathetic infatua-
tion with an apparent power that is essentially just a redundancy.
The highest we know is high for us, but its communication is an
interior, not an absolute, phenomenon. And I cringe to realize
that my own saying of my kind of truth is hazardous at best."[26]
Despite this reservation, it is a fact that Stafford is in pursuit of

truth in his poetry—probably not, however, a human truth. The other goal to his quest is for something we may label "home"—a multifaceted concept within the world of Stafford's poetry.

The ordinary, everyday sense of a home—involving a settled place to live and a family, with plants and pets perhaps included—appears in Stafford's poetry, not as something quested for, but as something already achieved, taken for granted. The "home" for which his character searches is a much vaguer, more spiritual entity, something that can be located, in differing manifestations, in both the past and the future. In order to distinguish these adequately, we must first carry a bit farther the pastoral distinction made above between the world of the city and the world of the countryside. The latter of these two landscapes actually embodies, not just one, but two types of locales—the specifically pastoral one combining small town and farm, and the further, less pastoral, and more extreme one of the wilderness. All three places exist on a scale ranging from the relatively decadent, distant-from-God city to the most unsullied, closest-to-God wilderness. The gardenlike middle range is a kind of golden mean, participating in the advantages of both extremes, but avoiding their dangers.

One of the homes for which Stafford's character searches is located in the past, on the farms and in the small towns of Stafford's own youth. Stafford—the closest thing to a folksy poet that serious contemporary literature has to offer—uses a great many of his poems, most of them occasional in nature, to celebrate the people and scenes, the events and values, of rural America. Because such material does not fit into the more substantial, more mythic pattern we are tracing, I do not intend to deal with it here in any detail.[27] It is the other search for "home," the one that carries Stafford's character toward the wilderness and into the future, that is of greater interest.[28] In "The Gift," Stafford defines this rather specialized concept of "home" as he applies it to the poet. The poem begins, "The writer's home he salvages from little pieces / along the roads" (*STCBT,* 164) and ends with these words of prophecy and exhortation, spoken by the imagined figure of the poet:

> "Some day, tame (therefore lost) men, the wild
> will come over the highest wall, waving
> its banner voice, beating its gifted fist:
> *Begin again, you tame ones; listen—the roads are your home again.*"

Again we see the image of the road, the path, the line—it is the lot of the true poet to be homeless; his "home" is on the road, on which he travels toward his destiny and the world's. (In "Vocation," another ars poetica, the poet's calling is defined this way: "Your job is to find what the world is trying to be"—*STCBT,* 107.) This road leads the poet ever westward, always away from the cities, through the small towns and across the farms, toward and into the wilderness.

Stafford attaches symbolic or quasisymbolic meanings to two of the four compass directions. In the north is located cold, harshness, winter, death, perhaps God; in the west is located nature, the pastoral world, eventually the wilderness. In fact, in titling his first volume of poetry *West of Your City,* Stafford was indicating his commitment to moving in this direction. The introductory poem, "Midwest," is an attempt to define what the west means, what it promises to one who would travel there:

> Cocked in that land tactile as leaves
> wild things wait crouched in those valleys
> west of your city outside your lives
> in the ultimate wind, the whole land's wave.
> Come west and see; touch these leaves.
>
> (*STCBT,* 29)

The last line, of course, is the book's invitation to the reader; "these leaves" are the pages that follow. It is in the West, away from the man-made landscape of the city and all its consequent delusions, that a person can confront a greater reality, a more fundamental level of experience. Even there, however, exist delusions to be avoided. Stafford is a relentless dualizer; having divided the world into city and country, having divided the country (preferable to the city) into small town / farm and wilderness, he then proceeds to divide the wilderness (ultimately more authentic than either town or farm) into its surface and its depths. This may be seen happening in many poems, but nowhere more tellingly than in "Bi-Focal," another poem from *West of Your City:*

> Sometimes up out of this land
> a legend begins to move.
> Is it a coming near
> of something under love?

Love is of the earth only,
the surface, a map of roads
leading wherever go miles
or little bushes nod.

Not so the legend under,
fixed, inexorable,
deep as the darkest mine
the thick rocks won't tell.

As fire burns the leaf
and out of the green appears
the vein in the center line
and the legend veins under there,

So, the world happens twice—
once what we see it as;
second it legends itself
deep, the way it is.

(*STCBT,* 48)

What Stafford is ultimately searching for is this hidden "legend," which can be found only beyond all roads, lines, and paths—we note that in the image of the leaf, the legend is, not the linelike vein that appears through fire, but something further, which "veins" even "under there."[29]

In a poem entitled "Earth Dweller"—appropriately placed in the book *Allegiances*—Stafford gives a clear indication of where he directs his faith, where he expects sacredness to be found. The first stanza praises the pastoral life—working on the land and the land itself. At the beginning, "all the clods at once become / precious," and at the end the world of the farm becomes sacred:

somewhere inside, the clods are
vaulted mansions, lines through the barn sing
for the saints forever, the shed and windmill
rear so glorious the sun shudders like a gong.

(*STCBT,* 196)

In the second and final stanza Stafford generalizes from this to a sense of earth worship:

Now I know why people worship, carry around
magic emblems, wake up talking dreams
they teach to their children: the world speaks.
The world speaks everything to us.
It is our only friend.

The more-than-human truth that Stafford seeks is essentially a
spiritual truth—located, however, not in church, but on the
land.[30] It is another example of that nature mysticism so preva-
lent in the poetry of America—wherein the profound religious
sense that our earliest settlers brought with them from the Old
World combines with a sense of the mystery of the wilderness,
that great empty continent out there, to produce a sense of the
mystic truths resident in the far reaches of nature.

Which is why, ultimately, Stafford's poet has to leave the road
behind him, wander from the path, venture away from all visible
lines onto the one that legends itself beneath the surface, unseen.
In William Faulkner's "The Bear," the young acolyte Ike McCas-
lin wishes to have a glimpse of the mythical beast in the forest. His
early forays end in failure. Then Sam Fathers, figure of the priest,
instructs Ike that he must leave behind him all man-made imple-
ments that would aid in his search—compass, watch, gun—and
rely instead on faith. Ike, we may say, must leave all roads behind
if he is to attain the mystical experience he seeks. This is precisely
the requirement that William Stafford discovers must be met by
the figure of the questing poet, the truth seeker, in his poetry. Staf-
ford has many poems in which the quest is the actual subject of the
poem, and always the lesson is the same—"finally in every can-
yon the road ends. / Above that—storms of stone," as he states it
in "The Research Team in the Mountains" (*STCBT,* 68). It is only
at this point, where the road ends, that the actual quest can finally
begin. The method to be followed is described in an early poem,
"Watching the Jet Planes Dive" from *West of Your City,* where Staf-
ford rejects the ways of modern man as superficial, guaranteed to
achieve only ignoble ends; if we are to attain the authentic, rather
than travel in planes and cars, "We must go back and find a trail on
the ground / back of the forest and mountain on the slow land"
(*STCBT,* 44). The poem concludes with these lines:

We must find something forgotten by everyone alive,
and make some fabulous gesture when the sun goes down
as they do by custom in little Mexico towns

where they crawl for some ritual up a rocky steep.
The jet planes dive; we must travel on our knees.

As the mention of customs in "little Mexico towns" makes
clear, Stafford looks for a paradigm of the kind of searching he
advocates, not in contemporary society, but in earlier, more
primitive societies, where the people were closer to and therefore
more in touch with nature and the land. Most often he locates
these qualities in the society of the American Indians: "I've al-
ways liked their way of life, living in the woods, close to the
animals. And the sense of freedom—I like a lot of space and
plenty of chance to let the impulses I have be predominant over
impulses imposed on me. Maybe that's a definition of freedom. I
take a step when I want to, not when the escalator tells me to. I'd
like to be able to go to the edge of town and just keep going, the
way the Indians did" ("Interview with William Stafford"). In
many of his poems Stafford uses the Indian as a kind of paradigm
for the man who is fully in touch with his environment, for
reasons noticed by Robert Coles: "The sense of continuity, the
faith in the ways of nature and at least a certain kind of man
(themselves) which Indians unselfconsciously have as a psycho-
logical possession and as elements in their cultural tradition."[31]
William Stafford commits himself imaginatively to the Indian
way of life in a great many poems, perhaps most fundamentally
in "Returned to Say," where he envisions joining a young chief
on what seems a mystical quest. Much of the language of the
poem echoes statements on this topic we have already looked at.

> When I face north a lost Cree
> on some new shore puts a moccasin down,
> rock in the light and noon for seeing,
> he in a hurry and I beside him.
>
> It will be a long trip; he will be a new chief;
> we have drunk new water from an unnamed stream;
> under little dark trees he is to find a path
> we both must travel because we have met.
>
> . . . .
> We will mean what he does. Back of this page
> the path turns north. We are looking for a sign.
> Our moccasins do not mark the ground.

(*STCBT,* 102–3)

The journey begins with a path that eventually disappears, leaving them to look "for a sign" on unmarked ground. We might speculate that when "the path turns north," it is turning from west; north is the ultimate direction in Stafford, the final direction, and leads into even more wild, more authentic territory than does west, leading at the end, in fact, both to death and to God.

The mystical thing sought for in Stafford's poetry may be metaphysical or spiritual, but it is not to be found in airy realms of ethereality. The quest for it carries Stafford's poet to the most basic, most physical, most elemental, even the most primitive realms. It is never quite attained in the poetry; the spiritual in Stafford's poems—as in those of the other "optimists" examined in [*The World's Hieroglyphic Beauty*], Richard Wilbur and Robert Penn Warren—is ultimately ungraspable by physical man within a material world. But he can gain glimpses of it, glimpses that foster and reinforce his faith that it does in fact exist and may some day be reached. In Stafford, such glimpses are gained in three different ways, each progressively less physical and more spiritual than the one before it—through touch, through sound, and somehow through the air. There is, of course, something frustratingly—but inherently, unavoidably— nebulous about a quest for a goal that can only be sensed, never reached. Stafford has, however, written several poems in which his speaker's goal is at least vaguely defined. "How to Get Back," a recent poem, appears in *A Glass Face in the Rain*. The first stanza describes the possibility of penetrating beyond time to a still moment of eternity:

> By believing, you can get there—that edge
> the light-years leave behind, where no one
> living today survives. You can get there
> where the lake turns to stone and your boat
> rocks, once, then hangs tilted a long time:
> in that instant you don't want to leave,
> where talk finds truth, slides near
> and away; where music holds its moment
> forever, and then forever again.
>
> (*GFR*, 29)

What Stafford describes is a frozen instant within time, which seems to open onto eternity; though the context is not specifically religious, the description resembles accounts of moments in

which mystical union was achieved by such writers as Saint
Teresa and Saint John of the Cross. The second, and concluding,
stanza of Stafford's poem closes the opening to eternity and
comments upon the process:

> You are only a wandering dot that fails—
> that has already failed, but you can get
> there. And you can come back—the boat
> moves; talk turns ordinary; music
> is hunting its moment again.
> Around you people don't know how you
> and themselves and the whole world
> hover in belief. They've never been gone.

Again we see the dualistic view, probably based on the pastoral
contrast. Although such perceptions are universally available,
Stafford believes, most people in the modern world do not
achieve them—the falseness of their lives isolates them from
such profundity.

While commenting upon the importance of nature imagery in
his poetry during an interview, Stafford alluded to a myth that
emphasizes the importance of touching, of establishing physical
contact with elemental reality: "nature . . . is important to me. I
think about the Greek hero, Antaeus—every time he touched the
earth he got stronger. For me, this myth is part of my life—to
touch something outside, to have things in your poetry, is a
healthy move. The world can save you, it can make you strong.
This . . . is a faith I live by" ("Interview with William Stafford").
The language used, with its talk of faith and hints of salvation,
does seem to promise that the avenue of touching the physical
world will lead somehow to a further world, a more than physical
world. For those specific connotations we will have to wait, how-
ever; although what is ultimately felt in the poems about "touch-
ing" does seem to hint at something more essential than mere
matter, the hints are teasingly vague. In "Touches," for example,
the speaker feels the wall of a real cave and imagines a more
elemental one, closer to the essence and source:

> You put a hand out in the dark of a cave and
> the wall waits for your fingers. Cold, that stone
> tells you all of the years that passed without knowing.
> You think of caves held in the earth, no mouth,
> no light. Down there the years have lost their way.

Under your hand it all steadies,
is the world under your hand.

(*STCBT*, 223)

"In the Deep Channel," an earlier poem, is even more indirect. It tells of "Setting a trotline after sundown" to catch a "secret-headed channel cat"; in the morning:

We would come at daylight and find the line sag,
the fishbelly gleam and the rush on the tether:
to feel the swerve and the deep current
which tugged at the tree roots below the river.

(*STCBT*, 31)

Here the speaker's sense of touch puts him in contact with a tension caused by movement, the current of the river that is pulling on the dead weight of the fish. Again, physical reality is as far as the poem reaches, but something seems alive, as though the speaker's hand felt the motion of nature's lifeblood.

While what we touch can be perceived in most cases by four senses—those of touch, sight, smell, and taste—sound is perceived only through the sense of hearing. It is for this reason that the "other" that is present in Stafford's poems based on sound seems a more spiritual "other" than that seen above in poems relying on touch. However, the sound in "A Sound from the Earth" still has only a physical origin:

Somewhere, I think in Dakota,
they found the leg bones—just the
big leg bones—of several hundred
buffalo, in a gravel pit.

Near there, a hole in a cliff
has been hollowed so that
the prevailing wind
thrums a note so low and persistent
that bowls of water placed in that
cave will tremble to foam.

(*STCBT*, 172)

Nevertheless, there is an implication that this hole somehow picks up the sound of mourning the earth makes over the death of the buffalo. Such a reading is reinforced by the rest of the poem, where "The grandfather of Crazy Horse" makes a sound in mourning for his grandson that in turn makes

> that thin Agency soup that they
> put before him tremble. The whole
> earthen bowl churned into foam.

In other poems a sound emanates from earth that seems to have a more distinctly mystical or spiritual source. In "Tornado," for example, Stafford describes the destructive passage of a storm through a town, and concludes with this observation:

> We weren't left religion exactly (the church
> was ecumenical bricks), but a certain tall element:
> a pulse beat still in the stilled rock
> and in the buried sound along the buried mouth of the creek.
>
> (*STCBT*, 71)

The "pulse" emanates from silent sources and is also loosely associated with religion; at the least it would seem to represent the spirit of power within nature, which we earlier saw manifested as winter. The poem "Believer" is both a subtle consideration of various levels of truth and a cunning testament of faith. In the first and third stanzas, Stafford suggests that even lies and tall tales tell a certain kind of truth:

> A horse could gallop over our bridge that minnows
> used for shade, but our dog trotting would splinter
> that bridge—"Look down," my father said, and there
> went Buster to break that bridge, but I called him back
> that day:—whatever they ask me to believe, "And
>   furthermore," I say.
>
> . . . .
> And scared as I am with my blood full of sharks, I lie
> in the dark and believe that whistle our dog's ears could hear
> but no one else heard—it skewers my dream; and in crystals
> finer than frost I trace and accept all of the ways
> to know:—they tell me a lie; I don't say "But"—
>   there are ways for a lie to be so.
>
> (*STCBT*, 122)

Stafford is essentially a narrative poet, though most of his important poems also function almost as parables, verging on homily. He clearly believes that the most important truths are best communicated through stories, narratives. At the level of literal fact, these may seldom be "true"—but at a higher, more illustrative, analogical, even allegorical or symbolic level, they are likely to be very true. This is why Stafford called his collected volume of poems *Stories That Could Be True;* it also clarifies why he has explained the authenticity of the material in his Indian poems in this way: "Well, it's authentic, but I make it up. In other words, it is authentic because I am an Indian, I have that Indian feeling, and not because I read it in some book" ("Interview with William Stafford"). If the spirit is authentic, then the story will be true whether the facts are right or not.

In the above stanzas from "Believer," then, Stafford is not so much saying he believes in the literal truth of everything he is told, but that there is a deeper level to every story, a level where the spirit of the story may always be said to be true. The "whistle our dog's ears could hear / but no one else heard" thus functions as an image for this deeper, this less easily seen, narrative level. The poem itself goes suddenly deeper in its fourth and concluding stanza, the meaning of which is structured upon the image of sound:

> You don't hear me yell to test the quiet or try to shake
> the wall, for I understand that the wrong sound weakens
> what no sound could ever save, and I am the one
> to live by the hum that shivers till the world can sing:—
> May my voice hover and wait for fate,
>   when the right note shakes everything.
>
> (*STCBT,* 123)

The aggressive sounds of the first two lines go against the nature of things, wherein an ultimate harmony is both desired and forthcoming. The language and imagery here associate that "song" and "note" with the millennium, when all things will hum in concert. The connotations of these lines seem distinctly religious. Meanwhile, "the hum that shivers" corresponds to the sounds the speaker now hears, the truthful notes residing in the "lies" he is told, the harmonic lyricism of the stories he himself tells in poems.

We now come to the third of three realms in which Stafford's quest for the absolute, the elemental, the spiritual seems to find

its goal. And in line with the progression we have been follow-
ing, this realm is the one in which the balance between physical
and spiritual is most heavily dominated by the spiritual. In the
realm of touch, the images carrying mysterious connotations are
the most certainly corporeal, available to as many as four of our
physical senses. In the realm of sound, those images are available
to only one of our senses—though often the connotative sounds
themselves are located by Stafford in convincingly physical
places—stone, mountains, water. In poems relying upon the
realm of air for their spiritual suggestion, the appeal is again to
one sense—that of feeling, a more vague version of the sense of
touch. Even more uncertain than the sensing of such images is
their source. In the poem "Things That Happen" (*STCBT*, 177–
78), Stafford begins by talking about the anticipation of "great
events," when an average person might say to himself, "A great
event is coming, bow down." The speaker, again a "believer,"
differentiates himself: "And I, always looking for something any-
way, / always bow down." He then proceeds to narrate one such
great event—not the arrival of a president, a pope, or Halley's
comet, but something that

> turned an unseen corner
> and came near, near, sounding before it
> something the opposite from a leper's bell.

The speaker and a companion are hiking in the mountains when
"one little puff of air touched us, / hardly felt at all." The final
two stanzas consist of a comment on this event:

> That was the greatest event that day;
> it righted all wrong.
> I remember it, the way the dust moved there.
> Something had come out of the ground
> and moved calmly along.
>
> No one was ahead of us, no one
> in all that moon-like land.
> Oh, I thought, how hard the world has tried
> with its wind, its miles, its blundering
> stumbling days, again and again, to find my hand.

This seeking world, of course, is not the everyday surface world
in which we all live, but the same world that, in "Bi-Focal," is

said to "legend" itself "deep, the way it is"; it is the world that, in "Earth Dweller," is said to speak "everything to us. / It is our only friend." Despite this distinction, this first puff of air definitely originates in the earth, comes "out of the ground"; its spiritual connotations are thus no stronger than those of the sounds thought to emanate from rocks or the strange vibrations with which a river current pulls on a fishing line.

Because the similar event that takes place in the poem "Space Country" does not originate with the earth, but comes instead from "out there" somewhere, its effect is more ethereal, its implications more spiritual. In fact, this event is not just a perturbation of the air but also involves a change in light:

As usual the highest birds first
caught it, a slow roll even the air
hardly felt; then the thick gold haze
that many filters of eyes found
fell deep in the desert country. Wells filled
and rocks—pooled in their own shadows—
lay at ease. People did not know
why they stood up and walked, and
waited by windows or doors, or leaned
by fences to look at far scenes.
The surface of all weathered wood relaxed;
even gravel and cactus appeared soft.

The world had passed something in space
and was alone again. Sunset came on.
People lay down, and the birds forgot
as they sleepily clucked and slept, close
on boughs, as well hidden as could be
in the air again clear, sharp, and cold.

(STCBT, 181–82)

The source of this event is left purposefully vague—indeed, it really does not matter exactly what has happened—the lie is both more interesting and more important than the truth. There was a moment of magic; something sacred came our way; somehow the world once again reached out to try and touch Stafford's speaker.

Stafford's goal in all of his poems is ultimately to achieve a sense of union with something absolute. In his cagey way, he will not define this something as being explicitly either spiritual or religious, nor does he refer to God when he is most serious in his quest. As I have said before, God usually appears in Stafford's poems at moments of convenience, times when God is what nearly anyone would rhetorically allude to. And yet the union that Stafford seeks sounds a lot like the sense of union with the godhead sought by mystics in more specifically religious texts and traditions. In the poem "Uncle George," Stafford is concerned once again to define life on a farm—now abandoned and falling to ruin—but in the midst of this he also defines the ultimate goal his questing poet figure seems to have as he journeys through the world:

> Trapper
> of warm sight, I plow and belong, send breath
> to be part of the day, and where it arrives
> I spend on and on, fainter and fainter
> toward ultimate identification, joining the air
> a few breaths at a time.
>
> (*STCBT*, 120)

Air is specifically used here as the connecting medium, the means of achieving union ("ultimate identification") with the world. Once again the context is entirely physical, but the language and narrative pattern together suggest the sacred mythology of mystical union with the spiritual realm.

NOTES

1. William Stafford, "Making a Poem / Starting a Car on Ice," in *Writing the Australian Crawl* (Ann Arbor: University of Michigan Press, 1978), 66.

2. Stafford, "A Way of Writing," in *Writing the Australian Crawl*, 17–18.

3. Ibid., 20, 18. Writing specifically about the function of myth in Stafford's poetry, George S. Lensing has noted as well the poet's "free-associative" method: "Stafford's poetry does not begin with a preconceived 'message' or even a formal method. To 'stumble' on myth necessitates a complete openness to the resources of the imagination" ("William Stafford, Mythmaker," *Modern Poetry Studies* 6 [1975]: 6).

4. Stafford, "A Way of Writing," 18–19.

5. James Dickey, "William Stafford," in his *From Babel to Byzantium: Poets and Poetry Now* (New York: Farrar, Straus and Giroux, 1968), 139.

6. From the "Interview with William Stafford," in *The World's Hieroglyphic Beauty: Five American Poets*, by Peter Stitt (Athens: University of Georgia Press, 1985). The poet William Heyen, a strong admirer of Stafford's work, has expressed his own reservations about the casual way Stafford writes his poems: "It may be . . . that Stafford has come to trust his way just a little too much. 'To me,' says Stafford, 'poetry is talk that is enhanced a little bit.' To me poetry is talk that is enhanced quite a bit. . . . Maybe the poet is less of an instrument, less of a receiver, and more of a shaper than Stafford believes him to be. Maybe just a little bit more critical consciousness, consciousness coming out of the cortex, would go a long way" ("William Stafford's Allegiances," *Modern Poetry Studies* 1 [1970]: 317). Similarly, Roger Dickinson-Brown has complained that "The quantity of what [Stafford] publishes is out of proportion to the really few things he has to say. . . . the excess has created a need for severe editing. Someone other than the poet will have to produce a 'definitive' Selected Poems, or he will be buried in the clutter . . ." ("The Wise, the Dull, the Bewildered: What Happens in William Stafford," *Modern Poetry Studies* 6 [1975]: 32–33).

7. From the "Interview with James Wright," in Stitt, *The World's Hieroglyphic Beauty*.

8. Those wishing further information on bibliographic matters are referred to James W. Pirie's outstanding *William Stafford: A Primary Bibliography, 1942–1979* (New York: Garland Publishing, 1983). Mr. Pirie is librarian emeritus of Lewis and Clark College, where Stafford taught for many years and where Mr. Pirie assembled what is by far the most extensive Stafford collection in existence.

9. On the way Stafford has collected his poems into books, George S. Lensing has written: "Stafford's finest poems are scattered almost indiscriminately over his career. One has little sense of major evolution and change in his work; both method and matter are relatively consistent from volume to volume" ("William Stafford, Mythmaker," 3).

10. William Stafford, "An Introduction to Some Poems," in *Stories That Could Be True: New and Collected Poems* (New York: Harper and Row, 1977), 201. Subsequent quotations from this volume will be documented parenthetically within the text, using the abbreviation *STCBT*. The other such abbreviation that I will use in this chapter is *GFR,* which stands for *A Glass Face in the Rain: New Poems* (New York: Harper and Row, 1982).

11. Stafford, "Finding What the World Is Trying to Be: An Interview with Sanford Pinsker," in *Writing the Australian Crawl*, 124.

12. The poem was first published as part of the essay "Making a Poem / Starting a Car on Ice," in *American Poets in 1976*, ed. William Heyen (Indianapolis: Bobbs-Merrill, 1976), 374. Stafford has since reprinted it (along with the essay) in *Writing the Australian Crawl,* 75.

13. In the only book-length critical study devoted to Stafford's work, Jonathan Holden makes a point similar to mine: "*Coldness* is . . .

199

a metaphor by which Stafford measures his sense of Nature's otherness. The cold aspect of the world is its threatening aspect, threatening because it is indifferent to human life" (*The Mark to Turn: A Reading of William Stafford's Poetry* [Lawrence: The University Press of Kansas, 1976], 18). Holden's point about the cold is part of his larger idea that there is a profound distance between man and nature in the poems of William Stafford. I do not think there is so radical a separation—indeed, I think the primary motivating passion in Stafford's poetry is man's desire to merge into the mysterious sacredness of nature.

14. The poem appeared first in Heyen's *American Poets in 1976* (373–74) and has since been reprinted in *Writing the Australian Crawl* (74).

15. John F. Lynen, *The Pastoral Art of Robert Frost* (New Haven: Yale University Press, 1960), 13.

16. Ibid., 9. In their book *Four Poets and the Emotive Imagination: Robert Bly, James Wright, Louis Simpson, and William Stafford,* George S. Lensing and Ronald Moran point out the negative poles of what I am calling Stafford's essentially pastoral vision: "The precarious world in which the poet finds himself is described through three principal categories. The first is composed of the dangers of the wilderness and nature itself, dangers that existed as much in the past as in the present, though they seem more acute now. The second category is made up of specific descriptions of modern, technological society. The poems here are concerned with the threats of nuclear war, of a ravaging industrial society, and of a mechanical existence that divorces the individual from authentic human values. Finally, some poems form a category which exposes the sham and vapidity of modern social behavior" ([Baton Rouge: Louisiana State University Press, 1976], 194). Lensing and Moran's discussion of Stafford is the best that I have seen in print.

17. Lynen, *The Pastoral Art of Robert Frost,* 11.

18. "Representing Far Places" illustrates in a mild way how easy it is for a pastoral poem to turn didactic. As long as Stafford makes his points primarily through the manipulation of images, he manages to avoid this failing. It is when he yields to the temptations of bald statement—overt sermonizing, some would call it—that a poem will go sour. Thus, the reader cannot help but feel that the homily with which this poem ends ("It is all right to be simply the way you have to be, / among contradictory ridges in some crescendo of knowing") is an unfortunate mistake. Roger Dickinson-Brown has described essentially the same failing as "a complacency of tone . . . that kills perception and what might be called perfectly true feeling." Too often, Dickinson-Brown continues, "I see a man seduced by his own habit of being very simple and very wise" ("The Wise, the Dull, the Bewildered," 34–35).

19. Stafford, "I Would Also Like to Mention Aluminum: An Interview with William Heyen and Al Poulin," in *Writing the Australian Crawl,* 129.

20. Holden, *The Mark to Turn,* 6. Indeed, Holden sees the imagina-

tion as the primary concern of Stafford's poetry: "The imagination—its resilience, its stubborn and playful instinct for deriving meaning and awe from the world—is the central theme of Stafford's work" (ibid.).

21. Stafford, "Writing and Literature: Some Opinions," in *Writing the Australian Crawl,* 12.

22. The comparison is certainly a startling one. Because of the country-bumpkinish stance he adopts in his poetry, Stafford is assumed by some readers to lack the cultural sophistication we generally expect from our authors. Jonathan Holden obviously disagrees: "In fact . . . his poems and his conception of poetry are extremely sophisticated. A deft, alert intelligence exhibits itself everywhere in his work—through his frequent etymological use of words, through puns, through the construction of deliberate but carefully limited ambiguities and through a scrupulous New-Critical attention to consistency" (*The Mark to Turn,* 6).

23. Lensing and Moran, *Four Poets and the Emotive Imagination,* 187–88. Similarly, John Lauber has written of the relationship between father and son in Stafford's poems: "Adolescent rebellion is absent; the father appears not as rival or oppressor, but as teacher, initiator, gift-bearer, and the gift he brings is a way of perceiving or of being in the world" ("World's Guest—William Stafford," *Iowa Review* 5, no. 2 [1974]: 90).

24. In his article on the importance of myth in Stafford's poetry, George S. Lensing has commented on the poet's use of narrative: "It is significant that Stafford's search for myth is conducted within the frame of 'some story.' His poems, though occasionally surrealistic in part, are founded on narrative, the imparting to the reader a human event in time" ("William Stafford, Mythmaker," 4).

25. The closely related notions of the path and the quest in Stafford's poetry have been noticed by other critics. Jonathan Holden, for example, has suggested that "Stafford's most common image for process is the image of a 'path.' This metaphor interlocks closely with both his metaphors of distance and place" (*The Mark to Turn,* 41). William Heyen introduces this idea into his discussion of Stafford's use of poetic form, which he metaphorically describes as "a road of words." He continues: "Stafford is fond of using what he calls 'an organized form cavalierly treated.' The room to follow impulse within outer strictness. The second line of Thomas Gray's 'Elegy Written in a Country Churchyard': 'The lowing herd winds slowly o'er the lea.' 'Winds,' the sense of a path, not necessarily the shortest, straightest line to the stable, but still a path within infinite possibilities of paths. The cattle of the imagination graze all over the place but, finally, the path winding homeward" ("William Stafford's Allegiances," 308). Finally, Dennis Daley Lynch points out that, in Stafford's poems, "undoubtedly the most striking thematic metaphor . . . is the motif of the journey. Trips of varying length and importance occur throughout [the] canon" ("Journeys in Search of Oneself: The Metaphor of the Road in William Stafford's *Traveling Through the Dark* and *The Rescued Year,*" *Modern Poetry Studies* 7 [1976]: 122).

26. Stafford, "Some Arguments against Good Diction," in *Writing the Australian Crawl*, 58.

27. In any case, other critics have paid adequate notice to this component of Stafford's work. Dennis Daley Lynch, for example, notes that "Much of William Stafford's poetry contains a painful, nostalgic longing for the way things were. . . . The remembrances usually center on the most basic and important elements of the past—namely, parents and the hometown" ("Journeys in Search of Oneself," 123). John Lauber makes essentially the same point, though more inclusively: "The poetry of William Stafford is rooted in a series of natural pieties rare in contemporary life or literature: piety toward the earth itself, toward the region, the home, the parents, toward one's total past" ("World's Guest—William Stafford," 88).

28. For George Lensing and Ronald Moran, the two quests for home become one, as they explain in a passage that states the thesis of their essay: "Stafford's poems reveal thematically a singular and unified preoccupation. The voice of his work speaks from a sheltered vista of calm and steady deliberation. The speaker looks backward to a western childhood world that is joyous and at times edenic, even as he gazes with suspicion and some sense of peril upon the state of modern American society. The crux of each volume by Stafford involves the search for that earlier age identifiable by certain spiritual values associated with the wilderness, values which can sustain him and his family as well as the whole of the technological and urban society which surrounds him" (*Four Poets and the Emotive Imagination*, 178).

29. As an introduction to their discussion of "Bi-Focal," Lensing and Moran comment on the hidden nature of the truth as Stafford presents it: "Stafford's depiction of the essential wilderness is set up through images—almost always in terms of a vertical hierarchy. The outer world is one of surfaces and shadows; it is available to everyone and yields many precious moments. The other world, concealed and far less accessible, is underground; its perception becomes the abiding vocation of the poet" (ibid., 204).

30. Speaking of the search conducted in Stafford's poems, Lensing and Moran point out that "while the journey involves the physical world of the wilderness, its reality is spiritual" (ibid., 193).

31. Robert Coles, "William Stafford's Long Walk," *American Poetry Review* 4, no. 4 (1975): 27. Lensing and Moran have also commented cogently on the role of the Indian: "Another character-type who corresponds to the father in the poetry of Stafford is the American Indian. Like the father, the Indians and their chiefs are dead; and their wisdom also derives from intimacy with the wilderness. . . . The qualities by which the Indian is most consistently defined are not ferocity and warfare, but reticence and concealment. . . . His life is enacted according to rituals and symbolic patterns which bring him into harmony with the wilderness" (*Four Poets and the Emotive Imagination*, 192).

JUDITH KITCHEN

Willingly Fallible
The Essays / The Art

When William Stafford retired from Lewis and Clark College in 1980, he had been teaching there for thirty-two years. Over those years he also led summer workshops at colleges and writers' conferences across the country, including the Breadloaf Writers' Conference. His essays on the teaching of writing have become well known—and often criticized as making a difficult process sound altogether too easy, as being too accepting of a given piece without demanding rigorous standards. It is easy to see how these criticisms could arise, but not so easy to see why the critics have not understood what Stafford has had to say. His theories of teaching come directly from his theories of writing, not the least of these what writing can, and should, do for the life of the writer. Given this specific context, his theories are consistent with his statements, not only on writing and revising but on living as well.

In 1970 an essay by Stafford appeared in one of the first issues of *Field,* a magazine produced at Oberlin College. Titled "A Way of Writing," the essay seemed to challenge the critical tenet of authorial intentionality by suggesting that the writer might not, after all, know exactly what he was doing. Or saying. He suggests that the writer might instead be trusting in something larger than himself, something he too must take on faith. Although this is no surprise to many writers, it certainly makes the discussion of poetry in the academic classroom much more equivocal. Stafford outlines his own process, emphasizing his spirit of receptivity:

> So, receptive, careless of failure, I spin out things on the page. And a wonderful freedom comes. If something occurs to me,

From *Understanding William Stafford* by Judith Kitchen (Columbia: University of South Carolina Press, 1989), 147–60. Copyright © University of South Carolina 1989.

it is all right to accept it. It has one justification: it occurs to me. No one else can guide me. I must follow my own weak, wandering, diffident impulses.

A strange bonus happens. At times, without my insisting on it, my writings become coherent; the successive elements that occur to me are clearly related. They lead by themselves to new connections. Sometimes the language, even the syllables that happen along, may start a trend. Sometimes the materials alert me to something waiting in my mind, ready for sustained attention. At such times, I allow myself to be eloquent, or intentional, or for great swoops (treacherous! not to be trusted!) reasonable. But I do not insist on any of that; for I know that back of my activity there will be the coherence of my self, and that indulgence of my impulses will bring recurrent patterns and meanings again.[1]

In this statement it is possible to detect the specific rules that guide Stafford's writing. First, the resistance to rules, the willingness to see what will happen. Second, the reliance on self as the ultimate authority and the confidence that that self will be the shaping force underneath every poem. Third, a responsiveness to language itself—the syllables that "happen along"—and the possibility that sound may shape meaning at least as effectively as sense. Fourth, a suspicion of what is "reasonable," or the converse, that resisting reason may in fact produce a deeper, more profound, kind of reason. Fifth, a willingness to fail, which implies a critical sense, one that can recognize the relative success or failure of the poem to produce a coherence. But the process itself is what is important; the insights to be gained in following this prescription go far beyond the possible "successful" poem. The recurrent patterns tell him something about what is important to him, about the nature of his imagination, about the world of language that he inhabits.

Stafford in prose is still the Stafford of the poetry. It is important to note the vagueness of the language he uses to describe this process—and the sureness of the tone. He is convinced of the rightness of his method (for himself), is certainly in tune with the process as he practices it, but cannot define with precision just what it is. Syllables "happen along." As a writer, he knows this. As a reader, he knows that critics talk as if this were not the case, as if every word were chosen for a particular purpose or end within the poem. In "Some Arguments against Good Diction" he carefully talks about the differences between practicing the craft and *talking about* the practice of the craft. Constantly aware that language distorts even as it tries to make clear, Stafford is trying to clarify an attitude, not a method. "Where words come from, into consciousness, baffles me. Speaking or writing, the words bounce instantaneously into their context, and I am victimized by them, rather than controlling them. They do not wait for my selection; they volunteer."[2] He makes this statement more explicit in an essay called "Capturing 'People of the South Wind,'" saying, "Intention endangers creation."[3]

Going on to assess the power of language to convey abstract ideas, Stafford concludes that communication is interior—not, in his phrase, an "absolute phenomenon." Therefore, he decides to trust the unconscious linkings (he calls them "logicings") that work through combinations of words. "Another way is to let the language itself begin to shape the event taking place by its means."[4] This statement may seem like a refusal to take responsibility for his meanings, but, read carefully, it is an insistence that meaning is discovered *in* language, not manipulated *by* language. To write in this way is to trust the process to reveal the importance of an event, a feeling, a particular word. It is also to be confident that the imagination is more interesting than the analytic mind. "For a writer, it is not the past or present of words that counts, but their futures."[5]

Stafford is unwilling to play by the "rules" because, for him, the rules do not provide a way of participating in art. The participatory aspect of art is what entices him. He would rather be alive in conversation, trying on new meanings and ideas, discovering the "unfound bonuses," risking and "frisking" at the party, than to miss the party entirely. "Technique used for itself will rot your soul," he says.[6] It is clear that William Stafford's poems employ a variety of technical skills—a strong iambic beat, careful use of rhythm or rhyme, cadence, formal structures—but for him these skills are all secondary to the receptivity that might bring something "new." In fact, the extensive use of slant and internal rhyme would indicate that he is exploring new ways to allow sound to manifest itself in the poetic line, and his quirky line breaks immediately demonstrate ways in which individual words can suddenly become important to the overall suggested meaning of the poem. All of these techniques are tools used to a larger end, and the end is not the individual work of art or its meaning; the end is the life of art and *its* meaning. The process of writing allows access to that life; through art the writer discovers just who and what he is: "The more you let yourself be distracted from where you are going, the more you are the person that you are. It's not so much like getting lost as it is like getting found."[7]

It is natural that Stafford's ideas on the teaching of writing center on this belief, and that his emphasis is on methods that might help the student find the person he is. In "A Witness for Poetry," Stafford makes the transition from speaking as a writer to speaking as a teacher:

One issue, "How the hell do you teach others to write poetry?" can be answered this way. One thing you do with others is try to encourage them, induce them and be company to them when they go ahead and follow the immediacies of experience. You tell them, "Don't be inhibited, don't be cautious, don't be correct; just go headlong into the experience."[8]

This same view was expressed earlier in a widely published and somewhat controversial essay called "Writing the Australian Crawl,"[9] which was interpreted by some educators (and even some writers) as an abandonment of standards. In that essay Stafford compares the process of writing to the process of swimming. He suggests that beginning writers should overcome their fear and reluctance much the way beginning swimmers must learn to trust the water. To do this, they must submit the body to the water and learn that it will hold them up. Language will hold the writer up. Enter it, learn to float. The prescription sounds so easy. And Stafford does make it sound as though language, that voluptuous being, will somehow help produce a fine result. English teachers, worried about syntax and diction and basic punctuation, do not believe it is as easy as he would make it sound. But his critics' interpretation is often superficial. Stafford at no time implies that the results will be good, only that they will be real, and sometimes surprising. They will come from that interior part of the student where imagination, or inventiveness, converges with a felt necessity to communicate. The result will be something that matters to the student. What better raw material for the exterior "rules" of grammar?

Asked the best thing he can do for his students, Stafford replies:

Be a listener . . . I think just being really alive to what they say, or write. And that there are all sorts of signals, only a very few of which are routine teacher-signals. My own conviction is—conviction is too strong a word, but the hunch I'm operating on at the moment in teaching writing—is that their moves are the important moves, and mine are sort of counter-moves or receiving moves. . . . This may seem too vague. And it leads to many vague sessions.[10]

The emphasis on listening comes as no surprise. As experts wrestle with the problem of writing in today's classrooms, on the elementary as well as the college level, more and more of them advocate the methods that Stafford has been using for over forty years. This does not mean a reduction in standards, but a revaluation of how those standards should be taught. Revision is the natural result of Stafford's way of teaching, but it comes from the student's urgent need to clarify or explore.

Since writing is a way of living, a means and not an end in itself, Stafford sees himself as teaching something that will be an ongoing resource in the life of the student: "You may find yourself in a continuing way of life that is enriched by the practice of art."[11] He also recognizes that his goal is difficult—and often misunderstood:

It was only far along in my teaching and writing—in the last ten years of my teaching, say, when I was deliberately withdrawing to half-time so as to save precious hours for writing— that I began to understand my way as simply incompatible with that of most others. It became apparent that many teachers, for instance, have forgotten how material begins to seek its own form, how a piece of wood, for instance, may like a certain curve when you are carving a gunstock like the one I admired in the corner of our living room, how a phrase when you speak it or write it begins to call up another phrase, or how a word suddenly finds another word that its syllables like to associate with.[12]

By offering this "relax in the water" approach Stafford has made writing a possibility for countless students. Few have become published writers, but it can be assumed that each of them has left the classroom with a better feeling of what it is to enter language, and a better sense of who he or she really is. The effect Stafford's approach can have on a genuinely talented writer is exemplified by the comments of a contemporary poet, Linda Pastan:

Bill Stafford . . . really made me start looking at writing in a different way. It loosened me up a lot. I used to think that a poem had its shape before you even began, and I knew ahead of time what I wanted to say. I'd come to the blank page with a specific idea. After talking a lot to Bill Stafford and hearing him talk, I really tried to follow a different path so that I wouldn't have any idea where I was going to end when I began—and that was really intoxicating. I mean, you really make discoveries that way—about yourself—and I think it leads to better poetry. [13]

While advocating writing as exploration, Stafford also says, with his special brand of wit, "Ideally for me, poems are nothing special. They are just the language without any mistakes." [14] The subliminal message here is that it is possible to achieve a kind of perfection. If so, it is a perfection that must reside in the reader, not the writer.

It is evident that Stafford believes in the capacity of the reader to complete the process. He assumes that the reader will enjoy the same associative play that he responds to as he is writing. In that meeting of minds, what Donald Hall refers to as "one man's inside talking to another man's inside," [15] there is room for tenuous connections to be made. Stafford asks the rhetorical question, "Can it be that poetry often allows both writer and reader to swing wide on allusion and hint and loose connection, just because only by such recklessness can one reach far out for meanings, with frail helps from language?" [16] By "taking his hands off the handlebars," [17] letting the poem make its own way for a time, he dares to follow its intuitive path. He trusts the poem implicitly; writer and reader will meet in that nebulous space the poem creates. A recent interview with the Brockport Writers Forum clarifies this further:

Kitchen: Is that your idea of the ideal reader—someone who will listen that hard?

Stafford: That's right. Superconductivity in the head is what I'm after. So that whatever comes is met with resilience, with initial acceptance; it doesn't mean that it isn't processed by your former experience and whatever kind of bounce you have in your own head, but it is, in the first instance, welcomed. That's what I try to cultivate in my writing, too. Whatever I start to write, I don't try to be hard on it—I try to welcome it, make it feel at home, see what it's going to say next.[18]

Although Stafford has written a few comments or articles on other writers (namely Brother Antoninus, Richard Eberhart, Robinson Jeffers, Thomas Hardy), he has carefully removed himself from the field of criticism. Stafford seems unafraid to judge the critics, however. His judgment comes from "inside," assessing any given comment to see if it helps or hinders the writer in his chosen task. "I'm afraid of the conditions under which students, for instance, are inducted into the idea of writing . . . that they are made to feel this obligation to be brilliant, to turn out things that are worthy, and that attitude is paralyzing, I think." He goes on to say he fears the loss of risk if he followed the prescriptions of the critics:

> The stance that some people take about doing art—which is a rigid stance, which is that it's got to make American Literature more dignified—is destructive to the recklessness or the willingness to be available to the now-ness of experience. . . . I believe the general public is not well served by critics and artists who make it seem that doing art is not available to human beings, that it is available only to those who are already accomplished. And when you do art you are not already accomplished—you are blundering in all over again. . . . I feel that the resultant of discussions about writing is that people who aren't in it get a distorted view of what it's like. I don't think that anyone is trying to distort this view, I'm just saying that in always focusing on successful works—the finished product—they don't realize that writers do a lot of dumb things. . . . Writers have wastebaskets.[19]

Stafford is not only writer and teacher; he is student as well: "I feel like a student all the time. Life is trying to teach me. Emerging experiences are giving me these opportunities."[20] "I think writing is itself educational, exploratory, and worthy of trust while you're doing it."[21] The reader instinctively feels that Stafford is learning as he is going. Thus the poems never seem to preach—or even teach—so much as to come to a natural conclusion. They embody Frost's adage, "No surprise in the writer, no surprise in the reader,"[22] and, in the case of William Stafford, the reader senses the writer's genuine surprise.

Whitman and Yeats spent their poetic careers revising and revising one long "book"—a central vision of the world. Such efforts as Hart Crane's *The Bridge* and William Carlos Williams's *Paterson* are lauded for a similar attempt. If William Stafford's work is viewed as an equally long "book," it too adds up to a vision of the world. His method of revision has been one of addition, of coming at the same material from a slightly altered perspective, of chipping away at the edges of things.

A carefully chosen "Selected Poems" would call attention to the complex vision in William Stafford's work, but the question still remains: In such elusive, illusive, allusive work, which poems should be chosen? So far he has left it to the individual reader to decide. William Stafford's body of work is certainly as important as that of those of his chronological generation—Robert Lowell, John Berryman, Elizabeth Bishop—and those of his poetic generation—Robert Bly, James Wright, Donald Hall. His vision is as broad and as all-encompassing as that of Yeats or Whitman. It is as tightly woven and as imaginatively complex as that of Stevens and as sensitive to the inner landscape as Roethke's. As with all truly great writers, his "generation" extends beyond the limits of time. We inherit not only the poems, but the attitude in which they were written: "I must be willingly fallible in order to deserve a place in the realm where miracles happen."[23]

NOTES

1. William Stafford, "A Way of Writing," *Writing the Australian Crawl* (Ann Arbor: University of Michigan Press, 1978), 18.
2. Ibid., 57.
3. Ibid., 33.
4. "Some Arguments against Good Diction," *Writing the Australian Crawl,* 59.
5. Ibid., 59.
6. "Whose Tradition?" *Writing the Australian Crawl,* 78.
7. Stafford, "A Witness for Poetry," *You Must Revise Your Life* (Ann Arbor: University of Michigan Press, 1986), 62.
8. Ibid., 62.
9. *Writing the Australian Crawl,* 21–34.
10. "Roving across Fields: A Conversation," *Roving across Fields,* ed. Thom Tammaro (Daleville, Ind.: Barnwood Press Cooperative, 1983), 22.
11. "Making Best Use of a Workshop," *You Must Revise Your Life,* 103.
12. "William Stafford: 1914–," *You Must Revise Your Life,* 20.

13. Stan Sanvel Rubin, "Whatever Is at Hand: A Conversation with Linda Pastan," SUNY Brockport, Brockport Writers Forum and Videotape Library, 4 November 1976.

14. "A Witness for Poetry," 58.

15. Donald Hall, *Goatfoot, Milktongue, Twinbird* (Ann Arbor: University of Michigan Press, 1978), 118.

16. "Breathing on a Poem," *You Must Revise Your Life,* 51.

17. "A Witness for Poetry," 59.

18. Stan Sanvel Rubin and Judith Kitchen, "A Conversation with William Stafford," SUNY Brockport, Brockport Writers Forum and Videotape Library, 22 March 1988.

19. Rubin and Kitchen, "A Conversation with William Stafford."

20. Ibid.

21. "Facing Up to the Job," *You Must Revise Your Life,* 74.

22. "The Figure a Poem Makes," *Robert Frost: Poetry and Prose,* ed. E. C. Lathem and L. Thompson (New York: Holt, Rinehart, 1972), 394.

23. "Some Notes on Writing," preface to *An Oregon Message* (New York: Harper and Row, 1987), 10.

PART THREE   *Essays on Particular*
                Poems or Articles

LEONARD NATHAN

From "One Vote"

What we cannot imagine but know somehow to be true—like
death or the possibility of nuclear war—affects us in ways that
are hard to define because the effects are often indirect, as when
otherwise harmless objects terrorize us in dreams and leave be-
hind echoes of the same terror when we awaken. Indirection
seems to be the only unhysterical way we can deal with the
terrible but true. That is why perhaps the best modern poetry
about death and cataclysm is indirect. The poem about nuclear
destruction I am most moved by is William Stafford's "At the
Bomb Testing Site."

> At noon in the desert a panting lizard
> waited for history, its elbows tense,
> watching the curve of a particular road
> as if something might happen.
>
> It was looking at something farther off
> than people could see, an important scene
> acted in stone for little selves
> at the flute end of consequences.
>
> There was just a continent without much on it
> under a sky that never cared less.
> Ready for a change, the elbows waited.
> The hands gripped hard on the desert.

The poem never alludes directly to its subject except in the
title. The awful potential is seen through the anticipatory behav-
ior of the lizard, and described with understated detachment.
Direct treatment of such subjects tends to be shrilly trite, hysteri-
cally accusing, and sometimes merely self-pitying, as though, in
search of terms congruent with the magnitude of the unspeak-
able, writers pass beyond the limits of what they can control by

New England Review and Breadloaf Quarterly 5 (1983): 521–24.

art and intelligence. I think it was the philosopher Adorno who, after World War II, proclaimed: "No poems about concentration camps!" Although I'm put off by his peremptory tone and his implication that there are subjects too serious for the self-indulgence of poets, I think I understand what prompted such an utterance. In a time when so much poetry contains, as a sort of authenticating credential, the personality of the poet, the treatment of really tremendous topics deserves something better than pathetic personal stance, more or less grandiose. In this century, American poets don't seem to have the powers for voicing serious public outrage, public grief or joy—the price we pay, I suppose, for our poetic tradition having rooted itself in subjectivity as the only authentic ground for poetry. One of the results of this aesthetic decision—which is part of the inheritance of the Romantic movement—is that whenever poets begin to write about some public issue, it is difficult for them not to conclude by assimilating it to their personal lives. This is as true of Carolyn Forché as it was for Wordsworth, though Wordsworth still had available to him poetic conventions that allowed him to generalize subjectivity into something like a public self. Most poets have long ago forsaken such conventions as being the mark of rhetorical bluster and eloquent mendacity. With the more modest instruments of a small lyric voice, contemporary poets do what they can, but what they cannot do very well, it seems, is move into the public domain without feeling self-conscious or clumsily defiant. And this, I think, is why a poem like Stafford's seems memorable. It is able to shift its subjectivity to another creature—a creature noted for its cold blood—and offer instinctual anticipation as a kind of measure for the unspeakable.

I am not against directness and my wincing at what seems to be the general badness of poems that directly address horror may only be the reflex of aesthetic bias. But I am against bad rhetoric in a good cause, that is, rhetoric which leaves untouched or alienates the very audience it meant to move to its view. The question to be asked here is: What can contemporary poetry do and to whom can it do it? It can, I think, make some see who don't and remind some who can, to look again. But this seeing takes considerable precision; otherwise, the poet is nothing more or less than a propagandist (and, I submit, usually an inferior one to those trained in the field). A trouble here is that not many people read poetry. I have received scratched-up ad hoc broadsides containing fifteen or twenty antinuclear poems, usually shoddy work, sometimes by good poets. I read them. Other poets read them. We all agree—

nuclear war is terrible. Something must be done. But the same effect can be, and often is, achieved in a newspaper editorial, which reaches a wider audience, some of whom do not agree or hardly think about agreement or disagreement. Between the value of the two kinds of protests, I'll pick the editorial every time. The antinuclear poems seem, next to a halfway decent newspaper article, hoarse sighs in the wilderness. It is as if American poets, in order to be believed, have to scream (lucky Russian poets; they can be hauled in for a subversive whisper). But American poets are *not* believed because they are not read—at least by the audience that their political poems aim to persuade. Since pupils, disciples, fellow poets are already persuaded, what then is the point, except to clear a heavy conscience or relieve a frustrated passion to DO something?

For all the dozens of antinuclear poems I have read and forgotten, Stafford's sticks in my mind (along with Karl Shapiro's wonderful "The Progress of Faust") not just as a clever handling of a difficult topic, but as some measure for the magnitude of the danger, a magnitude I can handle at least with some sense that I can act on it, in however limited a way, and can act, so far as it is in my power to, rationally. Direct poems on the topic usually leave me with one of two feelings, if they don't put me off altogether: either I feel helpless before what they prophesy or I feel like rushing out and doing *something* fast; since there is nothing useful like that to do, this latter feeling itself leads to a sense of futility and finally indifference. I begin to think of something else, something less paralyzing, and leave it to dreams to remind me of the unspeakable.

I do not rule out that ideal: a great public poem on this issue, speaking in powerful, widely understandable ways about nuclear war, a poem that, like Dostoyevski's *House of the Dead,* might significantly revolutionize behavior. But I doubt it. What I do not doubt is that effective poems can be written on the unspeakable. They may seem modest, perhaps innocuous, because they work through indirection, not startling us to mindless action like a siren charging through our sleep, but subtly shifting the way we see the reality, keeping our imagination alive to possibilities. And perhaps—though this may be wishful thinking—spreading through a wider consciousness than that represented by the tiny audience for poetry.

When I show those who are not poetry readers the Stafford poem, show it and try to explain how it works, they usually become thoughtful. I want them to be thoughtful, not to knock me down and run for the nearest exit. I think that's the best we can hope for—that a lot of people become thoughtful. Let them be scared too (and perhaps direct poems can have some effect here), but let them be thinking hard. That seems to me the first step toward serious argument and useful action. And I don't know what else or what better we can hope for out of all this.

CHARLES SIMIC

"At the Bomb Testing Site"

A political poem in which not a single political statement is made, what Stafford himself calls more "nonapparently political than apparently political."

Let me quote Nietzsche here: "The consequence of reverie which would borrow from intelligence the means to force upon the world its folly. . . . We are a race committed to the test of the act, hence pledged to the bloodiest fate."

In poetry a choice is made about the part that will represent the whole. Form, in its deepest sense, is selection. True form is the product of an extraordinary vision.

There's a lizard at the bomb testing site. The poem is an attempt to measure everything according to the duration and intensity of that little life.

A "weasel-worded" poem.

The naked world. The innocent lizard. A most primitive form of life. Ugly. Expendable—like those laboratory animals stuck inside a maze under the bright lights.

One assumes they're afraid too.

"How pure and great must be the cause for which so much blood is spilled," says Aleksandar Wat.

For now, just the timeless moment. Just the lizard, the desert. He's panting, trembling a little. Think of Elizabeth Bishop's "Armadillo," the fire raining on him. . . . That will come later.

History is marching. . . . Or, History is a throw of the dice . . .

Field 41 (Fall 1989): 8–10; reprinted in *Wonderful Words, Silent Truth: Essays on Poetry and a Memoir* by Charles Simic (Ann Arbor: University of Michigan Press, 1990), 126–28.

The poem is an attempt to convey certain old premonitions. The first lizard knew the world will end some day.

And at the heart of it—Incomprehension! Bewilderment!

Out there, perhaps, scratched in stone, there's the matchstick figure of the Indian humpbacked flute player. He is surrounded by other matchstick figures. They are enacting a scene, a sacred dance . . .

The sphinx is watching. An American sphinx waiting for history The hands grip hard, so we are on the very verge. It is the instant in which all past and all future wait suspended.

One should speak of Stafford's disappearing acts. As in "Traveling Through the Dark," he leaves us at the most crucial moments. At the end of his great poems we are always alone, their fateful acts and their consequences now our own to consider.

Solitude as an absolute, the only one.

The heavens above couldn't care less. The poet asks the philosopher in us to consider the world in its baffling presence.

An American sphinx in the desert of our spirit. Let us keep asking her questions.

In the meantime, we can say with Heidegger that poems such as this one open the largest view of the earth, sky, mortals and their true and false gods.

HENRY TAYLOR

"Thinking for Berky"

Millions of Intricate Moves

I

In "Thinking for Berky," many of the qualities that make Stafford's poetry what it is are at their best. The meter, strictly speaking, is unstable; some of the lines are iambic pentameter, and others stray from that toward fourteen syllables, yet the rhythmical rightness of each line is firmly there, not to be quarreled with. Similarly, the rhyme is the very opposite of insistent; though the rhymes between the first and fourth lines of each stanza are solid and true, there is enough between the rhymes to keep them from being more than a gentle and mysterious reminder that this is utterance weighed and wrought. Within this delicate scheme, the sentences move easily from immediate description to generalization and back again, the tone never modulating beyond the conversational. And yet there is something close to bravura in the calm statements of large truths: "there are things time passing can never make come true," "justice will take us millions of intricate moves."

Certain qualities of calmness and unpretentious gravity may create the impression that this voice is not easily modulated, or inclusive of various tones. But many of the qualities evident in "Thinking for Berky"—discursiveness, directness, delicacy of meter, specificity of description, definitiveness of general statement—are to be found in "Adults Only," a recollection of an evening at the state fair, in the tent reserved for the striptease act. The poem begins with a general statement: "Animals own a fur world; / people own worlds that are variously, pleasingly, bare." The rest of the stanza recalls how those worlds came clear to "us kids" the night they found themselves in that tent. The poem ends:

Field 41 (Fall 1989): 12–24.

Better women exist, no doubt, than that one,
and occasions more edifying, too, I suppose.
But we have to witness for ourselves what comes for us,
nor be distracted by barkers of irrelevant ware;
and a pretty good world, I say, arrived that night
when that woman came farming right out of her clothes,
by God,

At the state fair.[1]

Certain lines in this stanza—the first two, the last four—are quite clearly different from anything in "Thinking for Berky"; they are looser, more conversational. But only a few of the words—*pretty good,* for example—are foreign to the diction of the other poem. The use of the word *farming* in each poem is indicative of Stafford's unusual sensitivity to context: in "Thinking for Berky" the word has a hard and desperate sound, as if the parents farmed mostly with sickles and whips. In "Adults Only" the word is quirky but exact: the woman comes rolling out of her clothes like a combine out of a wheat field.

Along the spectrum from pure conversation to elaborate oratory, Stafford's poems occupy a relatively narrow range. But his acquaintance with that zone, and his sense of what context can yield, seem to have been, from the beginning, more than sufficient to the creation of explosions which many other poets would expend far more energy to bring about.

Stafford's first collection, *West of Your City* (1960), was published in an elegant limited edition by a small press; except for a few poems which have been widely anthologized, and fourteen which were reprinted in *The Rescued Year,* the work in it was unavailable for several years, until the appearance of *Stories That Could Be True: New and Collected Poems* (1977), which reprints Stafford's first two books, and three others: *The Rescued Year* (1966), *Allegiances* (1970), and *Someday, Maybe* (1973). *West of Your City* turns out to be a first book of great maturity, distinctiveness, and understated power; Stafford, it seems, is among those rare poets who do not publish a book before they have hit their stride. We are in danger now of taking Stafford's particular stride for granted, but it must have been earned courageously; most of the noisier proponents of this or that way of writing poems in the 1950s would have been reluctant to embrace these quiet, durable poems. In meters that are never too insistent, yet never out of control, the poems in *West of Your City* record the observations of a questing spirit—evoking the past, revealing in the present many small but significant signs of where we are, and heading westward, into the future. The tone is discursive, the diction conversational, but everywhere in these poems shines Stafford's amazing gift for arranging ordinary words into resonant truth and mystery: "Wherever we looked the land would hold us up."

Though *West of Your City* was out of print before it came to wide attention, *Traveling Through the Dark* (1962) immediately established Stafford as a poet of rare gifts and unusual productivity. As the citation of the poetry judges for the National Book Award put it: "William Stafford's poems are clean, direct and whole. They are both tough and gentle; their music knows the value of silence." True enough; and one is then awe-struck to realize that these splendid poems—seventy-six of them, enough for two collections—were published only two years after *West of Your City.* As James Dickey once said, poetry appears not only to be the best way for Stafford to say what he wants to say but also to be the easiest. This may be an exaggeration, but it is true that even in the most casual of circumstances, Stafford's utterances can have the distinctive and memorable flavor of his poetry, as when he closes a letter, "So long—I look toward seeing you everywhere."

In *Traveling Through the Dark,* the major advance over the first book is in breadth of tone. Looking at the ways in which his poems can break into humor, I begin to think that Stafford has a talent, never quite indulged, for self-parody. He is attuned to the effects he can create, and so sensitive to various modes of surprise, that even within a restricted range of word choices, he can be haunting, wistful, or slyly humorous.

In *The Rescued Year,* there are many poems which surprise only because they did not exist before; they are otherwise very much like Stafford's earlier work. As he says at the end of "Believer,"

> You don't hear me yell to test the quiet or try to shake
> the wall, for I understand that the wrong sound weakens
> what no sound could ever save, and I am the one
> to live by the hum that shivers till the world can sing:—
> May my voice hover and wait for fate,
> when the right note shakes everything.
>
> (*Stories,* 123)

But if the poems continue to sound exactly like the poems his earlier work led us to expect, there are among the subjects of these poems a few matters which Stafford had not previously staked out as his kind of territory. The title poem, longer and more leisurely than most of Stafford's earlier poems, is a fine evocation of a year of happiness lived in his youth, when his father had a job in another town and moved the family there. In "Following the *Markings* of Dag Hammarskjöld: A Gathering of Poems in the Spirit of His Life and Writings," Stafford fashions a moving long sequence of related poems, the more valuable because they do not depend too heavily on the inspiration acknowledged in the title. And in "The Animal That Drank Up Sound," he creates a myth of remarkable freshness, which has yet the flavor of folklore that makes it sound ancient. The first part of the poem tells how the animal came down and swallowed the sounds of the earth, until at last all sound was gone, and he starved. In the second section, a cricket, who had been hiding when the animal came by, awoke to a heavy stillness, and with one tentative sound, brought everything back:

> It all returned, our precious world with its life and sound,
> where sometimes loud over the hill the moon,
> wild again, looks for its animal to roam, still,
> down out of the hills, any time.
> But somewhere a cricket waits.
>
> It listens now, and practices at night.
>
> (*Stories,* 147)

The boldness of this poem and others in *The Rescued Year* is carried forward into *Allegiances* and *Someday, Maybe.* The strain of odd metaphor against discursive diction is rewardingly increased: "He talked like an old gun killing buffalo, / and in what he said a giant was trying to get out."

As always, any observation might start a poem, but in *Allegiances* Stafford seems freer to let the observation go either as far as necessary or to let it stop when it should. Several of these poems are tiny, fragmentary, but complete, like "Note":

> straw, feathers, dust—
> little things
>
> but if they all go one way,
> that's the way the wind goes.
>
> (*Stories,* 181)

Sometimes these small observations are gathered in bunches under one title, like "Brevities" or "Religion Back Home." In these clusters of short poems, the tension between their disparateness and their being gathered under one title reminds us of Stafford's sense of his vocation: "The world speaks everything to us. / It is our only friend."

More and more often in *Allegiances* and *Someday, Maybe,* Stafford evokes the spirits of those whose ancestors lived here before white people came. "People of the South Wind," for example, is a mythic explanation of where a person's breath goes after he dies; the tone is radically conversational, even for Stafford, but the effect is, magically, dignified. And the title poem of *Someday, Maybe,* "The Eskimo National Anthem," recalls a song, "Aleena, Al-wona," that echoes often through the speaker's daily life. The phrase is translated as "Someday, Maybe." (A small misfortune has befallen the version of the poem in *Stories:* "Someday" is misprinted as "Somebody.") The poem ends with the observation that the song might be to blame if the speaker's life never amounts to anything, though it is a comforting keepsake. The paradox is gracefully concealed; it is hardly possible, in the poetic world of William Stafford, to notice so much, and still live a life that amounts to nothing.

The gathering of previously uncollected poems, *Stories That Could Be True,* extends the range of Stafford's apparently boundless empathy. Many of the speakers in these poems are not the observer, but the thing observed—wind, seeds, trees, ducks—and they speak of how things are with them, in a voice that is of course truly Stafford's, but which is profoundly convincing; it is a lively extension of the myth-making tendency that began to be displayed in *The Rescued Year.* It is also noteworthy that in these more recent poems, Stafford often permits himself a strictness of meter and rhyme that is rare in his earlier work. He has usually preferred to suggest a form rather than commit himself fully to it; but there are poems here whose simplicity, memorability, and charm are like the verses people who speak English have had in their heads from childhood. It takes a lifetime of thoughtful and wide-ranging work to arrive at the stage where one can write a miniature masterpiece like "At the Playground," which in its way can speak for what Stafford has been up to all along, and for what he has been looking for in the books he has published since:

> Away down deep and away up high,
> a swing drops you into the sky.

Back, it draws you away down deep,
forth, it flings you in a sweep
all the way to the stars and back
—Goodby, Jill; Goodby, Jack:
shuddering climb wild and steep,
away up high, away down deep.

(*Stories*, 11)

II

In the past few years, Stafford has published a number of prose
pieces about how his poems come to be. Many of these have
been collected in *Writing the Australian Crawl* (1978) and *You Must
Revise Your Life* (1986), both published in the University of
Michigan's Poets on Poetry series. It is widely recognized by
now that Stafford presents himself as a poet for whom the pro-
cess is in many ways more important than the product. He wants
an openness to any possibility during the initial stages of—I
almost said *composition*. He is therefore suspicious of technique,
especially if it is used for its own sake, or used to force a poem in
a preconceived direction. His rhetorical stance toward these mat-
ters is exemplified in "Some Notes on Writing," a prose state-
ment at the beginning of his most recent collection of poems, *An
Oregon Message* (1987):

> My poems are organically grown, and it is my habit to allow
> language its own freedom and confidence. The results will
> sometimes bewilder conservative readers and hearers, espe-
> cially those who try to control all emergent elements in dis-
> course for the service of predetermined ends.
>
> Each poem is a miracle that has been invited to happen. But
> these words, after they come, you look at what's there. Why
> these? Why not some calculated careful contenders? Because
> these chosen ones must survive as they were made, by the
> reckless impulse of a fallible but susceptible person. I must be
> willingly fallible in order to deserve a place in the realm where
> miracles happen.
>
> Writing poems is living in that realm. Each poem is a gift, a
> surprise that emerges as itself and is only later subjected to
> order and evaluation. (10)

As direct as these paragraphs seem, there are certain questions
which they do not quite answer. Is Stafford describing a process

like automatic writing? Language must have "its own freedom and confidence," and "after they come," by "reckless impulse," the words "must survive as they were made." This is certainly suggestive of a method which involves little in the way of revision. On the other hand, the poems are "later subjected to order and evaluation," whatever "order" might mean here.

In "A Way of Writing," one of the essays collected in *Writing the Australian Crawl,* Stafford notes that others "talk about 'skills' in writing." He goes on to explain his difficulty with the concept:

> Without denying that I do have experience, wide reading, automatic orthodoxies and maneuvers of various kinds, I still must insist that I am often baffled about what "skill" has to do with the precious little area of confusion when I do not know what I am going to say and then I find out what I am going to say. That precious interval I am unable to bridge by skill. . . . Skill? If so, it is a skill we all have, something we learned before the age of three or four. (19)

It is statements like that last one, taken out of context—sometimes, admittedly, by Stafford himself—which have recently given rise to the notions that Stafford wants all poems to be equally valued, that writing teachers should not evaluate student work, and that a kind of open basking in possibility is more important than any talk of how to make a poem better than it is. "Well," we hear the teacher saying, "this might show us something important. Next?" I ponder the Zen of workshopping, the guru as wise ignoramus.

Again. In an interview with Cynthia Lofsness (in *Writing the Australian Crawl*) Stafford speaks suspiciously of technique:

> It's not a technique, it's a kind of stance to take toward experience, or an attitude to take toward immediate feelings and thoughts while you're writing. That seems important to me, but technique is something I believe I would like to avoid. (98)

In conversation on various occasions since that interview, which was first published in 1972, Stafford has said similar things; but in those contexts, the interviewer's definition of technique, included in her question, has not always been present as a background: "I would define technique as a belief on the part of the poet that there are certain rules or forms into which his ideas must be channeled for proper expression. A belief that there is a proper 'framework,' into which he must fit his specific feelings. . . ."

It is instructive to note the extremism of the positions Stafford opposes when he talks about these things. In one case, we have the desire to control absolutely every impulse, to work everything toward a predetermined effect or end; in another, we have a belief in rules, in a proper framework. The first method is obsessive, the second oversimplified and ignorant. Of course these ways of trying to write poems are doomed; and of course it is better to be ready for surprises. More conservative voices than Stafford's have been heard to say, for example, that a poem glides on its own melting, like a piece of ice on a hot stove, or that poetry should come as naturally as leaves to a tree.

Perhaps Stafford is increasingly concerned to address the notion that all one needs to be a poet is to learn the things that are taught in writing classes. It may be that his own extraordinarily prolific output has often brought him questioners who want to know exactly how he does it. It is certain that he falls rather easily into moods that inspire him to easily misunderstood pronouncements; he says what he means, most of the time, but the most audible part of what he says is the more radical part. In the passage about "skill" above, for example, he is careful to establish that he has "experience, wide reading, automatic orthodoxies and maneuvers of various kinds."

In a couple of passages from *You Must Revise Your Life* there are useful examples, first of the haste with which Stafford can sometimes say things which his poems contradict, and second, of the ease and friendliness with which he can discuss matters of great technical importance. In a short piece about a short poem, "Where 'Yellow Cars' Comes From," there are these sentences about sound:

> As for sound, I live in one great bell of sound when doing a poem; and I like how the syllables do-si-do along. I am not after rhyme—so limited, so mechanical. No, I want all the syllables to be in there like a school of fish, flashing, relating to other syllables in other words (even words not in this poem, of course), fluently carrying the reader by subliminal felicities all the way to the limber last line. (44)

The paragraph begins with the general and modulates toward the specific poem, but the dismissal of rhyme sounds general.

A few pages later, in another essay about the same poem, he writes:

And line breaks, too, happen along. By now, in my writing, many considerations occur to me in jotting down even first hints of a poem. I like to feel patterns—number of stresses, multi-unstressed or few-unstressed sound units, lines that carry over and make a reader reach a bit, pauses in the line that come at varying, helpful places: early in the line, middle of the line, later in the line. But I make the lines be the way they are by welcoming opportunities that come to me, not by having a pattern in mind. (47)

If we think of technique, not as some rigid belief in proper frameworks and rules, but as a partial and growing understanding of an enormous array of verbal effects and opportunities, some of them traditional and some of them more nearly unprecedented, then it becomes harder to entertain the idea that Stafford cares much less about it than Richard Wilbur does.

III

In the light of these remarks, it is useful to look more closely at "Thinking for Berky," and at one or two poems from Stafford's most recent collections. A sense of Stafford's skill, or technique, or outrageous good fortune, is barely suggested in the brief metrical description at the beginning of this essay.

For some readers, the metrical question will be difficult; for even more doctrinaire readers, it will be easy, or nonexistent. There are respectable people, in the school of J. V. Cunningham, who believe that lines either exemplify a strict meter, or that they do not, and that a mixture of both kinds of line in one poem is some sort of default on the contract. But Stafford has arrived at the contract, if any, with nearly evasive tact: the meter of the first three lines is so far from firmly established that it is purely a matter of opinion where to place stresses among the syllables "must have some" in the fourth. Yet, even veering as they do between nine and twelve syllables, and between four and six stresses, the first four lines arrive satisfyingly at their ends, and at the rhyme. Much of the satisfaction emerges almost unnoticed from rhymes and echoes elsewhere than at the ends of lines: *joined-kind-end, screaming-drama,* the march of four *l* sounds proceeding from beginning to end of words in the first two lines.

This kind of local sonic richness continues throughout the poem, even as a larger net is also being cast, to make connections among stanzas by means of end-words not included in the "official" rhyme scheme (*patrol-soul,* both connecting with the second stanza's rhymes; *come-came; wood-misunderstood*), and over the whole poem by the echo between *bed* and *beds,* and the repetition of *listening* and *night* in the first and final lines.[2] Meanwhile, another aspect of the poem's rhythmical balance is maintained by the tension between lengthening lines and shortening sentences.

Stafford's prose remarks seem intended to forestall the conclusion that these kinds of things are always calculated. Very inexperienced readers often want to know how many of a poem's effects could have been planned, and most practitioners know that many are not. But most practitioners also know that thinking about such matters, in one's own poems and in others', is a useful way to deepen acquaintance with them, and to grow toward recognizing them when an unpressurized knowledge, disguised as good luck, brings them into the lines we are writing.

The convergence of impulses—from the tradition and from the individual train of thought—can even result in a sonnet. The discovery that a sonnet is under way is usually made before all the rhymes are in place, so some searching and rephrasing must usually be done. During that process, I imagine, Stafford might constantly weigh the effects of either staying with tradition, or noticeably departing from it, perhaps to the point that strict readers might decide that the result is not a sonnet. Here, for example, is "Seeing and Perceiving," from *A Glass Face in the Rain* (1982):

> You learn to like the scene that everything
> in passing loans to you—a crooked tree
> syncopated upward branch by pre-
> established branch, its pattern suddening
> as you study it; or a piece of string
> forwarding itself, that straight knot so free
> you puzzle slowly at its form (you see
> intricate but fail at simple); or a wing,
> the lost birds trailing home.
> These random pieces begin to dance at night
> or when you look away. You cling to them
> for form, the only way that it will come
> to the fallible: little bits of light
> reflected by the sympathy of sight.

(46)

I believe it is possible to be drawn into this poem, to follow its sentences with enough absorption not to notice rhyme until the final couplet. It is unusual to find a sonnet, or near-sonnet, in which the form itself does not seem to constitute much in the way of a statement; these days, to elect the sonnet form is usually to make a gesture with something behind it. Here, the form seems gradually to evolve, as it might "come / to the fallible," so that the short ninth line has a rightness that outweighs its failure to meet rigid expectation.

Rhyme is infrequent in Stafford's most recent collection, *An Oregon Message* (1987). One of its more obtrusive manifestations is in "Brother," a mysterious poem which defies literal paraphrase:

> Somebody came to the door that night.
> "Where is your son, the one with the scar?"
> No moon has ever shone so bright.
>
> A bridge, a dark figure, and then the train—
> "My son went away. I can't help you."
> Many a clear night since then. And rain.
>
> I was the younger, the one with the blood.
> "You better tell Lefty what his brother done."
> They went off cursing down the road.
>
> A boy in the loft watching a star.
> "Son, your big brother has saved your life."
> He never came back, the one with the scar.
>
> (98)

The difficulty of assembling the details into coherence is emphasized by the self-contained lines, each of which is resonant with possibility. There is reference to what sounds like a threatening encounter, and possibly some catastrophe; but the details hang in the memory as they might in the mind of a traumatized victim of imperfect recall. Because it borders on the incomprehensible, in most prose senses of the term, the poem benefits immeasurably from the added mystery of regular rhyme. A line such as the fourth, with its assortment of three images which could add up in several ways concluding in departure, death, or rescue, becomes one of twelve beads on a string, attractive in itself; the same is true of the seventh, in which the phrase "the one with the blood" could suggest several paraphrases. The poem is reminiscent of certain ballads, like "Sir Patrick Spens," from which such usual narrative elements as motivation are absent, so that the events take on a stark necessity.

Some readers have called Stafford's poetry "simple," as if it had failed to comprehend our civilization's great variety and complexity. But the simplicity exemplified in "Brother" is exactly the kind that makes for complexity in contemporary life. None of us knows enough, it seems. William Stafford's many ways of reminding us of that, and of offering consolation, constitute one of the most secure and solid of recent poetic achievements.

NOTES

1. William Stafford, *Stories That Could Be True: New and Collected Poems* (New York: Harper and Row, 1977), 93. Subsequent citations of this book will be made in the text, to *Stories* and a page number; quotations from other collections, all published by Harper and Row, will be identified in the text and followed by a page number.

2. For a while in the early 1970s, Stafford read this poem aloud, and authorized reprinting it, with a slightly different last line: "While in the night you lie, so far and good." It has admirable qualities, but Stafford had reverted to the original ending by the time he assembled *Stories That Could Be True*.

JONATHAN HOLDEN

"With Kit, Age 7, at the Beach"

It was 1964 when I first encountered Stafford's little lyric "With Kit, Age 7, at the Beach," and I immediately liked it, especially the turn which its last line takes; but it wasn't until years later, rereading Martin Heidegger's *Introduction to Metaphysics,* that I could say that I had grasped the gist of the poem's argument, an argument built into the poem's very structure. The last time I saw Bill Stafford himself—at the Port Townsend Writers conference in July 1987, where we were both on the staff—I asked him if he had read the Heidegger. He said he hadn't, and this pleased me, because it meant that Stafford and Heidegger had independently discovered the same metaphysical ground. Or, put more precisely: they had discovered, on their own, strikingly similar metaphors by which to illuminate the same ontological vantage point, structures subtle enough to convince me that, as with mathematics, there are certain kinds of subject matter which can be accurately named (or "measured") *only* by means of certain metaphors. It is impossible, for example, to make certain kinds of scientific measurements—say to describe accurately, or even *to define the meaning of* the rate of acceleration of a particle—without a differential equation. It is similarly impossible to dramatize certain kinds of experience—say ontological intuitions—with utilizing the imagery and the structure of lyric.

What was especially pleasing about this "accidental" similarity between the Heidegger and the Stafford texts was that it constituted evidence that metaphysical intuition (and the metaphors to express it) is *not,* as it might sometimes appear to be, entirely subjective. Poetic metaphor, like the calculus, like chemistry, constitutes a body of knowledge.

The fundamental issue Heidegger grapples with in his *Introduction* he sets forth as follows:

Why are there essents . . . ? Why, that is to say, on what ground? from what source does the essent derive? on what

Field 41 (Fall 1989): 26–28.

ground does it stand? . . . The question aims at the ground of
what is insofar as it is. To seek the ground is to try to get at the
bottom.

A little later, Heidegger approaches this book's main question
phenomenologically, by means of imagery:

How does it stand with being? . . . We hear the flying bird,
even though strictly speaking we should say: a grouse is noth-
ing audible, it is no manner of tone that fits into a scale. And
so it is with the other senses. We touch velvet, silk; we see
them directly as this or that kind of essent, the one different
from the other. Wherein lies and wherein consists being? . . .
Is it situated anywhere at all?

Heidegger's quest for "being," like all religious quests, is for the
Absolute, and with this word—"the Absolute"—in mind we are
equipped to read Stafford's "With Kit. . . ."
    The first two stanzas set the scene of a dramatic lyric—father
and son climb a dune, to get a vantage point from which to
observe the world—and they end in a question, "What should
our gaze mean?" In the third stanza, with "*such* [my emphasis] a
hill,*"* the poem takes on allegorical overtones, and there is posed
the word *absolute,* on which the poem turns—a word which
retroactively is going to be, in the context of the poem's final
word, *swam,* radically enriched. The "vista" spread out before
the viewers, a vista not unlike the eighteenth-century Sublime, is
so grand, so menacing, dwarfs the viewers so totally that it
might as well be an absolute vista, be mistaken for The Abso-
lute. But the word *absolute* is double. Its Latin origins, *ab* (from)
+ *solvere* (to set free), suggest that the "absolute" is never out
there in a vista like the ocean seen from a dune. It is "set free"
from any boundaries. We are swimming in it *now.* We *are* it. In
fact, the very literal ground on which we are standing—"such a
hill"—in order to survey the world, no matter how "high," is
inherently unstable: it is a "dune." Terry Eagleton, in his para-
phrase of Heidegger's *Being and Time,* writes:

The world is not an object "out there" to be rationally ana-
lyzed, set over against a contemplative subject: it is never
something we can get outside of and stand over against. We
emerge as subjects from inside a reality which we can never

fully objectify, which encompasses both "subject" and "object," quite as much as we constitute it.

This is superb paraphrase. But it is only paraphrase. It lacks the agonized sense that we find in Heidegger of the philosophic mind in the very process of attempting to clarify. It lacks the concreteness, the drama, the sense of realization (through structural discovery) that we find in Stafford's poem. If we compare the lucidity of Stafford's poem to the turgidness of Heidegger or compare the narrative vision of Wordsworth's *The Prelude* to the psycholinguistic jargon of Jacques Lacan (who deals with the same issues which Wordsworth does), we are tempted to conclude that, when it comes to existential/phenomenological inquiry or psycholinguistic inquiry, achieved poetry is probably a mode of discourse that is conspicuously superior to that of systematic philosophy.

FRANK STEELE

William Stafford's "Mornings"

One of William Stafford's poems that I have not seen much comment on is "Mornings," from his book *Allegiances* (Harper and Row, 1970, 63). It's possible that the poem may seem so transparent that discussion is unnecessary. Someone, maybe Stafford himself, is up early in the morning, thinking, perhaps writing, watching it get light. Most readers who know anything about Stafford's published reports of his writing habits are familiar with this scenario, so they may take the poem as a kind of confession of process and move right along through the book. Yet there are things in the poem that have nagged at me for years. A probe or two may be useful. Here's the poem:

I

Quiet,
rested, the brain begins to burn
and glow like a coal in the dark,
early—four in the morning, cold, with
frost on the lawn. The brain feels
the two directions of window, and as if
holding a taper, follows the hall
that leads to the living room and silver
space; lets the town come close, the chains
of lights turned off, and purposeless feet
of chairs sprawled; lets it all rise and
subside, and the brain pulses larger
than the ordinary horizon, but deliberately
less than it wants to go. All benevolence,
the brain with its insistent little call
summons wraiths and mist layers near
from fields: the world arising and streaming
through the house, soundless, pitifully

Small Farm 9–10 (Spring–Fall 1979): 55–63.

elongated, inevitable, for review, like breathing,
quiet.

II

Waiting
in the town that flows for the brain, charmed,
weak as distance, no one can move or belong
till the brain finds them and says, "Live!"
There's one too far, the phantom beyond the brain
each day that can't hear the kindest call
(and kindness is volume in the brain's room)—
the stranger with the sudden face, of
erased body, who floats into my dream
again. Down the storm our lack of storm
implies I hear the lambs cry, every one
lost and myself lost by where I made our
home. I feel a wind inside my hand.
By a lack that our life knows, life owns its greatness:
we are led one thing at a time through gain
to that pure gain—all that we lose. Stranger,
we are blind dancers in two different rooms;
we hear the music both heard long ago: wherever
you dance, that music finds you. When you turn
I turn. Somewhere, whatever way you move
is ours; here, I keep our place,
repeat our turns, paced by my pulse,
waiting.

III

Lowly,
I listen as fur hears the air, and by will
I think one thing at a time while the world,
complete, turns—the farm where the wheat
votes, where they have already prayed the last day;
the glass of the ocean watching the storm;
all the extreme places; and I stand at the
prow of our house, an eye (for iris the attic window),
I gaze, and see so well my listening toes blur
on the rug and realize all the way to the island
of afternoon. My hands have given their gift,

then themselves. Can't the world see humility—my
trance, my face, the sober and steady spokes of my
bicycle? Many drive in piety and for the faith
an old car. Bishops in garages care, and presbyters
at the bank judge us—all that our shoes
and their crossed laces confess; angels behind
the counter inquire the name and send it up
the dizzying tube, and listen to the building
hum our estimation. Year by year the leaves
will come again, the suspicious grass, and the air
ever more tentative over the walls one color
at a time, fish of less than water, of evening;
shadows come and the bells get ready
before they sound, one part of a hum, like my self,
lowly.

IV

Light
comes inside the brain. It is early;
in the attic I hear the wind lie down.
"Stay!" I call, as we tell the dog. Sudden as
the telephone, day says, "I am here!" And
in that clear light the brain comes home, lost
from all it wandered in, unable to be
sure for questioners, caught again by needs,
reduced to its trouble with my tongue.
The frank sycamore is at the window;
dark trails sink and go backward;
the sun comes over the world, aiming
the trees at the day, hill by hill.
Light.

Jonathan Holden (in *The Mark to Turn: A Reading of William
Stafford's Poetry,* University of Kansas Press, 1976, 6) has sug-
gested that imagination is the theme of Stafford's work, as it is of
Stevens's. "Mornings" seems to be a poem about how the imagi-
nation behaves, although it is called "the brain" throughout, and
its productions are referred to as "my dream" or "my trance." A
lot of this poem, more than one section, uses the old Gothic
convention: the brain in the skull, the man in the house, the
house on the earth, the earth in the universe. So there's an aware-
ness all through the poem of things going out from a source and

things coming in from outside. That's what the "two directions of window" seem to mean, a reciprocity summarized at the end of the first section as being "like breathing."

Holden, whose book is a mine of insights, has also noticed that darkness, in Stafford's work as a whole, invites the imagination to act; whereas light, visually perceived, may be a brake to the imagination (20). This opposition reverses the usual literary polarity in which darkness is connected with ignorance or death, light with revelation or knowledge. There is certainly something paradoxical about the way darkness and light operate in "Mornings." In the first section the lights in the town, which are "turned off" at this hour, are thought of by the man as "chains / of lights." In view of what light does later in the poem, especially at the end, *chains* seem, at first, to suggest imprisonment, or at least limitation. The darkness, on the other hand, allows the brain, or imagination, to illuminate everything with a light of its own, "as if / holding a taper." The imagining man is aware of everything in the house, every room, every stick of furniture, but he's also aware, in this special morning state of mind, of everything outdoors, too.

A young man probably could not have written this poem about the cold outside and the brain (only) supplying warmth and benevolence. The poem is also, considerably, about getting older. The man himself seems at least as old as Stafford, but the brain is ageless, like remembered youth, putting out its warmth against the cold: precious, shy, generous, inviting, kind, even humble—especially humble. More about this quality later.

Section 2 is more complicated than the first section. It begins as if it's going to be a remembrance of one of the little towns that Stafford is always writing about. The people there are lost or dead or changed, until "the brain finds them and says, 'Live!'" The "phantom beyond the brain," whom the man can't quite get fully in touch with, the "stranger with the sudden face, of / erased body" is meant to be a little tantalizingly ambiguous. Although this may be an unknown ancestor or a lost love, several details in the poem make me believe he's a younger version of the man himself. There is, for example, a buried hint in the description at the end of section 1:

> wraiths and mist layers near
> from fields: the world arising and streaming
> through the house, soundless, pitifully
> elongated, inevitable, for review, like breathing. . . .

In quality, these lines echo (consciously or not) the famous sentence in *Heart of Darkness* describing Marlow's capture of Kurtz:

He rose, unsteady, long, pale, indistinct, like a vapor exhaled by the earth, and swayed slightly, misty and silent before me.

Later in this same section, the "phantom beyond the brain" is addressed directly:

> Stranger,
> we are blind dancers in two different rooms;
> we hear the music both heard long ago. wherever
> you dance, that music finds you. When you turn
> I turn. Somewhere, whatever way you move
> is ours. . . .

So the "phantom beyond the brain" is also very close to the narrator. A lot of overtones are here, although they are not all consciously made into allusions: Wordsworth's "child is father to the man"; Hemingway's "I wish I had the boy"; Conrad's "Secret Sharer"; Yeats's "Who can tell the dancer from the dance?" Words like *stranger, blind, wherever, somewhere,* and *whatever* make clear that the poem wants to emphasize the mysteriousness of the self-encounter. At the same time, however, the lines mean to create a resonant suggestiveness, a doppelgänger possibility, that every scholar is familiar with. The sense of the lost boy winds up being the one thing the man safely and protectively has, his main property. However, there is no self-pity in this section. Since the transaction between the two (a mutual but separate dance) is imaginative, there is, instead, a Keatsian hint, a Wallace Stevens moment.

The two people are separated but experiencing the same thing, as in another Stafford poem, "Watchmen." It's possible that the "blind dancers" are not just the older man remembering his youth but the older man thinking of the younger man reaching forward toward him. The younger man is still alive within the older, and it may be that the older man was implicitly present in the younger man's imagination. This idea is not merely a Wordsworthian allusion but also a suggestion that people create themselves, along with the other stuff they create: "the bells get ready / before they sound."

There are hard places. The first is that "kindness is volume in the brain's room." *Volume* may be a level of sound. It may also be mass or an amount of space. It is probably all three of these here, if emptiness can be taken as a personal lacking, or loneliness. *Volume* also connects with (and prepares for) the music that the mature man and the remembered youth hear later in this section. And, in a poem about the imagination, *volume* may, of course, suggest a book. (It needs remembering that Stafford is infinitely subtle, as well as humble.) The central paradox, however, is this: "By a lack that our life knows, life owns its greatness." The line means several things at once: (1) we all have a past that we have physically lost, and since it's lost, the imagination has to re-create it (like Frost in "Directive"); (2) wisdom through suffering; a man must lose his soul in order to gain it: Christian idea, and the lambs are crying just above; and (3) the implication of an after-life, possibly through art, which seems to hover over the human meanings here like an aura of belief. The "stranger" is, to some extent, also the reader.

It gradually becomes clear that "Mornings" is a poem about the paradoxical nature of creation: the relation of the temporal and the timeless, power and limitation, loss and gain. However, far from celebrating the imagination for its own sake or trying to make a secular religion out of it, as Stevens might have done, Stafford questions the autonomy of creative activity at every turn. Section 3 is about humility, about the limitation of human knowledge, including the poet's, and it employs both dramatic and situational irony.

Like the other three sections of the poem, this one makes a circle, beginning and ending with *lowly*. The man, who "by will" thinks "one thing at a time," sees himself in contrast to the larger world, which, "complete, turns." He can imagine it, but only through figurative language: metonymy ("the wheat / votes"; "Listen to the building / hum our estimation"); surrealization ("fish of less than water, of evening"); allegory (the house as a ship in a storm); metaphor ("the glass of the ocean"); or personification ("the suspicious grass"). All of these have as much to do with limitation and distortion as with knowledge, and the man in the poem knows this fact well.

Even so, he's capable of feeling sorry for himself, another kind of limitation, and of pleading for sympathy: "Can't the world see humility . . . my / trance, my face . . . ?" Unlike Robert Lowell or Sylvia Plath, William Stafford wouldn't be caught dead making such statements outright and autobiographically in a poem, but he might well put them into the dramatically ironic mouth of a character. Where now is the Old Testament–godlike tone of the second section ("the brain finds them and says, 'Live?' ")? No, the poem is not mainly a celebration of the imagination in the old Stevens-Yeats way.

The movement away from the narrator to bishops, presbyters, the bank, and "angels behind / the counter" in the middle of section 3 is puzzling. Perhaps the bishops, presbyters, and angels are connected to the apparently religious bells at the end of this section. But something odd is happening. The narrator, who wants to stress his own humility, rides a bicycle, a humbler means of transportation than even the "old car," which "Many drive in piety and for the faith." The means of travel here becomes an ironic index to the desired appearance of humility. There's a sort of progression of efforts at false humility—from the man's emotional outburst, "Can't the world see . . . ?" (it's pretty clear, as this section goes on, that the world *can't* see), to the bicycle, to the old car, to "Bishops" whose presence "in garages" is an expression of how much they "care." A bishop in a garage is automatically humbler than a bishop outside a garage. The progression winds up with the "presbyters / at the bank," who "judge" strictly by external appearances, and finally with the "angels behind / the counter," who judge by the amount of money the man has in the bank. So if the imagination is limited, on the one hand, to what it knows through figurative associations, which distort as much as they clarify, it's limited, on the other hand, by being forced to gauge the invisible by the visible, to deal with appearances. It is not surprising, therefore, given these limitations, that judgment, especially of people, is condemned as an activity throughout this section of the poem, or that the frame word *lowly* means considerably more the second time around than it does the first. Earning the right to say the frame word a second time in each section in a more intense and meaningful way is one of the poem's purposes, a demonstration of structural integrity.

Stafford may go around indicating that his poems are formless and casual, but that's modesty. They're intricately designed. Part 2 is mainly interior, the self and the remembered self. Part 3 is mainly exterior, the self in relation to other people and things. Part 2 relates the present to the past, part 3 the present to the future.

One means of dramatizing the theme of human limitation throughout the poem is by an emphasis on consecutiveness, or sequentiality. The phrase "one thing at a time" occurs twice. The air comes over the walls "one color at a time" and "year by year." The bells are "one part of a hum." The sun comes up at the end of the poem, "hill by hill." The limitation of thinking to consecutiveness is dramatized in subtler ways, too:

My hands have given their gift,
then themselves. Can't the world see humility—my
trance, my face, the sober and steady spokes of my
bicycle? Many drive in piety and for the faith
an old car. Bishops in garages care, the presbyters
at the bank judge us—all that our shoes
and their crossed laces confess; angels behind
the counter inquire the name and send it up
the dizzying tube, and listen to the building
hum our estimation. Year by year the leaves
will come again, the suspicious grass, and the air
ever more tentative over the walls one color
at a time. . . .

The complicated syntax is highly unusual for a Stafford poem, and the emphasis on sequentiality is present not only explicitly— "My hands have given their gift / then themselves," "year by year"—but also implicitly, through items in a series ("my / trance, my face, the sober and steady spokes of my / bicycle"); the prevalence of the coordinate conjunction *and* ("the sober and steady spokes . . . in piety and for the faith . . . Bishops . . . and presbyters . . . our shoes / and their crossed laces"); and an al-most mind-boggling compound predication—("angels behind / the counter inquire the name and send it up / the dizzying tube, and listen to the building / hum our estimation."). All through this part of the poem, the explicit content, the figurative devices, and the very grammar of the language perform a sort of fugue on a subject of limitation, and it's possible now to understand what the blind dancers and the music are doing at the end of section 2.

Sequentialness, which is associated with the limits of human perception and, since it involves time, with human mortality, also, paradoxically, implies a journey, or voyage. The allegoric possibility of the house as a ship which encounters storms is devel-oped throughout the poem. It originates, as such possibilities often do in poems, in a description of something else during the first section. "The brain . . . lets it all rise and / subside." There's an ambiguity about the *wraiths* and *mist layers* at the end of the first section—that they are suggestive of the aquatic is made explicit in the word *streaming,* a descriptive adjective leading to the verb *floats* early in the second section, in which the ambiguous material of the imagination is connected with dreaming.

The function of allegory is prophecy:

> I stand at the
> prow of our house, an eye (for iris the attic window),
> I gaze and see so well my listening toes blur
> on the rug and realize all the way to the island
> of afternoon.

The way out of human limitation, in this poem, is through meditation, or dreaming; but the escape occurs at the sacrifice of immediacy, another paradox: "I . . . see so well my . . . toes blur." To glimpse the future is to lose the present. The escape, like most of the other details in the third section, is false, and the reader is forced to look again at the theme: "By a lack that our life knows, life owns its greatness."

The imagination can go backward into remembered experience, repeating its turns, spatially outward places and people, or forward into glimpses of the future. All of these moves, however, are bounded or circumscribed (every section of the poem a circle) by the human condition of finiteness, which prevents any affirmations of the transcendent comprehensiveness of knowledge.

When "Light / comes" in the final section, it is clearly reductive. The imagination is "lost . . . unable . . . caught . . . reduced," as Jonathan Holden knew it would be. The "dark trails," which are the trails of the imagination, "sink and go backward." The sun appears: lucid, mundane, rational. Yet the conclusion is not bitter or pessimistic, because the man in the poem has seen through the illusions that the imagination may sponsor and has accepted both these temptations and his own limitations.

The acceptance is evident in a moment of pure Staffordian honor. Earlier, when it was still dark, the man had felt "a wind" inside his hand, which was associated with the storm imagery. Now, with the coming of light, he can "hear the wind lie down." He doesn't want it to stop but recognizes that it will:

> "Stay!" I call, as we tell the dog.

The juxtaposition of the words *lost* and *home,* with their contradictory connotations, which had first occurred in the second section, is repeated at the end to emphasize the theme: for the imagining man, to be at home *means* to be lost, uncertain, on a journey of his own making whose outcome is unknown.

As the sun rises, the light is seen "aiming / the trees at the day. . . ." *Aiming* may at first appear more sinister than it really is. It is a word which appears often throughout *Allegiances,* especially in such poems as "Return to Single Shot" (25) and "Montana Eclogue" (28–30). Like many other words, which Jonathan Holden has discussed as parts of Stafford's symbolic shorthand, *aiming* has its own rather specialized connotation, which it assumes through repetition. Since I don't have the space to discuss its uses in the other poems, I'll simply suggest that *aiming* is both threatening and creative at the same time, as Stafford uses it, implying both a challenge and a positive answer to challenge. In "Mornings" the sun is not merely sinister as it rises but also carries with it the meaning of newness, a different experience to respond to.

There is, of course, a whole literature of poems about the workings of the imagination, from the English Romantics and American Transcendentalists on through Poe, Tennyson, Arnold, and Swinburne, to Pound, Eliot, Yeats, Frost, Stevens, and many others. Poems about the imagination are most often celebratory and promise everything from political authority to philosophic serenity to personal fulfillment to religious sanctuary for those who partake of its enticements, especially through reading and writing poetry. Now, William Stafford, needless to say (after forty years of steady practice, a series of excellent books, important literary prizes, and prominent teaching and other positions), likes the imagination just fine. Yet "Mornings" is, finally, a qualifying footnote to an established literary tradition, a kind of testimony not to the blandishments of aesthetic engagement but to imaginative activity itself: its power to summon, its kindness and mystery, its suddenness and potential danger, and the benevolent humility with which it embraces bits and pieces of the human experience as they come along, without trying to reconcile them into a systematic guarantee of spiritual or other success. Despite his occasional use of conventional literary resources, Stafford is as different from most other American poets in this respect as night is from day. Of the poets now writing, he is the only one who has made a gentle skepticism and a tentative uncertainty central to his aesthetic program, and that in itself may be a kind of glory.

JOHN HAINES

A Comment on William Stafford's "A Way of Writing" in *Field* 2

What Stafford describes seems to me more or less what any poet does, and it *is* a kind of fishing. There may be differences among poets in the way they fish, but whether a poet fishes with a sheet of paper before him, or inside his head while taking a walk, doesn't seem very important. There are also differences in the pace of the poet's activity; for Stafford the pace may be far more rapid, and the work easier, than for another poet, myself, for instance—I am used to waiting longer and actually writing less.

Stafford's practice offers some advantages to a poet, along with a few disadvantages. Among the advantages is this: it allows him to keep up a continuing flow of thought, an inner speech, or dialogue, with the basic material of his writing, and to transfer that speech to the page with a minimum of interruption. But I think it also encourages him to make his poems out of material which is frequently secondary, of a low power, or a low order of thought. He cannot spend too much time on any one poem, on the details of that poem, or the energy might dissipate. This means that in practice he must write many poems, "say" much, in order to bring that sometimes small amount of genuine poetry to the surface and put it on paper.

Stafford's habit of writing may also lead him to write many lines in too ordinary a language, or to bridge vivid expression in a poem with language and material which is essentially filler; for example, the last two lines of the second stanza in the poem "Shadows":

> I looked up so hard outward that a bird
> flying past made a shadow on the sky

The implication is that because Stafford looks up hard the bird *must* make a shadow. But I find it difficult to believe in the

Field 3 (Fall 1970): 64–66.

relationship of the two phenomena; it seems too easy a correspondence. Similarly, the first two lines of the fourth stanza:

> Once I crawled through grassblades to hear
> the sounds of their shadows.

This *sounds* deep and mysterious, but if I really think about it, it begins to appear a little too smooth, not thought out enough; even substituting the word "in" for the "of" in the second line would make the lines clearer and more believable. There's a great deal of stuffing in Stafford's poems, and its presence weakens many of them. But this is plainly one of the hazards of his method, and it's obvious from reading his comments that he willingly takes such risks.

I think he is being deceptive when he says that a writer does not draw on a reservoir. Certainly we could get into an endless argument about this, but Stafford's poems themselves, and the poems of almost anyone, to the extent that they are real poems, do draw on a certain reservoir of experience and emotion. Stafford's description of how he writes merely tells us how he goes about drawing on that experience; how he is able by his writing activity to relate more immediate events to this deeper layer of thought and emotion. I mean that the activity he describes would all go for nothing, as it too often does with many younger men, if he did not have this, this *reservoir,* since we must call it something. Even what he is and is not receptive to may to a great extent be determined by things which happened to him before, perhaps long ago, and about which he once had similar emotions.

There is a freshness in Stafford's statement that if a thing occurs to him it is all right. But a noticeable characteristic of his poems is that they are apt to contain things which, though they undoubtedly occurred to him, have also occurred to others, and often in a manner and speech indistinguishable. This approach to writing may be partly responsible for the fact that in Stafford's work generally ideas seem to be weak and ordinary, or there are no ideas at all. Frequently only the inherent beauty of the expression saves his poems from banality. We expect a poet to tell us something beyond what we already know, and in Stafford's best poems this does happen.

Explicit in Stafford's account is the refusal to judge his own work; the same approach can be seen in his book reviewing as a refusal to judge other people's work. I make no comment on this further than to say that such an attitude tends to turn book reviewing, and ultimately, perhaps, all writing activity, into a series of endorsements, easy victories over whatever doubts a man might have about his own or another's writing. Beyond the present literary limits of this refusal we confront an increasingly familiar problem: To what extent may a man refuse to judge, not just his work, but his whole life, and the circumstances in which that life has been lived?

MARGARET ATWOOD

"Waking at 3 A.M."

Many of William Stafford's poems seem to me to be devotional in nature. But devotional in a muted, late-twentieth-century mode. When you listen to a Stafford poem spoken (and Stafford's is a poetry for the speaking voice, as distinct from the chanting voice or the singing voice), you hear, among other things, the other, earlier voices that may be shining through from behind it. What I hear behind this poem is Protestant, even Puritan, in tonality; a plainsong. There is something of the Henry Vaughan of "Eternity," matter-of-factly seen as "a great ring of pure and endless light"; the Blake of the "Songs"; George Herbert, with his metaphors for religious experience drawn from commonplace objects; but all of these with the central object of the devotional poem removed to a greater distance, made more problematic, and shorn of its name, and the mode transmuted from the ecstatic to the stoic.

The voice is serious, though personal and informal, like a New England Puritan's spiritual journal—again, transposed to our new sadder, less certain century. The speaker's notes to himself about how one remains alive; about the small affirmations that can be wrung from the too-large, too-cold, too-remote universe that surrounds us and in which we feel ourselves cut adrift, "free and lonely": a pairing familiar to us. Such small comforts will have to do, because they are the best thing available under the circumstances; and they may add up to a good deal, after all. Not salvation, exactly. But more than might be expected.

If "Waking at 3 A.M." were a piece of music, it would be (formally speaking) a congregational hymn, though sung by one voice; if a building, it would be a white wooden meeting house. But to say that a thing has a plainness and simplicity of line is not to say it lacks complexity or mystery. Often the simplest form is also the most enigmatic. Take the egg.

Like many of Emily Dickinson's poems—which spring from the same unornamented Protestant tradition—"Waking at 3

Field 41 (Fall 1989): 29–33.

A.M." proceeds by a series of riddles. These however are not so obviously riddles, and not so obviously answered.

The poem begins comprehensibly enough, with four lines about the experience of being awake and alone in the middle of the night. Fair enough, although we may pause to ask what sort of loving things belong in the category of "what doesn't matter." The "big room no one can see" is any child's room at night, but also the same as the "cave of night"; both are darkness, which encloses without offering a limit to the eye. Darkness can be as big as a room or as big as the sky, or as big as the impenetrably dark universe. Although it is big, this darkness is claustrophobic rather than comforting. It is the opposite of cosy.

But what are we to make of the next three lines?

> you push with your eyes till forever
> comes in its twisted figure eight
> and lies down in your head.

Pushing with the eyes captures exactly the feeling of what we do, with our eyes, in the dark. But what is this strange "twisted figure eight," and why is it the shape taken by "forever"?

A figure eight is the shape the Magician juggles with, in the Tarot Pack, and is supposed in some interpretations to be a symbol of Eternity. It is also the shape of the Möbius strip, that conundrum you can make by twisting a strip of paper once and glueing the ends together, the property of which is that it has only one side. Students are usually asked to prove this by running a finger along it; they find that their end is in their beginning. It is the Celtic snake with its tail in its mouth. "Twisted"? It does not exist in two planes, but in three; it's an eight taken by top and bottom half and twisted so that it separates at the intersection of the halves and becomes a single line which runs through three dimensions. It is imagined not as a static shape but as a dynamic one—it is "forever" because it *runs on* forever, around and around the line of the figure eight.

The next two images are suggested naturally by this flowing "forever": the water flowing in the river and the "tide" in the grain of the wood. (Trees have tides, as their sap travels up in spring and down in fall.) Through contemplating this flowing motion, the meditator becomes a kind of space—not a "cave" or a "big room," but a "storehouse." But what about this "secret storehouse that saves the country, / so open and foolish and empty"? How can a storehouse with nothing in it, not even wisdom—for it is "foolish"—save anything? And yet, we are told, the "country" is saved. Someone other than the meditator is saved; or something, because "country" can mean both a collectivity of nationals and an expanse of land.

Perhaps the storehouse (which is also the speaker) has the power to save because it *is* open; "foolish" (from the worldly point of view), because it has given all away; empty, because what was once in it has gone for the general welfare. "Secret," because its gifts were given in silence, and because they were held back until all other resources had been used up. Perhaps in the background of this paradoxical image are Pharaoh's storehouses in the biblical story of Joseph in Egypt, which held supplies stored up against famine and were opened and emptied in time of extreme need.

So the flowing figure eight of "forever" and the flow of river and tree move into a vision of another kind of flow—the flow of giving, which always moves out and away from the giver. The night meditator feels the flow of eternity moving through him, outward, toward the world. He becomes a vehicle—an empty space, because emptied; and empty also because one must be empty in order to receive such a flow, spiritual emptiness being a precondition for the reception of the mystical experience, as mystics from all faiths have testified.

In the third stanza the meditator experiences the result of his spiritual openness. "More than has ever / been found" arrives, to replace his initial feeling of being lost; the immensity of the universe, its inexhaustibility, its unnameability—it is just "more"—become a source of comfort rather than a trigger for Cartesian fears. The closed "cave" and "room" images, having transmuted themselves into the "secret storehouse," transform again, into an ever-expanding "vault that unlocks as fast / and as far as your thought can run."

As soon as this space has opened, it becomes closed again, although in a very different way. It is now "snug," and the loneliness and abandonment of the opening lines have been changed to a sense of security and comfort. "It is / a good world to be / lost in," partly because the speaker is not truly lost but cradled within a "great snug wall," which is apprehended as permanent.

The speaker is no longer orphaned, unloved, but parented by the universe, as the end of the poem makes clear. The last three lines have the simplicity and trust of a child's bedtime prayer. "It comforts you" and "It is / all right"—the second being what

every mother says, more or less, after a child's nightmare—
render the enclosing universe maternal and tender. The child-
likeness of the speaker, both as the initial orphan and as the
protected child of the last lines, is reinforced by the scarcity of
adjectives, and the choice of very plain ones: *big, secret, great,
snug, good.*

Incidentally, there are only two lines that don't rhyme (or off-
rhyme) with other lines in the poem, the ones terminating with
head and *sleep,* and, of these, *head* is a concealed off-rhyme with
tide in. So the last line of the poem does not connect back to any
of the previous lines and does not complete a sound pattern.
Instead it seems to point to something unfinished, beyond the
poem—to some other rhyme that will come later.

This poem is both an account of meditation and an object of
meditation itself. It does not merely lay out the result of the
experience, it forces the reader to undergo the process by at-
tempting to solve the riddles it poses. As with a New England
meeting house, it presents us with basic materials, elegantly put
together. And what you see, at first, is by no means all you get.

LINDA PASTAN

"Ask Me"

Writing about poems is not something that I am comfortable doing, so I have chosen Bill's poem "Ask Me" because it seems to give me permission to be almost silent, to stand with him a moment quietly at the edge of the frozen river and to just wait. In a way, this is something that I have been doing with him for years. In the mornings, alone in my study, when the blank page seems to stare malevolently up at me demanding a new poem, I have so often turned to his work, almost any page of it in any of his books. And I always find myself listening to a voice seemingly simple, addressing simply the most urgent of matters. ("Ask me whether / what I have done is my life.") Miraculously, and over and over again, I find myself wanting to engage with that voice, to talk back to it, to put something down on the empty page because he makes it seem at once so natural and so necessary to do so.

I do not mean to analyze "Ask Me" or to speculate on the answers to its several unanswerable questions. But I do want to say that this is a quintessentially Stafford poem and that the reader need go no further than the title itself to be invited in. "Ask Me," the writer says, and how can we fail to do so?

From time to time I meet someone who speaks of Stafford's poetry as kindly, benign, and full of homilies, and I am always mystified. Are we talking about the same poetry? In this particular poem we stand at the edge of a frozen place and are asked to contemplate some of the most devastating of possibilities. The mistakes hinted at here are clearly not typing errors. The acknowledgment that we may reach a place in our own lives where the strongest love or hate, where human intention, may not make any difference is one of the hardest things we have to think about, one of the most terrifying. This is only partly mitigated here, after a stanza break, by the possible comfort of shared conversation, by the possibility of some kind of eventual thaw.

American literature and landscape are full of rivers, and William Stafford is a very American poet. I won't speculate on whether these rivers are meant to stand for time or for the continuum of human life—analyze a river and you are in danger of ending up with hydrogen, oxygen, and assorted proteins. But I think it would be fair to say that much of the characterization of the river in this poem could also be a prescription for what a poem should be, what a Stafford poem so often is: a simple surface with hidden currents underneath, with comings and goings from miles away, and there right on the page, the stillness *exactly* before us, and the italics here are mine. "What the river says, that is what I say," the poet tells us.

I am deeply grateful to William Stafford not only because he himself will always listen to what you have to say but because he has rescued me time after time not only from the silence of the empty page but, with his wisdom and support, from the far more serious silence of desperation. What difference has his love made? My answer is that for me at least it has often made all the difference.

TOM ANDREWS

"Knowing"
Glimpses into Something Ever Larger

Anyone writing about William Stafford's poems has Stafford's uncanny example to aspire to. He has been so straightforward about his work, has said so many useful things (especially in the two University of Michigan Press books, *Writing the Australian Crawl* and *You Must Revise Your Life*), that I almost wonder if we shouldn't ask *him* to engage the poems celebrated in this symposium. He has also made it clear what he thinks about the practice of criticism—it's "like boiling a watch to find out what makes it tick." And, in a characteristic turn, he has offered a shrewd analysis of praise:

> You need to watch out, or a follower will
> praise you, and the stumbles you need for your life
> will be harder to take.

Still, I suspect Stafford wouldn't want his comments to get in the way of a "reckless encounter" with one of his poems; at least I'll assume that as I try to clarify what I find so valuable about "Knowing."

The story goes that when Kurt Gödel was a child his insatiable curiosity prompted his parents to nickname him "Mr. Why." When I ran across that anecdote recently in a biography of Gödel, I thought: Stafford! Who else among contemporary American poets has been as nakedly curious in poem after poem about the variousness of the world and the processes by which we discover it? I say "nakedly" because he seems able to approach the poem without anticipating in the least what he'll find there. It is this spirit of openness, this receptivity to whatever comes along, that quickens me as I read him. And perhaps Staf-

---

Field 41 (Fall 1989): 38–40. The symposium referred to in the first paragraph is in this issue of *Field*.

ford is able to make such good use of whatever comes along because his curiosity is so tenacious.

One of the things I love about "Knowing" is how that curiosity keeps turning on itself. The poem questions itself as it asserts itself; in Alberta Turner's phrase, Stafford "seems to assert but really invites." A precise prose rendering of "Knowing" is beyond me, and would seem to be contrary to the spirit of the poem. But I'm fascinated by the way the poem mimics a gesture of certainty—How do you know the other world? Well, "you turn / your hand . . ."—and, after the speaker's alert, respectful intelligence thoroughly interrogates that gesture, establishes a difficult rhythm of doubt, intuition, and affirmation.

"Knowing" is a model of efficiency. It says the needful and clears out. Again it's fascinating to watch Stafford take such a potentially "poetic" (or "Poetic") conceit as the opening lines and unfold from it a poem without the least bit of decoration or filigree. Each word is essential. A good example is the word *feels* in the third line. A hasty reader might dismiss the word outright as flat or unimaginative, but the careful echo of *angles* in the previous line combined with the torque and pull of the following word *pours* gives *feels,* to my ear at least, an unlikely solidity and presence.

Where does a poem like "Knowing" come from? It seems to come from a quiet center. Robert Hass has suggested that sensibility, finally, is the triumph of James Wright's poems, and I think that's true also of Stafford's work. A typical Stafford poem has the stamp, like a thumbprint, of sensibility—that shrewd, gentle, quizzical, ironic, playfully metaphysical yet firmly grounded quality of attention that gives him the sense that "everything is telling one big story." It may be that Stafford's most helpful contribution to our poetry and to other poets (if that's not too grand a phrase) is the example of this sensibility, its inner generosity. Analogously, in a review of Louis Simpson's *At the End of the Open Road,* published in *Poetry* in 1964, Stafford wrote that

the poems . . . lead again and again to an implied big story; the reader has a sense of living in a sustained pattern which works along behind the poems and makes of them a succession of glimpses into something ever larger. . . . In our time, this implied story is never embodied in a complete work—a *Paradise Lost* or a *Divine Comedy*—and apparently such an established story cannot be at this time convincingly delivered to us. But some writers do entertain hints that back of the shifting present there impends a meaning.

Stafford is such a writer, and he gives in his investigation of Simpson's poems an important insight into his own.

I said earlier that a precise prose rendering is at odds with the spirit of "Knowing." Reading the poem, and thinking of the ironic relation between the poem and the title, brings to mind a passage from the *Tao Te Ching* which may be emblematic: "He who thinks he knows, doesn't know. He who knows that he doesn't know, knows." But even that implies a measure of certainty that "Knowing" doesn't presume. The slippery world of a Stafford poem embodies, and provokes, a sense of alertness rather than assurance; as the speaker of "Knowing" puts it, "Your hand can make the sign—but begs for / more than can be told. . . ." "Knowing" is a prime example of a poem in which Stafford's sensibility takes things—"the shifting present" as well as the "glimpses into something ever larger"—as he finds them, leaving their mystery intact:

> even the world
> can't dive fast enough to know that other world.

ALBERTA TURNER

"Things I Learned Last Week"

When people have asked me why William Stafford is my favorite poet, I have heard myself say, "Because he is so comfortable inside his own skin." Yet just now, looking for a poem that epitomizes what I mean, I realize how misleading that statement can be. "In a Corner" shows a moment of despair, "Confessions of an Individual" shows self-reproach; "A Glass Face in the Rain" anticipates a bleak self-dissolution; "Epitaph Ending in And" shows an unassuageable anger; "When You Go Anywhere," a self-conscious selflessness; and "Why I Am Happy," a happiness so far and secret it is almost a brash defiance, as he "laugh[s] and crie[s] for every turn of the world, its terrible cold, innocent spin." These make "comfortable inside his own skin" sound insipid and untrue. Yet it is true. His comfort comes from his acute awareness of paradox and his faith that the world can be endured, even enjoyed, with all its paradoxes flying.

One of the poems that shows Stafford's awareness of paradox most clearly is "Things I Learned Last Week." Four of the seven stanzas are self-contained couplets, unusual for one who uses so much enjambment. None of the seven are linked by subject or syntax, and none, even the last one, interprets itself or any of the others or suggests a synthesis of tone or meaning for the whole poem. So we read this one with suspicion, our geiger counters clicking: (1) Ants passing on the right: Solid-state brains, creatures of habit? Creatures of courtesy? How dull, how safe, how frightening. (2) Sticky doors that elbows might open: Problems more easily solved by improvising? Serious problems made light of? Trifles made much of? (3) A man in Boston selling what everyone already knows: Funny? Not funny? (4) A pessimist playing the flute: to cheer himself up? A realist? An optimist fooling himself? (5) Yeats, Pound, and Eliot studying art as the source of art: Discovering where art really comes from? Elaborating the obvious? Making themselves important? (6) "If I ever die": Pretending death's OK? Selfless? Selfish? (7) The Pentagon

Field 41 (Fall 1989): 42–43.

preparing for the next war: Caring pins for it? Not caring pins for it?

When readers finish the poem, they dutifully ask what it adds up to. They try one answer after another but still have trouble fitting all the separate items under one theme. Nor does the order of the sequence seem climactic or inevitable. So—we have to suspect (I say *suspect* because I think Stafford doesn't want us to come to a single statable conclusion), that he wants us to bound on each separate statement as on a spring that will twang us off into a thicket of paradoxes, all harmless, all terrifying, most somehow amusing, and none canceling its apparent opposites.

The thing I like about this poem, Bill, is that it lets me admit that self-reproach is self-indulgence and that selves are quite as inept as they are crucl, and are often wonderfully funny. To lift the terrible *ought* off a quivering self is a generous boon. Thank you.

DAVID YOUNG

"1940"

Shivers of Summer Wind

Lots of our best poets since World War II have been heavy breath-
ers, characters with high energy, wild language, hectic lives, and
spectacular brands of individualism. One thinks of Roethke and
Lowell, Berryman and Dickey, Plath and Sexton, Ginsberg and
Bly. We wouldn't want to be without any of them, but we need a
countertradition. Our culture is too easily infatuated by hyper-
bole and hucksterism, even in the arts. We need poets who pick
up on the possibilities of plainness and understatement, who take
us into little noticed areas of rich simplicity and calm delight.
Many of *Field*'s symposia have reflected this need by celebrating
the likes of Robert Francis, Randall Jarrell, and Elizabeth Bishop.
It's a tradition in our own poetry that goes back through Wil-
liams and Frost to Dickinson, but it is reflected in many other
areas of life, in the Shakers and Quakers, in much of our music
and humor, our architecture and food.

But when I think of William Stafford, I don't just associate
him with Emily Dickinson and Shaker furniture. I also think of
Wallace Stevens and of jazz. That is because I think a big part of
his success lies in his willingness to improvise, to play, even to
fail deliberately at one moment in order to survive, artistically
and psychologically, for the next. No poet can wholly escape
being a rhetorician, a craftsman and manipulator, but every poet
needs to find a way to forget craft, to wring the neck of rhetoric,
to slip through the confines of his or her own style. Stafford has
proved to be a master at eluding the stiffening effects of success
and of infatuation with his own rhetorical accomplishments. A
pinheaded critic can always prove to you that every move you
come up with is just another bit of art, of craft, of rhetoric. To
make yourself forget what you know about form and technique
is, of course, just another way to arrive at them. But the argu-

Field 41 (Fall 1989): 45–52.

ment is sophomoric and tedious, like the ones about relativity and determinism and Zeno's paradox. Experience refutes the traps of logic, and art goes wild and free.

How clearly I remember the summer afternoon two years ago when I read through *An Oregon Message,* Stafford's newest collection, then in galley proofs. By the end of my reading I was breathless with emotion and gratitude. I felt refreshed and confident: about this country, about poetry, about my own life and its commitments. I wondered how it was that I could slip periodically into taking for granted things I ought to be daily praising and acknowledging: small things and large things all around my life, and the modest, deep-reaching poems of William Stafford.

But that taking for granted seems almost a part of Stafford's aesthetic. He wants to invoke rhythms of recognition and obliviousness. He has a larger public and a better claim to being our preeminent living poet than anyone else I can think of, but he is also deliberately self-effacing and offhand about what he does. His poems imply that poetry needs no special language. His persona and person and career seem to argue that the poet needs no special identity to justify a place among us. And he lives his life and writes his poems with remarkable and lovable consistency.

Going back to *An Oregon Message* now to select a poem to represent my delight of that day (as well as before and since), I find myself in a mild difficulty. Which poem to select? It was the entirety of the collection that moved and refreshed me. No single poem sums up that experience, partly because Stafford, in his playful and improvisatory aesthetic, his deep suspicion of final answers and summary statements, never allows a poem to carry the burden of saying and being everything, pretending to wholeness or permanence or authority or closure. One poem leads to the next, and as that happens you move along gradually, reading Stafford, into a spiritual affluence and openness to existence that you can't paraphrase and that no single poem need exemplify.

So I face a number of intriguing choices. Why not choose as exemplary a poem that fails in some respects, as for example I think this intriguingly titled piece does:

OWLS AT THE SHAKESPEARE FESTIVAL

How do owls find each other
in the world? They fly the forest
calling, "Darling, Darling."

Each time the sun goes out a world
comes true again, for owls:
trees flame their best color—dark.

At Shakespeare once, in Ashland,
when Lear cried out two owls
flared past the floodlights:

On my desk I keep a feather
for those far places thought
fluttered when I began to know.

I love the wit and rapidity of this, its juxtapositions, and I may
well be scorched by Stafford fans for calling it a failure, but I find
the last stanza disappointing. The next-to-last stanza gives us a
moment that might provoke a flood of insight, but the speaker
turns away from it, despite the colon that seems to signal its
arrival. He is left at his desk, with his token feather and his
somewhat lamely phrased thoughts about far places and begin-
ning to know. The poem fizzles out, abandoning its promise.

My point is not to show that Stafford is bad, but to indicate
that there is something exemplary and endearing about his less
successful moments. In this poem the distrust of big statements
and the instinct for self-effacement take over: this speaker isn't
going to tangle with owls and Shakespeare as a teller of truth.
He's going to let us know about his respect for mysteries, his
knowing how little he knows. And he ducks out of the poem,
clutching his feather, leaving us with the task of making more
sense of it than he has. This strategy, if that is the right word for
it, is in a sense what allows Stafford to survive. No ovens, no
jumping off bridges, no mental institutions for this fellow. He
can shrug and cut his losses right in front of us, without embar-
rassment, without betraying his rhetoric or his persona. His mod-
esty protects him like an invisible armor. "Owls" is not a bad
poem—it has great charm and imagination—but the limitations
of its ending might be used to illustrate Stafford's peculiar
strengths.

Another poem I might have picked is the sly and funny piece
called "Thinking about Being Called Simple by a Critic":

I wanted the plums, but I waited.
The sun went down. The fire
went out. With no lights on

I waited. From the night again—
those words: how stupid I was.
And I closed my eyes to listen.
The words all sank down, deep
and rich. I felt their truth
and began to live them. They were mine
to enjoy. Who but a friend
could give so sternly what the sky
feels for everyone but few learn to
cherish? In the dark with the truth
I began the sentence of my life
and found it was so simple there was no way
back into qualifying my thoughts
with irony or anything like that.
I went to the fridge and opened it—
sure enough the light was on.
I reached in and got the plums.

Just how ironic is the forswearing of irony here? The speaker is a
kind of simpleton who sits in the dark and tries to use clichés
about friends and enemies, light and dark, falsehood and truth,
to talk himself out of the depression that comes from unjust
criticism. He is more or less William Stafford, maybe reacting to
having someone like Paul Zweig accuse him of "strained simplic-
ity" and "deliberate naïveté."[1] But he's also the sly character who
thought of a poem that would allude, by way of defending itself
and its author, to a nursery rhyme (little Jack Horner), a cele-
brated poem of extreme simplicity by another William ("This Is
Just to Say"), and maybe to an old joke about a moron and the
light in the refrigerator. The poem is funniest at the end, when
the moment of illumination comes from the fridge and the de-
ferred grats of fame and praise take the form of a midnight
snack. It's all so open and self-deprecating that we are totally on
Stafford's side, and Zweig or whoever is completely refuted.
Simplicity shines forth as the great thing it is. Yet it is nearly
impossible to tell where the irony begins and leaves off. How do
you read the statement, "They were mine / to enjoy"? No irony
there? Okay, and the same for "Who but a friend" and "I began
the sentence of my life" and "anything like that"? I'm with you,
whatever you choose. I don't even know if there's irony built
into the design and structure of the poem, though I have to
suspect it. Understaters are famous for this, but Stafford is won-
derfully elusive, and we wouldn't have him any other way. Still,

I suppose this poem seems a little frivolous and specialized to stand for the excellences of a whole collection.

A better candidate would be the poem "Surrounded by Mountains." In its evocation of experience, its sense of wonder, and its diffidence about providing answers, it is quintessentially Staffordian:

> Digging potatoes east of Sapporo
> we would listen at noon to world news.
>
> The little radio was in one of the furrows,
> propped against a lunch bucket.
>
> We didn't make any judgments. Our fields
> were wide, slanting from wooded foothills.
>
> Religious leaders called for
> a revival of spirit in the world.
>
> Certain statesmen from important
> nations were considering a summit meeting.
>
> Old Mrs. Osaka, permanently
> bent over, stirred the clods beside her.
>
> Rice fields, yellow as sunflowers,
> marked off kilometers below us.
>
> The shrine where the crows lived
> had a bell that told us when rest was over.
>
> Goodby, old friends, I remember the Prime Minister
> talking, and the water jar in the shade.

The speaker could be Stafford, but he needn't be. His anonymity matches his technique of juxtaposing things, immediate and far, small world and big one, radio and furrow, without commenting on their significance to each other or in themselves. He represents a community that apparently preferred not to "make any judgments." If there's irony in the big world's representative, the little radio, being dwarfed by the furrows around it, he prefers to leave that inference to us. If statesmen and religious leaders and prime ministers dwindle before the reality of Mrs.

Osaka and a simple water jar, that's not something he cares to insist upon. The poem's openness is its source of attraction. We can mine values from it, but would we be able to tell the difference between what we found and what we brought? Stafford the artist has again and again disavowed total control, and his speakers follow suit, leaving readers a great deal of room to evaluate, interpret, and participate.

He has disavowed preoccupation with technique as well. It seems almost tactless to point out how well the choice of the couplet serves this poem, how neatly he pairs words and phrases that sound off each other—*potatoes/Sapporo, bucket/judgment, sunflowers/kilometers, remember/Prime Minister/water jar*—in a kind of offhand form of internal rhyme that is clearly more important than the end-of-line effects (e.g., six lines ending with *s* sounds, four with *r* sounds). Stafford doesn't have to measure and calculate such things. They are part of his working habit when he's attentive to words and sounds and sights. The little couplet about the shrine with the crows and bell has a kind of pun—*told/tolled*—but it's so lightly placed that you can't assume it's deliberate. Besides, what difference would that make? Stafford has offered you a quick-sketch pastoral, a chance to join, or rejoin, a peasant culture that will alter your perspective on history and power. You take it, and you trust him to get out of the way as much as possible. And he does.

So why did I finally choose "1940" over "Surrounded by Mountains"? In order to cite one more poem I liked? Partly, and partly because I think finally it has greater impact. I think it shows Stafford operating with all the same values and preferences that the other poems reveal, but reaching just a little farther and a little deeper. Perhaps comparisons are odious with this poet, but they necessarily surface when one is picking a poem to discuss and praise. I like "1940" because it plays a risky game with time, the second biggest mystery we live next to, and it can be heart-shaking if you let yourself be open to it.

If we could go back in time, what might we learn? What might it mean? Another powerful Stafford poem, "The Rescued Year," plays out that hypothesis too. Here the moment returned to is one of parting. As in "Surrounded by Mountains," history coexists with personal experience, but the parting of father and son, a final one, is what truly matters. If you could go back to that, the poem surmises, you would know so much more. And yet you would still know nothing, really. By saying "but you don't know" the poem makes you divide your consciousness between knowing and not-knowing. And you walk forward. Again as in "Surrounded by Mountains," particulars are all you have, are most of what you can know: cicadas, stones crunching, the little lights, your shoes. The distance of some forty-five years is also a distance from your observing eyes to your sometimes invisible feet as well as up to the overarching canopy of trees and cicadas. Ahead of you lies the partly known, the years you have lived since, and the unknown that even the wind turns back from, your mortality and the explanation, if there is any, of these rhythms of light and dark, knowing and not-knowing, the awesome movement of time.

Stafford handles all this in lightly rhymed triplets. He uses the second person to distance himself from his own experience and to offer it to us, in time, out of time. He uses the first and last stanzas for panoramic shots and the two middle stanzas for close-ups. One hundred and ten simple words. Lots of repetitions. Anticipations of the final line, with its repetitions and alterations, in effects like "you don't know. . . . You know" and "your shoes go brown, brown in the brightness." And again it feels a little bit beside the point to insist too much on the technique because Stafford himself would pooh-pooh it, refusing to take credit for the artful design of the experience, encouraging us to focus instead on the uncalculated, unmanageable life of the thing and its potential for touching our own lives.

Think what the poet has left out here! There is no mention of emotion, of the webs of experience that led Stafford to choose to be a conscientious objector during World War II, of when and how his father died. The choice is made to concentrate on the walk in the mysterious summer dark (I think of the middle section of "Ode to a Nightingale") in order to find out what meaning and illumination little things—fern, cicada, shiver of summer wind—will yield. The poet has gone back in time, defying its erasures and destructions, like Orpheus going down into hell. But he has refused to ask it to yield anything more than itself, the succession of moments by which we know and inhabit it. There is great mystery and depth of feeling here, and one can't help but admire the success of the poem's simple design and understated presentation. They make the walk from August to September a little easier. We step a little more lightly. Here they come: the depot, the dark, the light, the dark.

I reached for one plum and took four. Every time I opened the fridge the light was on. A reassuring experience. And I remember again my first, captivated reading of this book. I don't recall seeing any reviews of *An Oregon Message*. Not even ones that grumbled about "deliberate naïveté." But I may have missed them. Whether this essay constitutes a review or a salute, it will have served its purpose if it tempts some readers to put a few hours aside for that collection and be rewarded as I was.

NOTE

1. Zweig's review appeared in *Partisan Review* in 1974. It is cited by Judith Kitchen in *Understanding William Stafford* (University of South Carolina, 1989). Kitchen also discusses "1940" (121–23).

PART FOUR *Conclusion*

WILLIAM KITTREDGE, CHAIR; MARVIN BELL,
DENISE CHAVEZ, AND NAOMI SHIHAB NYE

Jurors' Citation, 1992 Western States Book Awards: Lifetime Achievement in Poetry

Allegiant to nature, story, and social values, receptive to verbal recklessness and luck, William Stafford's writing approaches the reader with considerate ease. In fact, without waving a flag he has long been among the most experimental and radical of our poets. His poetic idiom, conversant with natural speech, has been much imitated. But his special mixture of adventure, invention, keen senses, and intuition remains unmistakable and uncopied. As an international representative of poets, William Stafford's gentle attentions have encouraged free expression, while his intellectual jujitsu has caused many impulsive thinkers to reconsider. His confident and forgiving attitude toward daily writing and generous publication are the liberating talk of the town. Meanwhile, his poems—observant, engaged, resonant, and just plain irresistible—bear witness to both the care and disregard around us, naming the places, catching the shine of the ordinary, pulling the rug out from under vanity and pretension, giving fresh credit to the selfless and decent, acknowledging the inevitable, nudging us toward observant lives and peaceful interactions. His way of writing and of offering his work stands in silent rebuke to all that is loud, strident, assertive, and shallow. Yet close readers of Stafford's poetry know that there is a wildness at its center, by turns as gentle or tough as an undomesticated animal in an indifferent wilderness. He, of course, presents his poems and himself as if they should be taken for granted. We would like to say on this occasion that we do not.

Reprinted by permission of the Western States Arts Federation.

Selected Bibliography

Works by William Stafford

Down in My Heart (memoir). 1947. Reprint. Elgin, Ill.: Brethren Publishing House; Columbia, S.C.: Bench Press, 1985.
Winterward. Ph.D. diss. University of Iowa, 1954.
West of Your City. Los Gatos, Calif.: Talisman Press, 1960.
Traveling Through the Dark. New York: Harper and Row, 1962.
The Rescued Year. New York: Harper and Row, 1966.
Eleven Untitled Poems. Mt. Horeb, Wis.: Perishable Press, 1968.
Weather: Poems. Mt. Horeb, Wis.: Perishable Press, 1969.
Allegiances. New York: Harper and Row, 1970.
Temporary Facts. Athens, Ohio: Duane Schneider Press, 1970.
Someday, Maybe. New York: Harper and Row, 1973.
In the Clock of Reason. Victoria, B.C.: Soft Press, 1973.
That Other Alone. Mt. Horeb, Wis.: Perishable Press, 1973.
Going Places: Poems. Reno, Nev.: West Coast Poetry Review Press, 1974.
The Earth. Port Townsend, Wash.: Graywolf Press, 1974.
North by West, with John Haines. Seattle: Spring Rain Press, 1975.
Braided Apart, with Kim Stafford. Lewiston, Idaho: Confluence Press, 1976.
Late, Passing Prairie Farm. Northampton, Mass.: Main Street, 1976.
Stories That Could Be True: New and Collected Poems. New York: Harper and Row, 1977.
The Design on the Oriole. Mt. Horeb, Wis.: Night Heron Press, 1977.
Writing the Australian Crawl: Views on the Writer's Vocation (essays and interviews). Ann Arbor: University of Michigan Press, 1978.
Two about Music. Knotting, Bedfordshire: Sceptre Press, 1978.
All about Light. Athens, Ohio: Croissant and Company, 1978.
Tuned in Late One Night. Northampton, Mass.: Deerfield Press, 1978; Dublin: Gallery Press, 1978.
Passing a Creche. Seattle: Sea Pen Press, 1978.
Tuft by Puff. Mt. Horeb, Wis.: Perishable Press, 1978.
The Quiet of the Land. New York: Nadja Press, 1979.
Around You, Your House and a Catechism. Knotting, Bedfordshire: Sceptre Press, 1979.
Things That Happen Where There Aren't Any People. Brockport, N.Y.: BOA Editions, 1980.
Absolution. Knotting, Bedfordshire: Martin Booth, 1980.
Passwords. Seattle: Sea Pen Press, 1980.
Wyoming Circuit. Tannersville, N.Y.: Tideline Press, 1980.
Sometimes like a Legend: Puget Sound Poetry. Port Townsend, Wash.: Copper Canyon Press, 1981.

A Glass Face in the Rain: New Poems. New York: Harper and Row, 1982.
Segues: A Correspondence in Poetry, with Marvin Bell. Boston: David Godine, 1983.
Roving across Fields: A Conversation and Uncollected Poems, 1942–1982. Edited by Thom Tammaro. Daleville, Ind.: Barnwood Press, 1983.
Smoke's Way: Poems from Limited Editions, 1968–1981. Port Townsend, Wash.: Graywolf Press, 1983.
Stories and Storms and Strangers. Rexburg, Idaho: Honeybrook Press, 1984.
Listening Deep. Great Barrington, Mass.: Penmaen Press, 1984.
Wyoming. Bristol, R.I.: Ampersand Press, 1985.
You Must Revise Your Life (essays and interviews). Ann Arbor: University of Michigan Press, 1986.
Brother Wind. Rexburg, Idaho: Honeybrook Press, 1986.
An Oregon Message. New York: Harper and Row, 1987.
You and Some Other Characters. Rexburg, Idaho: Honeybrook Press, 1987.
Writing the World. Baltimore: Alembic Press, 1988.
Annie-Over, with Marvin Bell. Rexburg, Idaho: Honeybrook Press, 1988.
A Scripture of Leaves. Elgin, Ill.: Brethren Press, 1989.
Fin, Feather, Fur. Rexburg, Idaho: Honeybrook Press, 1989.
Kansas Poems. Topeka, Kans.: Woodley Memorial Press, 1990.
How to Hold Your Arms When It Rains. Rexburg, Idaho: Honeybrook Press, 1990.
Passwords. New York: HarperCollins, 1991.
The Long Sigh the Wind Makes. Monmouth, Oreg.: Adrienne Lee Press, 1991.
History Is Loose Again. Rexburg, Idaho: Honeybrook Press, 1991.
The Animal That Drank Up Sound (children's book, with illustrations by Debra Frasier). New York: Harcourt Brace Jovanovich, 1992.
My Name Is William Tell. Lewiston, Idaho: Confluence Press, 1992.
Seeking the Way. Minneapolis: Melia Press, 1992.

Secondary Sources

Books about William Stafford

Carpenter, David A. *William Stafford.* Boise: Boise State University Western Writers Series, no. 72, 1986.
Holden, Jonathan. *The Mark to Turn: A Reading of William Stafford's Poetry.* Lawrence: University Press of Kansas, 1976.
Kitchen, Judith. *Understanding William Stafford.* Columbia: University of South Carolina Press, 1989.

Essays and Book Reviews

Adams, Hazard. "Place and Movement." Rev. of *The Rescued Year. Poetry* 110, no. 1 (April 1967): 42–44.
Almon, Bert. Rev. of *Roving across Fields* and *Smoke's Way. Western American Literature* 19 (February 1985): 319–20.
Altieri, Charles. *Self and Sensibility in Contemporary American Poetry.* Cambridge: Cambridge University Press, 1984.
Andrews, Tom. "'Knowing': Glimpses into Something Ever Larger." *Field* 41 (Fall 1989): 38–40.
Atwood, Margaret. "Waking at 3:00 A.M." *Field* 41 (Fall 1989): 29–33.

Barnes, Dick. "The Absence of the Artist." *Field* 28 (Spring 1983): 27–34.

Bartlett, Lee. *The Sun Is but a Morning Star: Studies in West Coast Poetry and Poetics.* Albuquerque: University of New Mexico Press, 1989.

Benediktsson, Thomas E. "Montana Eclogue: The Pastoral Art of William Stafford." In *World, Self, Poem: Essays on Contemporary Poetry from the 'Jubilation of Poets.'* Edited by Leonard M. Trawick. Kent, Ohio: Kent State University Press, 1990.

Benoit, Raymond. "The New American Poetry." *Thought* 44 (Summer 1969): 201–18.

Berke, Roberta. *Bounds out of Bounds: A Compass for Recent American and British Poetry.* New York: Oxford University Press, 1981.

Biggs, Mary. *The Gift That Cannot Be Refused: The Writing and Publishing of Contemporary American Poetry.* Westport, Conn.: Greenwood Press, 1990.

Bradley, Sam. "An Approach to Seven Poets." *Approach* 36 (Summer 1960): 3–10.

Brand, Millen. "New Pastorals." Rev. of *The Rescued Year. Book Week,* 13 November 1966, 15.

Brown, Laurie. Rev. of *Roving across Fields. Library Journal,* 1 June 1983, 1140.

Burke, Herbert. Rev. of *West of Your City. Library Journal,* 1 March 1961, 1004.

Burns, Gerald. "A Book to Build On." Rev. of *Allegiances. Southwest Review* 55, no. 3 (Summer 1970): 309–10.

———. "Editors Cloth, Poets Paper." Rev. of *Going Places. Southwest Review* 61, no. 1 (Winter 1976): 98–100.

Burns, Richard K. Rev. of *The Rescued Year. Library Journal,* 1 October 1966, 4671–72.

Carruth, Hayden. "In Spite of Artifice." Rev. of *The Rescued Year. Hudson Review* 19, no. 4 (Winter 1966–67): 689–700.

Cavitch, David. "Lonely Poet, Mellow Poet." Rev. of *Someday, Maybe. New York Times Book Review,* 9 December 1973, 45.

Chappell, Fred. "Two Views of the Lone Man." *Small Farm* 9–10 (Spring–Fall 1979): 52–54.

Christensen, Paul. "William Stafford." *Contemporary Poets.* 5th ed. Edited by Tracy Chevalier. Chicago: St. James Press, 1991.

Claire, William. "Contemporary American Poetry at the Crossroads." *American Studies International* 18 (Winter 1980): 5–18.

Coblentz, Stanton A. *The Poetry Circus.* New York: Hawthorn Books, 1967.

Cole, William. "Nature and Man's Nature." Rev. of *Stories That Could Be True. Saturday Review,* 7 January 1978, 42.

Coles, Robert. "William Stafford's Long Walk." *That Red Wheelbarrow: Selected Literary Essays.* Iowa City: University of Iowa Press, 1988.

Corey, Stephen. "Lives on Leaves." Rev. of *Things That Happen Where There Aren't Any People. Virginia Quarterly Review* 57, no. 4 (Autumn 1981): 732–43.

Cotter, James Finn. Rev. of *A Glass Face in the Rain. America,* 27 August 1983, 92.

Creeley, Robert. "'Think What's Got Away. . . .'" Rev. of *Traveling Through the Dark. Poetry* 102, no. 1 (April 1963): 42–48.

Davison, Peter. "The New Poetry." Rev. of *Traveling Through the Dark. Atlantic Monthly,* November 1962, 88.

Dickey, James. "William Stafford." Rev. of *West of Your City.* In *Babel to Byzantium: Poets and Poetry Now.* 2d ed. New York: Ecco Press, 1981.

Dickinson-Brown, Roger. "The Wise, the Dull, the Bewildered: What Happens in William Stafford." *Modern Poetry Studies* 6 (Spring 1975): 30–38.

Engel, Bernard F. "From Here We Speak." *Old Northwest* 2 (March 1976): 37–44.

Fitts, Dudley. "A Varied Quintet." Rev. of *West of Your City*. *New York Times Book Review*, 26 February 1961, 10, 12.

Flint, R. W. "Feeding the Hunger for Stories." Rev. of *Segues*. *New York Times Book Review*, 8 April 1984, 14.

Fowler, Albert. "Two Books by William Stafford." Rev. of *West of Your City* and *Traveling Through the Dark*. *Approach* 47 (Spring 1963): 40–42.

French, Warren. "'Sunflowers through the Dark': The Vision of William Stafford." In *Late Harvest*. Edited by Thomas Killoren. Kansas City: BkMk Press, 1977.

Galler, David. "Description as Poetry." Rev. of *The Rescued Year*. *Kenyon Review* 29, no. 1 (January 1967): 140–46.

Garber, Frederick. "On Richard Hugo and William Stafford." *American Poetry Review* (January–February 1980): 16–18.

Garrison, Joseph. Rev. of *Stories That Could Be True*. *Library Journal*, 15 December 1977, 2503.

Garrison, Steve. "William Stafford." In *Dictionary of Literary Biography: American Poets since World War II*. Edited by Donald J. Greiner. Detroit: Gale Research, 1980.

Gibbons, Reginald. "Poets on Poetry: The Ann Arbor Paperbacks." Rev. of *Writing the Australian Crawl*. *Ironwood* 24 (Fall 1984): 183–91.

Giles, Ronald K. "William Stafford's 'Traveling Through the Dark.'" *Explicator* 43, no. 3 (Spring 1985): 44–45.

Gioia, Dana. "Poetry and the Fine Presses." Rev. of *The Quiet of the Land*. *Hudson Review* 35, no. 3 (Autumn 1982): 483–98.

Gitzen, Julian. "The Listener: William Stafford." *Modern Poetry Studies* 11 (1983): 274–86.

Greiner, Charles F. "Stafford's 'Traveling Through the Dark': A Discussion of Style." *English Journal* 55 (November 1966): 1015–18.

Haines, John. "A Comment on William Stafford's 'A Way of Writing' in *Field* 2." *Field* 3 (Fall 1970): 64–66.

Hall, Donald. "Some American Poets." *Review* 9 (October 1963): 43–52.

———. "William Stafford: Eight Notions." *The Weather for Poetry: Essays, Reviews, and Notes on Poetry, 1977–1981*. Ann Arbor: University of Michigan Press, 1982.

Hansen, Tom. "On Writing Poetry: Four Contemporary Poets." *College English* 44, no. 3 (March 1982): 265–73.

Hartley, George. *Textual Politics and the Language Poets*. Bloomington: Indiana University Press, 1989.

Hartman, Geoffrey H. "Beyond the Middle Style." Rev. of *Traveling Through the Dark*. *Kenyon Review* 25, no. 4 (Autumn 1963): 751–57.

Haskell, Dennis. "The Modern American Poetry of Deep Image." *Southern Review* 12 (1979): 137–66.

Hazo, Samuel. "The Experience of the Idea." Rev. of *Stories That Could Be True*. *Hudson Review* 31, no. 3 (Autumn 1978): 536–47.

Heller, Michael. "Owls, Monkeys and Spiders in Space." Rev. of *An Oregon Message*. *New York Times Book Review*, 12 June 1988, 15.

Heyen, William. "William Stafford's Allegiances." *Modern Poetry Studies* 1 (1970): 307–18.

Hoffman, Daniel, ed. *Harvard Guide to Contemporary American Writing*. Cambridge, Mass.: Harvard University Press, Belknap Press, 1979.

Holden, Jonathan. "Landscape Poems." *Denver Quarterly* 20–21 (Spring–Summer 1986): 159–76.

———. *Style and Authenticity in Postmodern Poetry.* Columbia: University of Missouri Press, 1986.

———. Rev. of *An Oregon Message. Choice* 25 (January 1988): 770.

———. "With Kit, Age 7, at the Beach." *Field* 41 (Fall 1989): 26–28.

———. *The Fate of American Poetry.* Athens: University of Georgia Press, 1991.

Holland, J. Gill. "Stafford's 'Traveling Through the Dark.'" *Explicator* 45 (Fall 1986): 55–58.

Howard, Ben. "Near and Far." Rev. of *A Glass Face in the Rain. Prairie Schooner* 57, no. 4 (Winter 1983): 81–85.

———. "Together and Apart." Rev. of *Passwords. Poetry* 160, no. 1 (April 1992): 34–44.

Howard, Richard. *Alone with America: Essays on the Art of Poetry in the United States since 1950.* 2d ed. New York: Atheneum, 1980.

Howes, Victor. "Quiet as All Books." Rev. of *Allegiances. Christian Science Monitor,* 28 September 1970, 9.

Huff, Robert. "Design and Matter." Rev. of *West of Your City. Prairie Schooner* 36, no. 1 (Spring 1962): 80–83.

Hugo, Richard. "Problems with Landscapes in Early Stafford Poems." *Kansas Quarterly* 2 (Spring 1970): 33–38.

Juhasz, Suzanne. Rev. of *Segues. Library Journal,* 1 November 1983, 2087.

Kaufman, Ellen. Rev. of *Passwords. Library Journal,* 15 May 1991, 86.

Kelley, Patrick. "Legend and Ritual." *Kansas Quarterly* 2 (Spring 1970): 28–31.

Kiernan, Robert F. *American Writing since 1945: A Critical Survey.* New York: Frederick Ungar, 1983.

Kizer, Carolyn. "Poetry of the Fifties in America." In *International Literary Annual No. 1,* edited by John Wain. London: J. Calder, 1958.

Kramer, Lawrence. "In Quiet Language." Rev. of *Stories That Could Be True. Parnassus* 6, no. 2 (Spring–Summer 1978): 101–17.

Krauth, Leland. "'A Visioned End': Edgar Lee Masters and William Stafford." *Midamerica: A Yearbook of the Society for the Study of Midwestern Literature* 11 (1984): 90–107.

Kuntzelman, Jackie. "William Stafford: A Poet for All Reasons." *Prism* (Oregon State University) (Spring 1975): 2–5.

Kyle, Carol A. "Point of View in 'Returned to Say' and the Wilderness of William Stafford." *Western American Literature* 7 (Fall 1972): 191–201.

Lauber, John. "The World's Guest—William Stafford." *Iowa Review* 5 (Spring 1974): 88–100.

Leavens, Dennis. "'What the River Says, That Is What I Say': The World as Parable in William Stafford's Poems." *Paintbrush* 17 (Spring–Autumn 1990): 52–60.

Lensing, George S. "William Stafford, Mythmaker." *Modern Poetry Studies* 6 (Spring 1975): 1–17.

Lensing, George S., and Ronald Moran. *Four Poets and the Emotive Imagination: Robert Bly, James Wright, Louis Simpson, and William Stafford.* Baton Rouge: Louisiana State University Press, 1976.

Lieberman, Laurence. *Unassigned Frequencies: American Poetry in Review, 1964–1977.* Urbana: University of Illinois Press, 1977.

Love, Glen A. "William Stafford." In *Fifty Western Writers: A Bio-Bibliographical*

Sourcebook, edited by Fred Erisman and Richard W. Etulain. Westport, Conn.: Greenwood Press, 1992.

Lynch, Dennis Daley. "Journeys in Search of Oneself: The Metaphor of the Road in William Stafford's *Traveling Through the Dark* and *The Rescued Year.*" *Modern Poetry Studies* 7 (Autumn 1976): 122–31.

Lyon, Thomas J. "Western Poetry." *Journal of the West* 19 (January 1980): 45–53.

Marcus, Adrianne. "Five Poets." Rev. of *The Rescued Year. Shenandoah* 18, no. 3 (Spring 1967): 82–84.

Martz, Louis L. "Recent Poetry: Visions and Revisions." Rev. of *Allegiances. Yale Review* 60, no. 3 (Spring 1971): 403–17.

McDowell, Robert. "The Mum Generation Was Always Talking." Rev. of *Writing the Australian Crawl. Hudson Review* 38, no. 3 (Autumn 1985): 507–19.

McFee, Michael. "Just Being." Rev. of *A Glass Face in the Rain. Carolina Quarterly* 35 (Spring 1983): 88–91.

Mersmann, James F. *Out of the Vietnam Vortex: A Study of Poets and Poetry against the War.* Lawrence: University Press of Kansas, 1974.

Miller, Tom P. " 'In Dear Detail, by Ideal Light': The Poetry of William Stafford." *Southwest Review* 56, no. 4 (Autumn 1971): 341–45.

Mills, Ralph J., Jr. "Like Talk." Rev. of *Stories That Could Be True. New York Times Book Review,* 1 January 1978, 11, 21.

Milton, John. "From Artifact to Intuition in Great Plains Writing." *Prairie Schooner* 55 (Spring–Summer 1981): 131–40.

Mitchell, Mark. "A Poet for Brethren." *Messenger* 130 (September 1981): 10–11.

Moss, Stanley. "Country Boy." Rev. of *The Rescued Year. New Republic,* 19 November 1966, 23–24.

Mullenneaux, Lisa. Rev. of *An Oregon Message. Library Journal,* August 1987, 130.

Murray, G. E. "Poets on Poetry." Rev. of *Writing the Australian Crawl. National Forum* 60, no. 4 (Fall 1980): 50–51.

Myers, Jack, and David Wojahn, eds. *A Profile of Twentieth-Century American Poetry.* Carbondale: Southern Illinois University Press, 1991.

Narita, Michiko. "William Stafford: His Aura of Revelation." In *Traditional and the Anti-Traditional: Studies in Contemporary American Literature,* edited by Kenzaburo Ohashi. Tokyo: Tokyo Chapter, American Literature Society of Japan, 1980.

Nathan, Leonard. "From Our Balloon over the Provinces." *Practices of the Wind* 3 (combined issue for 1981–83): 231–32.

———. "One Vote." *New England Review and Breadloaf Quarterly* 5 (1983): 521–24.

Nordstrom, Lars. *Theodore Roethke, William Stafford, and Gary Snyder: The Ecological Metaphor as Transformed Regionalism.* Uppsala: Studia Anglistica Upsaliensia 67, 1989.

Odean, Kathleen. Rev. of *The Animal That Drank Up Sound. School Library Journal* (June 1992): 125–26.

Orfalea, Greg. "The Warm Stoic: William Stafford." In *A Book of Rereadings in Recent American Poetry: Thirty Essays,* edited by Greg Kuzma (triple issue of *Pebble,* nos. 18–20). Lincoln, Nebr.: Best Cellar Press, 1979.

Parisi, Joseph. Rev. of *A Glass Face in the Rain. Booklist,* 15 October 1982, 290.

———. Rev. of *Segues. Booklist,* 15 November 1983, 466.

Pastan, Linda. "Ask Me." *Field* 41 (Fall 1989): 35–36.

Pearson, Michael. Rev. of *A Glass Face in the Rain. Southern Humanities Review* 19, no. 1 (Winter 1985): 82–83.

Perelman, Bob. "The First Person." In *Talks,* edited by Bob Perelman. Published as *Hills* 6–7 (Spring 1980): 147–65.

Piccione, A. Rev. of *You Must Revise Your Life. Choice* 24 (July–August 1987): 1697.

Pinsker, Sanford. *Three Pacific Northwest Poets: William Stafford, Richard Hugo, and David Wagoner.* Boston: Twayne, 1987.

Powers, Edel. "Stafford Wins National Book Award." *Publishers Weekly,* 18 March 1963, 30–31.

Pritchard, William H. "Expressing the Difference." Rev. of *Stories That Could Be True. Poetry* 132, no. 4 (July 1978): 230–38.

———. "Aboard the Poetry Omnibus." Rev. of *Smoke's Way* and *Segues. Hudson Review* 37, no. 2 (Autumn 1984): 327–42.

Prunty, Wyatt. *"Fallen from the Symboled World": Precedents for the New Formalism.* New York: Oxford University Press, 1990.

Quinn, Sister Bernetta. "Symbolic Landscapes." Rev. of *Allegiances. Poetry* 118, no. 5 (August 1971): 288–90.

Ramsey, Jarold. "Shades of Regionalism: Three Northwest Poets." *West Coast Review* 9, no. 2 (October 1974): 48–51.

———. "Introduction" to *Coyote Was Going There,* edited by Jarold Ramsey. Seattle: University of Washington Press, 1977.

———. "The Indian Literature of Oregon." In *Northwest Perspectives: Essays on the Culture of the Pacific Northwest,* edited by Edwin R. Bingham and Glen A. Love. Seattle: University of Washington Press, 1979.

Ramsey, Paul. "What the Light Struck." *Tennessee Poetry Journal* 2 (Spring 1969): 17–20.

———. "American Poetry in 1973." Rev. of *Someday, Maybe. Sewanee Review* 82, no. 2 (Spring 1974): 393–405.

Ratner, Steven. "Poetry by Post Seals Friendship, Explores Nature of Verse." Rev. of *Segues. Christian Science Monitor,* 4 November 1983, B5.

Rev. of *Allegiances. Publishers Weekly,* 16 March 1970, 53.

Rev. of *The Animal That Drank Up Sound. Publishers Weekly,* 20 January 1992, 64.

Rev. of *A Glass Face in the Rain. Virginia Quarterly Review* 59, no. 2 (Spring 1983): 61.

Rev. of *An Oregon Message. Publishers Weekly,* 24 July 1987, 182.

Rev. of *An Oregon Message. Virginia Quarterly Review* 64, no. 2 (Spring 1988): 63.

Rev. of *Passwords. Publishers Weekly,* 29 March 1991, 87.

Rev. of *The Rescued Year. Virginia Quarterly Review* 43, no. 1 (Winter 1967): xvi.

Rev. of *Roving across Fields. Small Press Review,* October 1983, 8.

Rev. of *Segues. Publishers Weekly,* 9 September 1983, 52.

Rev. of *Smoke's Way. Choice* 21 (March 1984): 980.

Rev. of *Stories That Could Be True. Publishers Weekly,* 31 October 1977, 55.

Rev. of *Stories That Could Be True. Choice* 15 (June 1978): 550.

Rev. of *Traveling Through the Dark. Virginia Quarterly Review* 39, no. 3 (Summer 1963): xvi–xvii.

Rev. of *Writing the Australian Crawl. Choice* 15 (October 1978): 1054.

Ricou, Laurie. "Prairie Poetry and Metaphors of Plain/s Space." *Great Plains Review* 3 (1983): 109–19.

Roberts, J. Russell, Sr. "Listening to the Wilderness with William Stafford." *Western American Literature* 3 (Fall 1968): 217–26.

———. Rev. of *A Glass Face in the Rain. Western American Literature* 18 (November 1983): 253–54.

————. "William Stafford." In *A Literary History of the American West*. Fort Worth: Texas Christian University Press, 1987.

Rosenthal, M. L. "A Quartet of Singers: Voices Pitched in Varied Keys." Rev. of *Traveling Through the Dark*. *New York Times Book Review*, 21 April 1963, 38.

————. *The New Poets: American and British Poetry since World War II*. New York: Oxford University Press, 1967.

————. "A Common Sadness." Rev. of *A Glass Face in the Rain*. *New York Times Book Review*, 13 March 1983, 6, 18–19.

Shapiro, Janet D. "William E. Stafford: Consultant in Poetry in English to the Library of Congress." *Special Libraries*, September 1970, 353–56.

Shetley, Vernon. "Short Reviews." Rev. of *An Oregon Message*. *Poetry* 152, no. 2 (May 1988): 98–112.

Simic, Charles. "At the Bomb Testing Site." *Wonderful Words, Silent Truth: Essays on Poetry and a Memoir*. Ann Arbor: University of Michigan Press, 1990.

Simpson, Louis. *A Company of Poets*. Ann Arbor: University of Michigan Press, 1981.

Slater, Joseph. "Immortal Bard and Others." Rev. of *The Rescued Year*. *Saturday Review*, 31 December 1966, 24–25.

Smith, Virginia E. "Taking the Reader's Hand." Rev. of *Things That Happen Where There Aren't Any People*. *Southwest Review* 65, no. 1 (Winter 1981): 114–16.

Smith, William Jay. "The New Poetry." Rev. of *Traveling Through the Dark*. *Harper's*, September 1963, 106–15.

Sollid, Karen. "William Stafford's Sunflowers through the Dark." *Organon* 2 (Fall 1970): 64–70.

Spector, Robert D. "Betwixt Tradition and Innovation." Rev. of *Allegiances*. *Saturday Review*, 26 December 1970, 24.

Squires, Radcliffe. "Three First Books." Rev. of *West of Your City*. *Northwest Review* 4 (Summer 1961): 81–85.

Steele, Frank. "William Stafford's 'Mornings'." *Small Farm* 9–10 (Spring–Fall 1979): 55–63.

Stepanchev, Stephen. "Eight Poets." Rev. of *Traveling Through the Dark*. *Shenandoah* 14 (Spring 1963): 58–65.

————. *American Poetry since 1945: A Critical Survey*. New York: Harper and Row, 1965.

Stitt, Peter. "'Looking at an Old School Album': Bonuses in a Stafford Poem." *Practices of the Wind* 3 (combined issue for 1981–83): 218–20.

————. "A Remarkable Diversity." Rev. of *A Glass Face in the Rain*. *Georgia Review* 36 (Winter 1982): 911–22.

————. "The Poetry of Realism." Rev. of *Smoke's Way*. *Poetry* 144, no. 4 (July 1984): 231–37.

————. *The World's Hieroglyphic Beauty: Five American Poets*. Athens: University of Georgia Press, 1985.

Stranahan, Martha. "Poet Laurete William Stafford: Making Mud-Pies." *Ruralite* (Forest Grove, Oreg.) (September 1976): 16–17.

Stuart, Dabney. Rev. of *Someday, Maybe*. *Library Journal*, 1 June 1973, 1824.

Sumner, D. Nathan. "The Poetry of William Stafford: Nature, Time and Father." *Research Studies at Washington State University* 36 (September 1968): 187–95.

Taylor, Henry. "'Thinking for Berky': Millions of Intricate Moves." *Field* 41 (Fall 1989): 12–24.

Turco, Lewis. *Visions and Revisions: Of American Poetry.* Fayetteville: University of Arkansas Press, 1986.

Turner, Alberta. "A Second Bite of the Muskrat: Further Pursuit of Excellence in Contemporary Poetry." *Midwest Quarterly* 15 (January 1974): 177–89.

———. "William Stafford and the Surprise Cliché." *South Carolina Review* 7 (April 1975): 28–33.

———. Review of *A Glass Face in the Rain. Field* 28 (Spring 1983): 69–76.

———. "Things I Learned Last Week." *Field* 41 (Fall 1989): 42–43.

Venn, George. "Continuity in Northwest Literature." In *Northwest Perspectives: Essays on the Culture of the Pacific Northwest,* edited by Edwin R. Bingham and Glen A. Love. Seattle: University of Washington Press, 1979.

Wagner-Martin, Linda. *American Modern: Essays in Fiction and Poetry.* Port Washington, N.Y.: Kennikat Press, 1980.

Walkup, Kathleen. Rev. of *Sometimes Like a Legend. Fine Print* 9 (April 1983): 77–79.

Waskowsky, Nicolaus. "The Permission of the Snow." *Practices of the Wind* 3 (combined issue for 1981–83): 239–40.

Weatherhead, A. K. Rev. of *Traveling Through the Dark. Northwest Review* 6 (Winter 1963): 121–26.

———. "William Stafford's Recent Poetry." Rev. of *A Glass Face in the Rain. Concerning Poetry* 16 (Spring 1983): 71–78.

Womack, Judy. "Daniel Boone—'Over the Velvet Falls.'" *Kentucky Folklore Record* 18 (1972): 21–22.

Young, David. "The Bite of the Muskrat: Judging Contemporary Poetry." In *A Field Guide to Contemporary Poetry and Poetics,* edited by Stuart Friebert and David Young. New York: Longman, 1980.

———. "'1940': Shivers of Summer Wind." *Field* 41 (Fall 1989): 45–52.

Zweig, Paul. "The Raw and the Cooked." Rev. of *Someday, Maybe. Partisan Review* 41, no. 4 (1974): 604–12.

Bibliographies

Macmillan, Samuel H. "On William Stafford and His Poems: A Selected Bibliography." *Tennessee Poetry Journal* 2 (1969): 21–22.

Murphy, George E., Jr. "William Stafford: A Bibliography." *Small Farm* 9–10 (Spring–Fall 1979): 64–68.

Nordstrom, Lars. "A William Stafford Bibliography." *Studia Neophilologica* 59 (1987): 59–63.

Pirie, James W. *William Stafford: A Primary Bibliography, 1942–1979.* New York: Garland Publishing, 1983. .

Tammaro, Thom. "A Chronology of Books by William Stafford." In *Roving across Fields: A Conversation and Uncollected Poems, 1942–1982,* edited by Thom Tammaro. Daleville, Ind.: Barnwood Press, 1983.

POETS ON POETRY   Donald Hall, General Editor

Poets on Poetry collects critical works by contemporary poets, gathering together the articles, interviews, and book reviews by which they have articulated the poetics of a new generation.